Empowering Adolescent Girls:

Examining the Present and Building Skills for the Future with the Go Grrrls Program

Also by the Authors:
The Go Grrrls Workbook
(Norton)

Empowering Adolescent Girls:

Examining the Present and Building Skills for the Future with the Go Grrrls Program

Craig Winston LeCroy and Janice Daley

W. W. Norton & Company
New York • London

The text and display of this book is composed in Janson Text
Manufacturing by Haddon Craftsmen
Book design and composition by Paradigm Graphics
Production Manager: Leeann Graham

Library of Congress Cataloging-in-Publication Data

LeCroy, Craig W.
Empowering adolescent girls : examining the
present and building skills for the future with the
Go Grrrls Program / Craig Winston LeCroy and Janice Daley.
p. cm. – (A Norton professional book)
Includes bibliographical references and index.
ISBN 0-393-70347-9
1. Teenage girls—United States—Life skills guides. 2. Go Grrrls Program.
I. Daley, Janice. II. Title. III. Series.

HQ798 .L437 2001
305.235–dc21   2001018336

W. W. Norton & Company, Inc., 500 Fifth Avenue, New York, N.Y. 10110
www.wwnorton.com
W. W. Norton & Company, Ltd., Castle House, 75/76 Wells St., London W1T 3QT

1 2 3 4 5 6 7 8 9 0

Contents

Acknowledgments

The Go Grrrls program has evolved over many years. We want to acknowledge the countless M.S.W. students from Arizona State University who have participated in the development or field testing of this program over the years. In particular, Velia Leybas and Angela Chintis provided significant contributions. The program has been vastly improved thanks to the valuable feedback we have received from over 60 group leaders who contributed their time and effort. Thank you, Will and Kerry for the love and constant encouragement. And, of course, we thank the hundreds of girls who participated in the program, helping us refine it and keep it interesting and pertinent.

Introduction

As of this writing, over 60 programs based on the Go Grrrls curriculum have been conducted. We recently attended the final session of one of these programs. The young women who led the group distributed graduation certificates and expressed heartfelt thanks to the participants for their enthusiasm and hard work. They praised each graduate for a specific personal quality that helped everyone in the group: Jennifer for her sense of humor, Eileen for her sense of fair play, Kathy for her leadership. When the girls finished their program evaluation forms, they feasted on pizza, danced to their favorite music, and shared their impressions of the program with us.

"What did you like best about Go Grrrls?" we asked several participants.

"I liked that you get to be who you are and not who other people want you to be," reported Ellen, an outspoken, articulate 11-year-old.

"We got to start putting positive thoughts into our minds," Anne shared. "And we got to talk to the leaders about our problems."

Other girls chimed in: "It was very cool and fun." "We got to know more people and learn about ourselves." Marilyn, one of our most ardent fans, said, "You have a great program. It makes me want to come back a third time."

As we left the session, we felt an enormous sense of satisfaction. While the Go Grrrls program has now served hundreds of girls (with more requests for services rolling in all the time), there was a time when we were just beginning to sell school administrators on the need for prevention services geared specifically for girls.

Six years ago we could not find one comprehensive book that provided a professional review of the literature on the many varied issues girls face today. Similarly, while we found some articles suggesting prevention or treatment for single issues, we did not find an entire program designed to help equip girls with the strength and range of skills they need to make their way to a healthy adulthood. In response to this gap, we began conducting groups for early-adolescent girls and used the substantive and practical knowledge accumulated in those groups to design an effective program tailored to the needs of this unique population. Since we began this project, the girls' movement has exploded, producing material that we have benefited from enormously: the emerging voices of girls themselves, parental-advice and social-understanding books, self-help books targeting girls, and burgeoning social science research on girls' issues. It is virtually impossible to keep up with all the new developments. This movement was and continues to be critical to our study and understanding of adolescent girls. After many years of designing the Go Grrrls program, we developed a more specific curriculum and began to pilot test the intervention.

Research and evaluation of the Go Grrrls project is an ongoing process. Initially we conducted assessments looking at changes that occurred from a pretest at the beginning of the program, to a posttest at the end of the program. We also conducted a series of focus groups to learn more about what program elements the participants wanted and thought were most useful. Eventually, we were able to set up a quasi-experimental evaluation using a comparison group of girls who completed the tests but did not receive the program. Results were promising. We saw positive changes across multiple measures of outcome and significant differences between the treatment group (i.e., Go Grrrls participants) and the comparison group on most of the measures. More refinements were made to the program. Last year we completed the process by launching a randomized trial to further assess program outcomes. Again, the results were positive and are described in Appendix B of this book.

Go Grrrls participants have helped us revise the curriculum so that it is both fun and informative and have encouraged us by expressing their thanks for this program. They have shared their stories and taught us much about what it is truly like to be a girl in today's world. The many young women who have facilitated these groups also have contributed immeasurably to this project by offering suggestions, relating group anecdotes, and sharing their enthusiasm. All of these experiences helped forge our vision of helping girls adapt to a challenging society and make positive changes for themselves. Because we are confident that Go Grrrls is on track and producing clear outcomes, we decided to help disseminate the program by writing this book.

This book is presented in two parts. Part I is intended to help readers understand the full scope of unique risks young girls face during adolescence. Each chapter in this section begins with girls' quotes culled from a variety of sources. These quotes highlight the personal, individual effects of the broader issues we address. The bulk of the chapter consists of a review of current and classic literature on the topic addressed. We hope that this information will help potential Go Grrrls program directors and group leaders gain a solid understanding of the issues. Without such an understanding, curriculum implementation would be hollow. This information is also extremely useful for community and school presentations, as well as for grant applications.

Part II provides one model of a broad-reaching, programmatic solution that addresses the risks detailed in Part I and promotes positive development. We believe that much has been said about the difficulties adolescent girls face but little work has been done to remedy those difficulties. Chapter 10 offers practical suggestions for program implementation. Each chapter begins with quotes from Go Grrrls participants. Brief dialogs adapted from Go Grrrls sessions introduce the detailed descriptions of how to conduct the various group sessions. Each description contains the following information:

- Session number and name.
- Rationale: This is a very brief reminder of why the session is being conducted.
- Goals: This is intended to be a quick, "at a glance" list of goals for leaders to check just before launching a session.
- Materials: This is a checklist for group leaders to consult before beginning the group.
- Overview: This section briefly describes the activities that will occur during the group.
- Procedure: These are the detailed, step-by-step instructions for conducting the session.

We expect all group leaders to actively consult their copy of the curriculum during the group. We have had some ambitious but misguided group leaders who tried to memorize the sessions and conduct them without the curriculum handy. This is definitely not recommended, as it is too easy to leave out important points or activities. It is also important to use the guide during groups to ensure that the pacing is right. The sessions are intentionally fast-paced (girls who have been through the program helped us develop this pacing) and leaders will find the time recommendations extremely useful. Paragraphs are kept short so that group leaders can quickly glance at and act on the directions. Of course group leaders must read the entire curriculum before implementing a group, but quick glances at the curriculum during a session are also necessary.

Most sessions conclude with some sort of brief game. While these games do not always reflect on the topic of the session, they are still important. Because Go Grrrls is generally implemented as a voluntary, after-school club, we have found that including some lighthearted games or small creative projects at the end of the session helps establish and maintain girls' enthusiasm for the entire program. This "game time" also provides an opportunity for group leaders to deepen rapport with the club members. Game prizes and incentives certainly do not hurt the girls' morale, either!

The Go Grrrls Journal/Workbook

The Go Grrrls program works in tandem with a specially designed workbook that is available for purchase. This workbook includes all the journal assignments, the handouts and information sheets for each session, and supplemental activities, exercises, and information for girls to peruse. The workbook reinforces material that is presented in the program by following the same major topics (e.g., body image, friendship), and introduces different formats for the material such as slumber party dialogues, "advice columns," and worksheets. For example, the chapter on body image has a slumber party dialogue in which girls discuss pressure to be thin and look good, and the advice column is a response to a girl who has developed an eating disorder. While we recommend that participants use the Go Grrrls workbook as their journal during the club meetings, it is also possible to purchase and distribute notebooks or plain paper journals to fill this purpose.

Girls are assigned journal exercises at the end of every meeting. These exercises are included for several reasons. Overall, journal writing is a wonderful means of self-expression and -exploration—activities near and dear to the hearts of early-adolescent girls. The journal assignments in Go Grrrls are specifically designed to help girls prepare for upcoming club topics, and in this way they tie the curriculum together. For example, the journal assignment preceding the session on positive self-image asks girls to list five things they like about themselves. During the session, they consult these lists and share some of their responses. The quality of group discussion is enhanced by the preparation work the journals promote.

To encourage girls to complete the journal assignments, we offer special incentives. For each journal assignment she completes, the girl's name will go into a drawing for a prize at the last club meeting. Thus, if a participant completes ten assignments, her name is entered in the drawing ten times. During the final club meeting, we hold a drawing for a small prize.

Useful Tools: The Appendices

By scanning the list of items included in the appendices, you will gain a quick understanding of how simple we have made it to plan, establish, implement, and even evaluate a Go Grrrls group in your school, agency, community center, or other venue. We have included the parent curriculum, materials lists, and sample permission slips. And because we know the importance of evaluation on so many levels (from understanding the strengths and growth areas in implementation to securing and maintaining funding) we have even included potential tools for program evaluation.

Ready, Set, Go Grrrls!: Changing the World One Group at a Time

As many educators, counselors, and parents already know, students often turn out to be superb teachers. Girls in this program teach us about the strengths, struggles, and triumphs of growing up female in today's world. They inspire us to help make changes in the world. They infect us with their energy and enthusiasm. We welcome you to use this book as a reference and resource, but we truly hope that you will use that knowledge to start a Go Grrrls group of your own. The experience will be rewarding for you, for your community, and, most importantly, for the group of girls you will meet.

Empowering Adolescent Girls:

*Examining the Present and Building Skills
for the Future with the
Go Grrrls Program*

PART I

THE ISSUES

Chapter 1
A Framework for Understanding Girls

It's hard enough being young, but being a girl, and then there's where you live and the color of your skin, it can be really hard growing up. I would never trade who I am, I'd just make society hear us better. Youth have a lot to offer this world, but sometimes girls aren't taken that seriously. But just watch me. Me and my girls are making something of ourselves.

—Tara, from *The Girls Report: What We Need to Know about Growing Up Female* by Lynn Phillips (1998, p. 10)

Little girls learn to split their consciousness, filtering their dreams and ambitions through boy characteristics while admiring the clothes of the princess. The more privileged and daring can dream of becoming exceptional women in a man's world. The others are being taught to accept the more usual fate, which is to be a passenger car drawn through life by a masculine train engine. Boys, who are rarely confronted with stories in which males play only minor roles, learn a simpler lesson: girls just don't matter much.

—K. Pollitt, *New York Times Magazine* (1991, p. 22)

What image comes to mind when you think of adolescence in the 21st century? A pregnant teenage girl? An emaciated teenage body? A bottle of whiskey? A teenager with a semiautomatic gun? Researchers have tried for years to correct the mistaken notion that all adolescents experience psychological turmoil. The stereotype of adolescents as maladjusted rebels or delinquents is fueled by widespread generalizations drawn from a smaller, more visible group of adolescents. Still, the images conjured above do represent some of the risks young people face in today's society. We believe that while many more adolescents can successfully navigate the transition to adulthood than contem-

porary images would have us believe, adolescents in today's culture are not provided with the needed support and opportunities to develop competencies for
successful adulthood.

Compared to their parents' teen years, contemporary adolescence is a
period of far greater risk to young people's current and future health (Takanishi,
1993). A significant difference is that today's adolescents are exposed to risky
behavior at a much earlier age than adolescents of the past. Many youth begin
experimenting with drugs before age 15 and the majority of high school seniors
have used alcohol and smoked cigarettes (Gans & Blyth, 1990). Mental disorders are quite prevalent among today's youth. Some estimates suggest depression affects up to 30% of adolescents (Petersen et al., 1993). Suicide rates
among 15- to 24-year-olds have increased 154% since the 1960s (Weiten &
Lloyd, 1997). An often-quoted statistic of the 1990s is the rapid increase (up
111% between 1985 and 1990) in homicide deaths to African American males
aged 15 to 19. For females in the United States, pregnancy is a major health
risk. The vast majority—up to 87% (Moore, 1994)—of births to adolescent
females are unintended. Of course, sexual activity carries many other serious
risks: We are seeing increases in AIDS and epidemic proportions of sexually
transmitted diseases such as chlamydia and gonorrhea. One in seven adolescents has had a sexually transmitted disease (Santrock, 1996). In fact, the Office
of Technology (1991) classified one fourth of all adolescents as high-risk. An
exhaustive survey of adolescent risk behavior estimated that 50% of youth are
at moderate to high risk for engaging in problem behavior (Dryfoos, 1990). And
even those young people who are not considered high-risk must navigate
through a playing field of obstacles and barriers to healthy development.

Concerns about problem behaviors are increasingly directed at girls.
Current estimates are that this year or next, girls will surpass boys in tobacco
and alcohol use and will equal boys in marijuana use. Some argue, however, that
it isn't girls but rather the way society responds to girls that is getting worse.
Whatever the cause, there is an increasing awareness that we need gender-
specific programs with a new approach tailored to the unique issues adolescent
girls face.

The approach outlined in this book is consistent with the trend away from
remediation of single problems and toward promoting positive development.
Several researchers (e.g., Elliott, 1993; Millstein, Petersen, & Nightingale,
1993) have attempted to move away from interventions for single problems like
substance abuse, suicide, and adolescent pregnancy, and instead suggest interventions that focus more generally on positive adolescent development and
health. These efforts have grown out of the understanding that specific
problem behaviors can be better understood as a constellation of interrelated

problems. Resisting peer pressure, for example, is a skill young people need to acquire to confront substance use, avoid pregnancy, and maintain friendships.

Protective Factors and Risk Reduction: The Best of Both Worlds

Most preventive interventions focus on reducing risk factors, increasing protective factors, or some combination of both. Risk factors are variables that can be identified and are associated with increased risk. Protective factors emphasize personal and social competence leading to adaptive outcomes such as coping skills. The Go Grrrls program attempts to reduce risk factors and promote protective factors. Because it is a primary prevention program intended to be of value to all early-adolescent girls, the emphasis on prevention is broad. Risk factors such as negative body image are targeted and addressed but protective factors such as coping skills and problem solving are also included in the program.

Kazdin (1993, p. 136) argues that "large-scale universal programs for young adolescents in the schools are . . . important to promote positive social competence and resistance to internal and peer pressures that might lead to at-risk behavior (e.g., unprotected sex, experimentation with hard drugs, use of alcohol while driving)." It is increasingly recognized that a range of interventions is necessary to respond to the needs of adolescents. More targeted interventions are required to respond to specific problem areas; however, preventive interventions are often the gateway for young people to access those targeted or treatment-focused interventions.

The Go Grrrls program can be an important component in the integration of primary prevention and treatment efforts. Depression, for example, is a common concern among many adolescent females. While Go Grrrls addresses depression and has been shown to reduce levels of depressed mood (LeCroy & Daley, 2000), our program may not be sufficient for the higher-risk cases. However, it can teach basic skills and refer girls who need more help to programs aimed at high-risk groups. As Petersen and colleagues (1993) point out, prevention and intervention efforts could be coordinated by addressing common aspects of cognitive functioning, skills for coping with stress, and strategies to address relational problems that are often at the center of dysfunctional cognitive processing. These themes could be addressed in primary prevention, secondary prevention, and treatment programs to contribute to the development of a core set of competencies. In this framework, the groundwork for such competencies would be established by the primary prevention program. The Go Grrrls program can serve as a beginning point for the establishment of many critical competencies and skills that can be built upon in later programs as girls transition to adulthood.

Developmental Tasks of Early-Adolescent Girls

Girls' transition to adulthood now seems to be more challenging than ever. Havighurst's (1953) notion of developmental tasks is a useful organizational framework for Go Grrrls and for understanding the challenges girls face. A developmental task is one that "arises at or about a certain period in the life of an individual, successful achievement of which leads to . . . happiness and to success with later tasks, while failure leads to unhappiness in the individual, disapproval by the society, and difficulty with later tasks" (p. 2). This focus on tasks stresses the competencies and abilities that contribute to successful adaptation to and mastery over demands placed on individuals in the environment. Healthy development for early-adolescent girls is defined according to these tasks, which include physical, social, emotional, and self-development factors. Development is conceptualized as a process in which young people attempt to learn to adapt to the necessary tasks placed on them by the social environment. Havighurst believed that individuals go through a sensitive period when they are most ready to learn new competencies, and he referred to these sensitive periods as "teachable moments."

The Go Grrrls Curriculum

Our framework conceptualizes tasks somewhat differently than Havighurst in order to reflect new information and research about adolescence and to acknowledge gender specificity. The Go Grrrls program is built around tasks that are considered critical for the healthy psychosocial development of early-adolescent girls in contemporary society. As tasks are mastered, new competencies are acquired and individuals can engage in more complex social relationships. A successful prevention program for girls must emphasize competencies that help participants learn what they need to know to successfully meet the demands being placed on them. This is why we believe a broad-based prevention program must be gender specific—there are unique tasks that early-adolescent girls need to master in order to transition successfully to adulthood. The following list presents the developmental tasks we have identified for early-adolescent girls. Each of these categories constitutes a curriculum section in the Go Grrrls program.

1. Achieve a competent gender-role identification
2. Establish an acceptable body image

3. Develop a positive self-image
4. Develop satisfactory peer relationships
5. Establish independence through responsible decision making
6. Understand sexuality
7. Learn to obtain help and find access to resources
8. Plan for the future

Gender-role identification

Early adolescence is a time for developing one's gender-role identity. This task is particularly critical in today's society, where social forces exert a powerful and early influence on how individuals view their gender identity. In early adolescence, girls experience dramatic physical and social changes and must reconcile their gender role and identity (Belansky & Clements, 1992). The widely accepted "gender intensification theory" suggests that as girls and boys reach puberty they experience an intensification in gender-related expectations. The differences between girls and boys become more pronounced because of increased socialization pressures to conform to traditional masculine and feminine roles during puberty (Lynch, 1991). At the onset of puberty, girls sense others' expectations that they should behave in an increasingly "feminine" way. Research studies (Galambos, et al., 1985) have found that during early adolescence, boys and girls begin to approve of gender-based differences.

It is also during early adolescence that girls become acutely aware of how they appear to others. This concern often directs their attention more intensely to images and gender stereotypes portrayed in the media. The messages adolescent girls receive from the mass media have a significant influence on their gender development (Condry, 1989). Pipher (1994) describes how girls experience a conflict between their autonomous selves and their "need" to be feminine. Studies have found that early adolescence is a period of heightened sensitivity to television messages about gender roles (Huston & Alvarez, 1990). Young adolescent girls need to understand how to cope with life as a girl in today's society. In the first two Go Grrrls sessions, leaders promote awareness of the profusion of negative images of women and girls that abound in popular media. Girls are given the skills and confidence to challenge cultural stereotypes. Group activities for this session include creating a collage culled from popular teen magazines and evaluating lyrics from hit songs.

Establishing an acceptable body image

Adolescent girls are likely to develop a negative body image, which tends to be related to low self-esteem and depression. Relentless media images of gaunt models bombard girls, who are experiencing a developmentally natural accumulation of fat, with an unattainable beauty standard. Early-maturing girls are at very high risk for tripping over the developmental task of establishing an acceptable body image, but all girls are exposed to some risk in this area. It is important to help girls confront the unrealistic beauty standards set for them by society and to help them redefine beauty as a combination of unique physical and character traits that they alone possess. In the curriculum relating to this topic, girls embark on a series of image-boosting activities. In one such activity, girls are asked to make a list of five things they like about themselves and to share some of these items aloud in the group. Next, girls work in pairs, tracing one another's body outline on cloth. They decorate these self-images and write some of their positive qualities (physical, character traits, skills and abilities, etc.) onto the cloth. Discussion then centers on the fact that each girl has a unique set of strengths.

Developing a positive self-image

Another critical developmental task for early-adolescent girls is to achieve a positive self-image in response to the many biological, psychological, and social changes they are confronting. Adolescent girls need to develop acceptance of the self as a stable person of worth (Simmons & Blyth, 1987). But many girls set themselves up for failure by aspiring to unattainable goals and self-criticism. While it seems to be culturally acceptable for girls to put themselves down, many girls believe that if they speak highly of themselves they will be seen as "stuck up." Go Grrrls teaches girls how to recognize the signs of self-abasement, how negative self-statements can lead to a "downward spiral" of emotion, and how to encourage themselves to do their best and achieve an "upward spiral" of self-acceptance. Girls play a game to practice identifying positive and negative self-statements and learn how to boost their own self-confidence.

Developing satisfactory peer relationships

Peer relations are also critical in the developing adolescent. Newman and Newman (1997) identify membership in the peer group as the central process that must be successfully achieved for early adolescents. Within peer relationships, adolescents develop a group identity that emphasizes membership and connection with other peers. Early adolescents launch a search for group membership with the expectation that they can learn more clearly who they are and with whom they belong (Newman & Newman, 1997). Adolescents who do not develop positive peer relationships are at greater risk for developing problems like delinquency, substance abuse, and depression (Simmons, Conger, & Wu, 1992).

Few discussions of adolescent problems take place without consideration of peer pressure and conformity. We know that early adolescence is the time when the greatest degree of conformity and susceptibility to peer pressure occurs (Leventhan, 1994). Even with good peer relationships and friendships young people must learn to confront peer pressure as their exposure to social problems increases. The Go Grrrls curriculum helps girls identify desirable qualities in a friend and teaches them basic social skills (e.g., how to start and end conversations) that will facilitate the process of connecting with peers. Girls participate in role-plays, play a specially created board game, and create a "friendship toolbox" to help them fix problems that arise in friendships.

Establishing independence through responsible decision making

In early adolescence, girls come to a critical juncture where they experience increased interest in relationships and intimacy but begin to recognize that society undervalues the type of qualities that allow intimacy to flourish (Brown & Gilligan, 1992). In American culture, assertiveness and independence are valued above cooperation, for example. It is important to help girls appreciate the relationship skills they possess, but it is also necessary to help them develop assertiveness and problem solving skills so that they can speak up for themselves in a culture that is all too willing to relegate them to silence. Go Grrrls leaders teach girls a five-step problem-solving model and help them work through real life problem scenarios to ensure that they grasp the process. Assertiveness training in the Go Grrrls curriculum includes a series of role-plays designed to give girls practice and confidence in speaking for themselves.

Understanding sexuality

The physical and social changes girls undergo during early adolescence are accompanied by a burgeoning curiosity about sex and sexuality. While girls are exposed to media messages that encourage them to acquire a highly sexualized appearance, they are also met with many adults' reluctance to discuss sex in a forthright manner. Statistics on teen pregnancy and sexually transmitted diseases testify to our national failure to adequately inform and instruct young people about their bodies and their decisions about sexual behavior. Girls need to be taught that they have the right to develop as healthy sexual beings. They must also learn to understand that they have the right to set sexual limits for themselves that are respected by partners. Go Grrrls combines elements of understanding gender-role stereotyping, establishing a positive body-image, and learning problem solving and assertiveness skills to help girls develop an understanding of their own sexuality. Go Grrrls leaders review the "basics" of reproductive physiology so that girls have a reasonable understanding of their own bodies and the mechanics of intercourse. Sexual myths are dispelled and questions are answered. Group leaders teach girls that they have the right to refuse unwanted sexual advances and give them practice in refusal skills. Girls learn the relationship between substance use and unwanted sexual activity, and facts about sexually transmitted diseases are taught. Finally, girls who already are sexually active, or who plan to be in the near future, are given referrals to qualified sources for additional information on birth control methods and supplies.

Learning to obtain help and find access to resources

Our program is designed to help girls understand and cope with the society they live in. But it is important to note that we are not stating that girls must change because they are to blame for this toxic environment. The message is that girls are not responsible for the society they live in but they can develop solutions to address the problems they are likely to confront. Along those same lines, it is important to teach girls that not every problem they encounter can be solved using a five-step process. Sometimes it is absolutely essential to reach out for help. We teach girls that seeking help is not an admission of defeat but rather a valuable skill. We help girls understand some of the issues with which they may need outside help (e.g., addictions, domestic violence, depression) and show them where and how to seek help. Girls create a personal resource "yellow pages" to use when serious problems arise.

Planning for the future

During early adolescence young people begin to adopt a more serious attitude about plans for the future. Whether adolescents begin to think about their educational future and attend college or not has implications for future career opportunities (Klaczynski & Reese, 1991). Sadly, during their early-adolescent years, many young girls experience a "crisis in confidence" that can seriously undermine their chances for educational and career success later in life. Lack of support for girls' educational attainment, particularly in math and science, can restrict their access to technological careers. Pressures to identify less as a competent, intelligent being and more as a sexualized, fashion-conscious follower can sidetrack girls from developing their full potential. Girls need encouragement in reaching their goals and practical instruction about how to plan for long-term success. In the Go Grrrls program, girls are encouraged to forge goals in the realms of education, career, and adventure. They learn to set long-term goals and short-term objectives to achieve those dreams.

Chapter 2

Being a Girl in Today's Society: The Media is the Message

In American society, wimmin are novelties. Objects. A body part. Something to use for convenience. Wimmin need to learn that power is not given, we have to take it. We need to realize that we don't have to stand around and be treated like this. Don't let anyone control you or dictate your life to you. Wimmin's bodies are sold everyday—whether we realize it or not. On tv, in magazines, in movies, on billboards—open your eyes—it's everywhere you look. We need to break free of our own stereotypes. No one can save you from your oppression except yourself. GIRLS UNITE!

—Misty, from *Girl Power: Young Women Speak Out*
by Hillary Carp (1995, p. 58)

It's about standing up for our rights and about knowing we have them. We are taught to be passive, to look the other way, and boys will be boys, to cross our legs, to desire a family, to play with dolls, to open our legs, to shut our legs, to smile as we die inside (so as not to upset anyone). We are taught to value makeup and diets and fashion models and high heel shoes, thats what grrrls grow up to feel, think, be, understand.

—Dawn, 19-year-old, from the zine *Function*
cited in Carp (1995, p. 34)

Girl babies wear pink. Boy babies wear blue. Girls are cooperative, sensitive, and patient while boys are boisterous, physically active, and competitive. These statements reflect gender-role stereotypes common to our culture. A gender role is a set of expectations about how females or males should think, act, and feel. By early adolescence, children have already acquired vast amounts of information about their expected gender roles through, among other

9

sources, language, toys, television, peers, and parents (Richmond-Abbott, 1992).

There is abundant evidence to suggest that many gender-role traits and behaviors are mediated by cultural dictates. While it is important to acknowledge that *both* girls and boys are limited by acceptance of stereotypical feminine and masculine roles, we will specifically be discussing gender-role messages and stereotypes that appear to negatively affect the healthy development of early-adolescent girls. And because stereotypical male traits have tended to be more valued in our society, girls appear to be at a particular disadvantage in the gender difference debate. Discussion of gender-role differences does not presuppose that there are no biological sexual differences. We are not attempting to weigh the potential biological versus cultural influences on gender perceptions, but we do assume that societal influence is a strong factor in the development of sex-role differences.

No one has summarized what being a girl in today's society is like better than Mary Pipher in her book *Reviving Ophelia: Saving the Selves of Adolescent Girls*. This *New York Times* bestseller struck a deep chord within our society about what life is like for many teenage girls. An often-quoted phrase summarizes the issues: "Today's girls come of age in a dangerous, sexualized, media-saturated culture" (p. 12). Girls, notes Pipher, are pressured to be sophisticated, which is defined by peer culture as rejecting parental values, smoking, using chemicals, and being sexually active. Pipher believes that there are new pressures on today's young girls that parents and other adults don't understand. It is not so much that girls have changed but that the world around them has changed. She points to the loss of family and community relationships, the media barrage, and the easy access to cigarettes, drugs, and guns, all of which have contributed to making contemporary society a dangerous place for adolescent girls.

A key thesis in Pipher's book is that girls ultimately deny their true selves and assume false selves. The pressure that splits the girls' true and false selves comes from the culture. During adolescence, girls experience social pressure to set aside their true selves and display only a small part of who they really are. Nancy Friday remembers this process in her book, *Our Looks, Our Lives*:

> I'd buried and mourned my eleven-year-old self, the wall walker, and had become an ardent beauty student. From now on I would ape my beautiful friends, smile The Group smile, walk The Group walk, and, what with hanging my head and bending my knees, approximate as best I could The Group look. But I was very, very angry; not then, not consciously, but I can recognize it now. How could I not be, me and every other girl who doesn't fit the mold? (pp. 290–291)

The mold that society has constructed to shape girls' identities can be damaging to their emerging selves. The cultural reality of growing up as a girl carries significant burdens not present for boys. While boys are certainly influenced by gender stereotyping, the "male mold" seems to be far less constricting. Indeed, to be a boy is to *not* be a girl. A serious insult to an adolescent boy is to be called a "girl." The reverse is not true. To call a girl a "boy" suggests that she is tough, assertive, and aggressive, but the epithet is not hurled as a calumnious insult. There are many inconsistencies and contradictions for adolescent girls that lead to greater stress and fewer coping resources.

Being a girl in today's society may lead to the development of a negative sex-role self-image. Past research studies found that girls regard their own sex role with less favor than males do. Indeed, studies found that females are more likely to wish they had been born a member of the opposite sex, to feel it is better to be a male than a female, and to denigrate the characteristics that stereotype their own gender (Wylie, 1979). Surprisingly, these findings have been replicated over time despite expectations that progress has been made in obtaining equality between the sexes. Simmons and Blyth (1987) summarize their findings regarding adolescent gender roles this way:

> Girls rate themselves and their sex less highly than do boys; girls value appearance and same-sex popularity more; boys are allowed earlier independence and are expected by parents to act in older ways; girls view a job as a temporary activity to be halted when they have young children; boys conform less to adult prescriptions related to school. (p. 135)

Clearly, any effort to help girls develop a more positive attitude about being a girl will be beneficial. Efforts toward influencing a girl's self-image must take into consideration the strong gender messages girls receive from society.

Building a Girl: Social Construction

Researchers explain the difficulties that adolescent girls face in society as being part of the social organization of adolescence and gender, pointed out by Chodorow in her classic book, *The Reproduction of Mothering* (1978). Girlhood has been socially constructed in a manner that allows for different treatment of girls and boys. In Western society, feminine behavior is perceived as being expressive, nurturing, and emotional, while masculinity is perceived as being instrumental, competitive, and rational (Chodorow, 1978). A major aspect of this theory is that society defines gender differences based on women's traditional responsibilities in nurturing and raising families. Chodorow suggests that women have developed the capacity for intimacy and strong relationships because generations of women have been responsible for child rearing and nurturing, while men have developed the capacity for independence and instrumentality. The female need for connection leads women to emphasize husband, children, and close friendships. The perception of women as "nurturers" leads to social inequity for women because such "feminine traits" are considered less valuable or even inferior to alleged "masculine traits."

In early adolescence the gender-role intensification that takes place creates additional stress on girls. This is when gender inequity begins to accelerate. The differences between boys and girls become more pronounced—occupational aspirations for girls contract into a more narrow range of traditionally female-dominated occupations, girls value popularity more than boys do, and girls begin to develop expressive values while boys develop instrumental values. Erikson's (1950) developmental theory suggested that identity formation is more difficult for adolescent girls because the future roles to which they aspire are devalued by boys and the culture. In our society girls have greater difficulty coping with this particular life transition than boys in part because the major roles girls are prepared for in adolescence are less valued than the roles boys are groomed to fill (Bush & Simmons, 1988). Although, in Western society, many occupational opportunities have increased for women, there are striking disparities in some careers. Still, only ten to twenty years ago, women did not initiate dates, rarely ran for public office, and few were responsible for major corporations. The feminist movement has made great gains in reducing sexist behavior; however, many people believed such gains would be realized more rapidly.

Gender Role and Self-Concept

Developmental theorists have posited that gender-role differences increase at puberty due to adolescents' emerging sexuality and search for identity (Hill & Lynch, 1983; Richmond-Abbott, 1992). As females experience the physical and social changes that accompany adolescence they must formulate a new definition of their gender role. As noted in chapter 1, the gender intensification theory suggests that at the onset of puberty girls experience an intensification of gender-related expectations. Puberty appears to signal others that the female is approaching adulthood and needs to act in more stereotypical ways. Some studies have demonstrated that gender-role attitudes become more stereotypical as children grow older (Hill & Lynch, 1983; Schnelmann, 1987) but begin to shift back in the late teenage years (Fabes & Laner, 1986). The effect of gender-role attitudes on adolescents has been studied in several realms. The first realm to be considered here is that of general self-concept, including self-esteem and self-efficacy.

Lerner, Sorell, and Brackney (1981) believed that because masculine traits and behaviors are more highly regarded than feminine traits in American culture, adolescents who place greater value on their masculine traits would rate higher in self-esteem. Several studies support this hypothesis. Researchers have found that adolescents classified as masculine or androgynous scored higher on measures of self-esteem than those classified as feminine or undifferentiated (being low on masculine and low on feminine traits) (Lamke, 1982; Mullis & McKinley, 1989). In a study examining the relationship between gender-role orientation and self-esteem in 12- to 15-year-old adolescents, Lamke (1982) found that masculinity significantly predicted self-esteem, particularly in early-adolescent females. Mullis and McKinley's (1989) results also demonstrated that girls with masculine and androgynous gender-role orientations scored higher on measures of self-esteem, with junior high girls showing the strongest correlation between masculinity and high self-esteem.

In another study (Rose & Montemayor, 1994) female and male students from sixth to twelfth grade were given tests measuring gender-role orientation and self-competency. Results indicated that students who endorsed an androgynous gender orientation scored highest on all measures of self-competency. For girls, high endorsements of masculinity were significantly correlated with perceived global self-worth, romantic appeal, and close friendship, social, and scholastic competency. Femininity was not significantly correlated with any of the scales.

One potential explanation for the apparent advantage of possessing a masculine or androgynous self-concept suggests that traditionally "masculine" characteristics include instrumental qualities such as independence, assertiveness, and ambition—all qualities that would conceivably boost feelings of self-competency (Rose & Montemayor, 1994). The Go Grrrls program places major emphasis on the development of independence, assertiveness, and goal setting (related to ambition) in the session entitled "Establishing Independence." Teaching these skills is a necessary and empowering component of the program. In fact, much of the value in discussing the role girls play in society is to focus efforts toward their own sense of empowerment, which can be applied to psychological functioning and has implications for correcting girls' position in society. Often, powerlessness is seen as a "state of mind" and is associated with learned helplessness, where one's control of situations is perceived as external rather than internal. Empowerment is emphasized because it is linked to beliefs of self-efficacy and competency. Self-efficacy is characteristic of individuals who are more persistent, less depressed and anxious, more skillful, and generally more successful (Bandura, 1991). One way to empower girls is to teach them how to develop instrumental skills such as assertiveness, independence, and goal setting.

We must be particularly careful, though, not to devalue the traditionally "feminine" characteristics of cooperation, communication, sharing, and nurturing. Being an authentic self is a key theme in Gilligan's work on adolescent girls (Brown & Gilligan, 1990; Gilligan, 1982). According to Gilligan, girls come to a critical juncture in their development, especially in early adolescence. Part of the message girls begin to hear from the culture is that intimacy is not important in a male-dominated society. This leads to a fundamental conflict: girls can be selfish and pursue independence and self-sufficiency or they can be selfless and pursue caring and responsiveness to others. The result is that girls may end up "silencing" their "different voice."

Some researchers believe the self-doubt girls experience is the determining factor in explaining their high rates of depression and eating disorders. In response to Gilligan's theory, some critics have noted that her view may reinforce stereotypes of females as nurturing and sacrificing. However, consensus exists that we need to create more opportunities for girls to reach higher levels of achievement and self-determination. In the Go Grrrls program, efforts are made to reinforce the importance of skills related to both "nurturing" and "instrumental" attributes. But if girls are to truly break free of the stereotypes that constrain their growth and development, they need more than these tools. Girls need to develop the ability to think critically about the stereotypical messages they receive. One of the main sources of these stereotypical messages is the media.

Image for Sale

In order to help girls overcome the barriers of gender-role stereotypes, we must also help them identify factors that contribute to the stereotype of females as passive and dependent. Media influences exert an ever-increasing influence on the way young women and men view their lives. From the early time spent in front of the television, to exposure to magazines and novels, billboards and advertisements, and the Internet, we are all bombarded with images and sound bites that prompt us to live our lives in a particular way.

Gender-role socialization can be directly linked to influences from the media, beginning with television (Luecke-Aleska et al., 1995). Developmentally, early adolescents have highly idealized thoughts and this may lead to strong identification with television personalities. Television has traditionally presented images of boys and girls in highly stereotypical ways. Turn on the TV during afternoon soaps or prime time and you'll find women who are largely submissive, passive, and emotional. Men, on the other hand, are portrayed as assertive, competent, and independent. Studies have confirmed the influence of television on formation of gender-role ideas. One such study (Morgan, 1987) found that children who watched the most television had the most traditional gender-role development.

Commercials also contribute to the construction of gender roles (Bretl & Cantor, 1988). In many ads, women appear deeply concerned about trivial matters: *Are these sheets as white as I can get them? Are there spots on the glasses when I take them from the dishwasher?* Even in commercials, men are seen in more professional roles than women (Geiss et al., 1984; Lovdal, 1989).

The impact of advertising has been referred to as unintentionally imposing a "sense of inadequacy" on women (Pollay, 1986). Studies (Downs & Harrison, 1985; Martin & Gentry, 1997; Myers & Biocca, 1992) have found that advertising and the mass media contribute to a preoccupation with physical attractiveness. Furthermore, girls compare their bodies and physical attractiveness with those of the models in the ads (Martin & Kennedy, 1993, 1994). Many early-adolescent girls even develop a strong desire to be a model (Martin & Kennedy, 1994). From a social-comparison theoretical perspective, girls compare themselves with the advertised models and their self-perceptions and self-esteem are subsequently affected. The impact can be particularly devastating in early adolescence, when the media calls for women who are beautiful and thin, just when girls are experiencing a developmental, pubertal fat spurt.

Because they are so exposed to media influences, girls need to be equipped with "advertising discounting" skills. A series of studies (Cash, Cash, & Butters, 1983; Stice & Shaw, 1994; Thornton & Moore, 1993) found negative effects on self-perception when women were exposed to ads or photographs with highly attractive females. Another study found self-perception and self-esteem were unaffected when girls discounted the beauty of models (Martin & Gentry, 1997). Hence, a critical skill for girls in today's society is learning how to discount advertising images.

Television shows and advertisements are clearly not the only media influence on youth. Early-adolescent girls, who have already absorbed years of stereotypical messages from television, are then exposed to even more stereotypical content and advertising in teen magazines. Given their popularity and distribution, it is important to consider what these magazines communicate to girls about the concept of being a girl. The majority of popular magazines aimed at the teen girl audience are focused on beauty and fashion topics, and the accompanying advertisements (which often comprise nearly 50% of the publications) further support the appearance-oriented content. Using a sample of three years of *Seventeen*, Pierce (1990, 1993) found most of the articles were about fashion, beauty, food, decorating, and relationships with the opposite sex. Evans and associates (1991) analyzed ten issues each of three major magazines (*Seventeen, Young Miss,* and *Sassy*) and found that over one third of their content focused on fashion, while even so-called feature articles overwhelmingly dealt with fashion and beauty issues. Even the fiction content in these magazines presented girls in largely stereotypical roles. In a series of qualitative interviews with 48 adolescent girls in the 13 to 17 age range, Currie (1997) explored the way readers of fashion magazines interpreted content and advertising. Jasmine, a 15-year-old reader, made the following comments:

> *They (magazines) teach you a lot of things, like what you should do, what you should think. Sometimes they're really helpful—like your Mom dies, right? They might have advice on how to struggle through this. Like problems and things like that. And maybe makeover. Like you know, "how to do a makeover." I mean you can just look at those for suggestions.* (p. 464)

Unfortunately, Jasmine is far more likely to find articles about makeovers than articles about how to deal with grief and loss. Pierce (1993) summarizes the overall message from these magazines, that a "girl learns that her job is to look good, find a boyfriend, and take care of home and hearth" (p. 61).

Recently, an effort to reject teen magazines has been embraced by nontraditional girls with the creation of magazines by and for teenage girls or young women. These small, amateur publications, referred to as "zines" with material provided by "grrrls," are created out of interest and passion and without regard for profit (Green & Taormino, 1997). In addition to the amateur zines, some alternatives to *Sassy* and *Seventeen* have recently been established. *New Moon*, a mainstream alternative magazine for 8- to 14-year-old girls, presents material for positive and healthy living without any of the gender stereotypical advertising. Unfortunately, the distribution rate of the larger, commercial magazines far exceeds these small publications for now.

Messages in popular music contribute further to the message that girls are to be valued as physical and sexual commodities. According to the *Journal of the American Medical Association*, the average teenager listens to 10,500 hours of rock music between the 7th and 12th grades—slightly fewer hours than they spend in school (Mann, 1994). Rock and rap music have been mentioned frequently as culprits in the media attack on the popular image of girls and women. Mann (1994) states that lyrics of some songs are "rife with sexual sadism" and provides the following examples:

> "Body Dismemberment," by Rigor Mortis, which Capitol Records brought out in 1989, describes a scene in which a woman—described merely as "bitch"—is dismembered by an axe-wielding man as she reaches sexual climax. He wants to know why she made him do this and concludes by calling her a "stupid fuck" . . . at the same time, the music dwells on the idea that women are constantly available for sex and that

they just can't get enough oral sex. The title of the 2 Live Crew song tells the story: "Dick Almighty." The lyrics are puerile penis worship for the truly insecure. (p. 256)

Not all rock and rap music lyrics are negative, nor should those two genres be singled out as the only popular music categories in which gender-role stereotypes can be transmitted. The Go Grrrls curriculum encourages girls to listen critically to one rap song (with far less offensive lyrics than those quoted above) and one country song to extract gender-role stereotypes in lyrics. One participant's comments follow:

> *Some stuff that we thought they are saying is, like, you've gotta be sexy . . . and you're supposed to be easy, but then you're bad, like a "hoochie mama" if you do stuff. Then you're supposed to take care of your house and your husband and kids . . . but you got to look good and put your makeup on while you do.* (personal communication, 1999)

Perhaps nowhere is stereotypical programming more evident and more damaging to adolescent girls than in music videos and on MTV. Popular shows like "Beavis and Butthead" and "Wayne and Garth" are not only stereotypical but also very male-oriented (Santrock, 1996). Furthermore, a random viewing of music videos is likely to show females dressed provocatively—twice as often as in prime-time programming (Sherman, 1986). Jhally (1990) aptly describes MTV as a teenage boy's dreamworld comprised of beautiful and aroused women who outnumber men, who seek out or even assault men to have sex, and who always mean yes even when they say no.

Girls assimilate gender-role messages from media sources. Obviously, parents and other concerned adults can limit exposure to some of the most blatantly offensive messages. But many of these messages may be more insidious, and even the most concerned and involved parent cannot prevent a child from hearing all of the myriad messages that reinforce stereotyped notions about girls and women. Instead, it is essential to equip adolescent girls with the knowledge that these negative stereotypes do exist, to encourage them to carefully analyze the messages they receive, and to teach them ways to think critically and "talk back" to depictions of their gender that they find unrealistic and offensive.

Lean on Me: Girls and Support

In her book *Slut: Growing Up Female With a Bad Reputation* (1999), Leora Tanenbaum recommends girls' groups as one means of fighting the sexual double standard girls must endure. In this way girls can change the way they relate to one another. As she describes it, "girl groups are not intended to shut out boys; they are simply meant as a forum for girls to discuss the issues that affect them—everything from slut-bashing to how they feel about the *Sports Illustrated* swimsuit issue" (p. 250). The purpose of such groups is described by a member:

> *I realized that I'm not the only girl who's had problems. I learned through the group that some others were called bitches, too. Next year we're going to talk about body image and sexism and sexual harassment. We're going to have Awareness Days where we put up posters about these issues. I hope to make some friends through the group.* (Tanenbaum, 1999, p. 250)

Making friends through the group can truly help girls to identify and challenge gender-role stereotypes. Enhancing relationships between people helps maximize the potential of individuals' socialization (Bronfenbrenner, 1977). By bringing girls together in a mutual aid group they can benefit from the social support that becomes part of the process. In fact, "received support" is associated with the need for support (Coyne, Ellard, & Smith, 1990). In other words, girls are more likely to offer support when they believe others are in need of it.

A rallying point for girls is often the recognition that they have important rights in society. Such rights are aptly described in the Girls' Bill of Rights (Girls Incorporated, 2000):

> Girls have the right to be themselves and to resist gender stereotypes.
> Girls have the right to express themselves with originality and enthusiasm.
> Girls have the right to take risks, to strive freely, and to take pride in success.
> Girls have the right to accept and appreciate their bodies.
> Girls have the right to have confidence in themselves and to be safe in the world.
> Girls have the right to prepare for interesting work and economic independence.

The Go Grrrls program is designed to help girls take advantage of these rights as they learn skills to change the way they interact in the world. Also, the group setting is an ideal place for this learning, given the importance of peers in adolescent development.

Developmentalists point out that support from friends increases dramatically from middle childhood to adolescence. In a complex longitudinal study using network analysis, Garbarino and colleagues (1978) documented how early adolescents create a social world that is largely composed of peers. However, this does not displace the importance of the family (Youniss, 1980). Still, peers can be critical in addressing adolescents' psychosocial needs. Peers, for example, provide needed support for developing identities, offsetting feelings of loneliness, boosting self-esteem, and providing a sense of belonging and group identity (Gottlieb, 1991). This, coupled with the early adolescent's growing capacity for perspective taking and intimacy, gives peers an important function in the healthy development of adolescents.

There are significant gender differences in intimacy, suggesting peer support as a unique protective factor for girls. Studies suggest that girls seek more help and support from peers than boys do (Belle, 1988). Given girls' predilection and developmental readiness for peer helping, this is a natural period of time to build social support networks by organizing girls' groups. Bringing individuals together in groups also helps counteract some of the isolation commonly ascribed to early adolescents.

Working together to create a vision about how to help one another in a group is a powerful experience. The girls and those they help in the group become more positive and the group culture can change. Their own thoughts and behaviors become more responsible and the experience can be a basis for developing and maintaining self-respect and meriting the respect of others. Girls' groups allow girls to learn that they are not alone in their efforts to confront society's pressure to pursue outward beauty. They are not alone in their efforts to raise their self-esteem and to desire and construct relationships that promote growth. They discover that other girls have shared experiences of harassment and the like. Over time, they even learn that what appears to be "normal" may in fact be oppressive. With encouragement, they learn that together they can work toward long-term goals to create better conditions for girls in today's society.

Chapter 3

Girls and Body Image: A Lifelong Struggle

I was 13 when I first sat in a brown padded chair in a dimly lit office while a psychologist with domino-sized sideburns said softly, "Wouldn't you like to be thin, Laurie? You'd be a pretty girl you know."

—From *Hopes, Fears and the Architecture of Adolescence* by Fraser (1997, p. 46)

i used to have fantasies about taking a razor and shaving off my face and when it grew back it would be perfect. no flaws, no points of interest whatsoever. i know i'm stepping out of line here. this is secret, private stuff. shame shame shame. what a pitiful way to live, not having the ability to see beauty in myself. i'm trying. i really am. i want to stop with all these standards of beauty anyway and i know i need to start with my own reflection. it just hurts though to never like what you see when you look at yourself. that's all.

—Ericka, 18-year-old, from *Girl Power,* p. 52

Body mania, the diet trap, unhappy bodies—whatever the name, the phenomena is sweeping America as the fear of fatness becomes an everyday reality for women and girls in the 21st century. One need only stand in any grocery store checkout line to be assaulted by headlines crowding the covers of women's magazines: "How to Get Thin and Stay Thin," "The 90-Day Diet," "What Type of Women's Body Most Men Like," "Summer Slim Down Strategies," and the list goes on. In today's media-saturated culture one message stands out: Thinness equals beauty. And so begins a lifelong battle that American women wage against their bodies. Striegel-Moore and colleagues (1986, p. 247) sum up the dilemma: "The more a woman believes that 'what is fat is bad, what is thin is beautiful, and what is beautiful is good' the more she will work toward thinness and be distressed about fatness."

Thompson (1990) suggests that the body-image disturbances so prevalent today are rooted in sociocultural understandings of behavior. This theory postulates that societal standards for beauty influence women's obsessive desire for thinness. As Silberstein and colleagues (1987, p. 92) claim: "From birth, females are indoctrinated with the message that they should be pretty—which in this sociohistorical moment means being thin." Striegel-Moore and Cachelin (1999, p. 86) note that "the combination of the cultural prescript for girls to care about others' opinions and to define themselves through their physical appearance, and the particular beauty ideal of extreme thinness, creates a powerful motivational force for girls to pursue thinness."

Not surprisingly, when asked to describe their physical forms, males identify themselves as being of normal weight or thin, while females are more likely to identify themselves as heavy or of normal weight (Desmond et al., 1986). Indeed, most girls perceive themselves as overweight even when their weight falls within "normal" standards. In one study (Fisher et al., 1991) 80% of high school girls felt they were above the weight at which they would be happiest. Studies also find a substantial percentage of women who are classified as thin but are still dieting.

What these studies tell us is that normal, healthy girls often perceive themselves as overweight and thus develop negative body images. Such concern with body image has led to an epidemic of dieting among early-adolescent girls. Recent surveys have estimated that as many as 80% of early-adolescent girls are dieting at any given time (Berg, 1992).

Feingold (1990) conducted a meta-analysis of 222 studies and found that compared to men, the number of women who have a poor body image has risen drastically since the 1970s. For three decades women have been increasingly preoccupied by how they look (Garner, 1997) and women's body preferences have moved toward a thinner and thinner ideal. The cultural icons for feminine beauty demonstrate this: today's Miss America contestants weigh less than ever before. And examination of any recent Playboy centerfold model quickly reveals that the stylish body of today is dramatically thinner than those in the days of Marilyn Monroe.

One body-image study (Cash, 1997) recently found that half of all Americans dislike their overall appearance compared to 36% in the 1980s and 19% in the 1970s. Another study found that a large majority (78%) of teenage women, ages 13 to 19 are dissatisfied with their weight (Eisele et al., 1986). Figure 3.1 on page 22 dramatically illustrates the results of a survey of women's dissatisfaction with their bodies from the years 1972, 1985, and 1997. The sizable increases in dissatisfaction from decade to decade reflect the increasingly thin body ideal that has emerged over time, as well as women's accelerat-

FIGURE 3.1
WOMEN'S DISSATISFACTION WITH THEIR BODIES
Adapted from Garner (1997)

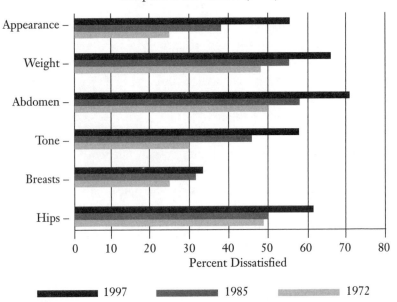

ing perception that they cannot achieve this cultural ideal. Notable increases in dissatisfaction are most apparent in the categories of women's appearance, weight, and abdomen. These results show that while a large percentage of women experienced dissatisfaction with their bodies in 1972, in 1997 a *majority* of women experienced body dissatisfaction. Evidence suggests that these increases in dissatisfaction can be traced to the influence of the media on women.

Thin is In: Mass Media and Body Image

One likely culprit in the soaring rates of body dissatisfaction is the impact of magazines and television on women's self-image. How much influence does the media have in promoting women's dissatisfaction with their bodies? Mounting evidence suggests it has a lot. First, the trend of using increasingly emaciated-looking models to promote products is linked with the rise in women's body dissatisfaction over historical time. Recently *Vogue* magazine acknowledged the serious nature of the new gaunt, heroin-addicted look of the models. The look has become so extreme that it may have prompted a backlash against the advertising industry. Eating disorders—the most extreme expressions of body dissatisfaction—have also increased over a similar period. A recent survey found that 67% of women who are dissatisfied with their bodies report that very thin or muscular models "very often" or "always" make them feel insecure about their weight (Garner, 1997). These women also report that models displayed in magazines and on TV make them want to lose weight. One study (Anderson & DiDomenico, 1992) analyzed the number of articles on weight loss and body shape in 10 popular magazines that target either young men or women. Not surprisingly, the women's magazines contained over 10 times as many advertisements and articles on weight loss as the men's. These results parallel research that finds women have a stronger tendency to worry about their weight and suggest that media has a very direct impact on women's body dissatisfaction.

The media's construction of the ultra-thin ideal female figure negatively affects both females and males. One study (Furnham & Radley, 1989) examined perceptions of the ideal female and male body shape among 16-year-olds. Using sketches of naked males and females, salient body features such as thighs, shoulders, and stomach were displayed. The adolescents rated several sketches on sixteen bipolar indices such as "attractive-unattractive." The results document both sexes' bias toward the thin, "perfect" female body. Overall, female figures were perceived much more negatively than were male figures by both females and males. For example, female figures in the normal range were perceived negatively while male figures in the normal range had a greater latitude of acceptability.

Relentless media messages about the importance of "being attractive" and "having a perfect body" exert a powerful influence on young girls, who learn to equate attractiveness with popularity and success. During early adolescence, girls tend to look for guidelines that can shape their transformation to young women. This search for standards may be, in part, why girls are so vulnerable to the overwhelming cultural preference for thinness. For growing girls, weight control is the clearest avenue to the ultimate but illusory path toward "successful thinness." Any discussion of adolescent health must acknowledge these facts.

Negotiating New Curves

At puberty, girls become increasingly preoccupied with their bodies. They often spend a lot of time looking at and thinking about their bodies. Developmental psychologists consider acceptance of one's body a basic task of adolescence (Havighurst, 1972). During this critical time girls develop their own image of what their bodies are like. In general, girls are less happy with their bodies and have more negative body images than boys (Brooks-Gunn & Paikoff, 1993). Adolescents are more dissatisfied with their bodies during puberty than they are in later adolescence (Hamburg, 1974).

Normal, early-adolescent physical development plays a critical role in the struggle most young girls have with obtaining an acceptable body image. As young girls sexually mature they develop what is often referred to as a "fat spurt"—an accumulation of large amounts of fat in the subcutaneous tissue, which is indicated by increased skin-fold thickness (Young, Sipin, & Roe, 1968). This change in physical appearance is both normal and dramatic, adding an average of 11 kg or 24.25 lbs of weight in the form of body fat (Brooks-Gunn & Warren, 1985). Rather than understanding and accepting these physical changes as a part of normal development, the adolescent girl often becomes focused on the desire to be thin and may begin a lifetime struggle for weight control (Dornbusch et al., 1984). Brooks-Gunn and Reiter (1990, p. 45) state that "perhaps the most maladaptive response to pubertal growth involves the devaluation of the mature female body."

Penalty for Early Puberty

With respect to these physical changes, an important developmental consideration is whether girls mature early or late. Early maturers are more likely to develop eating problems and negative body images due, in part, to the fact that they are more likely to be heavier than average- or late-maturing peers (Attie & Brooks-Gunn, 1989; Brooks-Gunn, 1988). Early-maturing girls' bodies tend not to match society's image of the beautiful woman: thin, long-legged and fundamentally *prepubertal* (Faust, 1983). This coltish image is more consistent with late-maturing girls. Recent research has documented other difficulties that early-maturing girls face in addition to poor body image, including: poorer emotional health (Brooks-Gunn, 1988), depressive affect, and a smaller network of intimate friends (Brooks-Gunn & Reiter, 1990). The practical implications of these results suggest that practitioners may want to identify and target early-maturing girls for prevention and intervention efforts, although all girls will benefit from the type of activities described in this book.

Unfortunately, identification of early maturers is not a simple process. The assessment of pubertal timing is complicated and researchers have used a variety of methods including age at peak height velocity, body fat, hormones, age at menarche, skeletal age, and self-report (Graber, Petersen, & Brooks-Gunn, 1996). With the exception of self-report, most methods of assessment are not practical for practitioners. Petersen (1988) developed the Pubertal Development Scale (PDS), which is a pubertal status report obtained through an interview or questionnaire. Adolescents are instructed to rate their level of development on indicators from 1 (not begun) to 4 (development complete). This method of assessment has been found to be reliable and valid (Petersen, 1988).

Simmons and Blyth (1987) assessed girls as early developers if they had reached menarche by the seventh grade and late developers if they had not. This method of assessment is limited in that it does not differentiate stages of development. At the age a girl has reached menarche she can be defined as having reached an advanced level of pubertal development. While not perfect, this may be the simplest and most practical method of assessment.

Toward an Equal Opportunity Disorder: Body Image and Ethnic Considerations

While it has long been believed that race plays a major role in eating disorders and body-image problems, such differences may be overstated. Many people believe African American and Hispanic women experience less body-image dissatisfaction than Anglo women because the cultural body ideals include women of heavier weights. The specific protective factors often identified are: more family and cultural acceptance of a fuller body size, less emphasis on physical appearance, and less emphasis on weight (Root, 1989). However, a study by Striegel-Moore and Cachelin (1999) that included over 1,500 African American women found eating disorder rates and emotional issues concerning weight similar to those of Anglo women. Other studies (Levinson, Powell, & Steelman, 1986; Parker et al., 1995) have found significant differences between African American women and Anglo women, with Anglo women having a higher percentage of body dissatisfaction than African American women. Perhaps the more recent study reflects a shift in African American women toward preference for a thinner body ideal.

If non-Anglo cultural body ideals are truly protective factors for Hispanic women, then it stands to reason that the most acculturated members of that group would have the highest level of eating disorders. But a recent study of Mexican American adolescent girls found that acculturation levels were not related to anorexic or bulimic symptoms or body dissatisfaction. Sadly, the old notion that Anglo American values of beauty and thinness are impacting only Anglo girls may be giving way to a new cultural order of thinness that is spreading across ethnic groups.

Body Image and Psychosocial Problems

Several studies have documented the need to help girls and women with eating disorders learn acceptance of their bodies as a key component to treatment (Wilson, 1996). This is because developing a positive body image involves more than just addressing physical appearance and attractiveness—body image reflects one's overall feelings about identity and impacts day-to-day thoughts and interactions. Furnham and Greaves (1994) identify three primary components of women's body image: sexual attractiveness, weight concern, and physical condition. The different ways a woman perceives her body are integrally related to positive feelings about herself in general, and females who perceive themselves as overweight are more likely to have low self-esteem (Tiggemann, 1994).

One heartbreakingly commonplace experience for girls is to be teased about their appearance. Research studies by Thompson and others have found that there probably is a causal relationship between teasing and the development of a negative body image (Fabian & Thompson, 1989; Thompson et al., 1991). In a study of appearance teasing, Cash (1995) found that 72% of the women surveyed had experienced appearance-related teasing/criticism. Furthermore, most of the women reported that the teasing occurred during middle childhood to early adolescence. Facial characteristics and weight were the two most frequently noted areas of teasing.

Overall, negative body image can have serious psychological implications for girls. Many young girls develop the belief that there is nothing they can do to achieve the perfect body and therefore develop feelings of helplessness and hopelessness, with associated low self-esteem and depression (Furnham & Greaves, 1994). In general, dissatisfaction with body image has been found to be associated with higher levels of depression (Fabian & Thompson, 1989). Normal developmental changes in female physique and concomitant dissatisfaction with body image may partially explain the finding that postpubertal girls have a high prevalence of depression (Hodges & Siegel, 1985).

A few treatment programs have documented positive results for helping women become more accepting of their bodies. Rosen (1990) conducted a study with college women who were unhappy with their bodies and found that participants' dissatisfaction with their appearance dropped from a clinical range to a normal range after participating in the program. In our studies we found that early-adolescent girls who participated in the Go Grrrls curriculum showed significant improvement from pretest to posttest on ratings of their body image. They also showed a significant improvement when compared to a control group (LeCroy & Daley, 2000). However, the potential impact of such programs on the perceptions and feelings of young adolescent girls is only now being investigated. While treatment programs suggest that women can change their body image such changes do not come easily—as one woman describes:

> i am not a size 6, or 8 or 10 or 12. i am a size 14. i am 5'11" and i weigh 178 lbs. no matter how hard i try, i will never be super model skinny. (And i have tried.) Nor do i want to be. i have "big" thighs. i have stretchmarks. i have a big belly. and i am finally learning to like it. i am finally trying to accept myself. after all the pain, and the fat torment i finally don't care. i am beauti-

ful. beautiful to nobody's standards but my own. i will never do ads for victoria's secret. i bet her secret is that she can't wear her own designs without feeling gross. call me fat, whale, cow, whatever. i'll eat it up. because i don't count calories, and your words are zeros anyway. i'll wear hot pants, and you can deal with it. i did. (Carlip, 1995, p. 55)

From Malcontent to Malady:
Body Image and Eating Disorders

Sara F. describes the beginning of a life trajectory that for many girls involves major preoccupations with food, weight, and control:

There is something horribly, terribly wrong when so many girls suffer from eating disorders. I'm not talking about the clinically-diagnosed anorexics and bulimics—i'm referring to me, perhaps you, and i believe most middle and high school girls in this country who have made food our best friend and worst enemy. On several occasions, i have gathered with other girls in various situations, and, usually as part of a late-night bonding session, each girl relates her own eating disorder story . . . i used to be one of these girls. A look at my diary from seventh to ninth grade is truly frightening. on these pages, i ripped myself to shreds, with stinging self-inflicted insults and pleas for "just 10 more pounds" on every page. (Green & Taormino, 1997, p. 31)

These issues are so common that body-image problems plague a large percentage of women and can lead to a number of different disorders. Referred to as body-image disorders, they vary from mild to life threatening. A description of common body-image problems is presented in Table 3.1.

Eating disorders are briefly discussed here because they are a serious matter for many girls and young women. Eating disorders can be considered the extreme consequence of developing a negative body image. Girls with eating disorders develop an overriding preoccupation with their "weight" or perceived "fatness" and engage in dysfunctional behaviors to control their weight. Eating disorders are classified as one of two types: anorexia bulimia and anorexia nervosa.

Bulimia is characterized by obsessive eating where the individual gorges herself. This is often done in secret, as is the characteristic purging behavior that tends to follow gorging. Bulimics attempt to control their weight through a variety of methods such as vomiting, fasting, and the use of laxatives, enemas, weight control drugs, and exercise. These behaviors are indicative of bulimia; however, such "weight control" methods are becoming socially accepted as normal behaviors among the growing number of girls seeking body perfection

TABLE 3.1
COMMON BODY-IMAGE DISORDERS

Benign discontentment	Unhappy with appearance, but such feelings do not impact one's day-to-day life or quality of life (up to 40% of Americans affected).
Subclinical body disturbances	Dissatisfaction with one's looks that leads to depression or anxiety. Often diagnosed as depression but such feelings are related to body-image concerns (up to 45% of Americans affected).
Body-image disturbances	Clinical disorders such as depression, anxiety, and linked to clinical disorders phobias that are directly related to body disturbances (incidence difficult to determine).
Eating disorders	Includes anorexia and bulimia where one's self-worth is related to body image. Dieting patterns can be life threatening (anorexia affects 1% of women and bulimia affects up to 5% of women).
Binge-eating disorder	An eating disorder that is becoming more prevalent. It includes binge eating without the purging behavior. Frequently associated with obesity (up to 4% of women affected).
Body dysmorphic disorder	Characterized by a hyperexaggerated focus on a specific body part that the person believes is undesirable and socially embarrassing. For example, a wrinkle could be perceived as horribly deforming. Often extensive treatment is sought out to correct the "deformities" (incidence not determined at this time).

Compiled from American Psychiatric Association (1994), Attie & Brooks-Gunn (1989), Fabian & Thompson (1989), and Thompson (1990)

(Garner, 1997). Hall and Cohn (1988) found that 25–33% of female first-year college students were using vomiting as a method of weight control. Although bulimics are often of normal weight they suffer from negative body images. When compared with control subjects, bulimics have lower self-esteem, a more negative body image, higher self-expectations, higher need for approval, and greater propensity toward dieting (Katzman & Wolchik, 1984). The diagnostic criteria for bulimia nervosa and anorexia nervosa (American Psychiatric Association, 2000) are as follows:

Bulimia nervosa

1. Recurrent episodes of binge eating characterized by
   a) large intake of food (more than what most people consume) usually within a 2-hour period.
   b) sense of loss of control during the eating binge.
2. Recurrent inappropriate compensatory behavior. Main aim is to reduce weight gain. Methods may include self-induced vomiting, laxatives, enemas, fasting, excessive exercise.
3. Binge eating and compensatory behavior occur about twice per week for 3 months.
4. Body shape and weight are crucial in self-evaluation.
5. This experience does not only occur during a period of anorexia nervosa.

Anorexia nervosa

1. Refusal to maintain minimal normal weight. Body weight is less than 85% of that expected for age and height.
2. Fearful of becoming fat or gaining weight.
3. Disturbance in body weight and shape perceptions. Body image linked to self-esteem.
4. Absence of at least three consecutive normal, non-drug-induced menstrual cycles.

Anorexia nervosa is characterized by extreme dieting provoked by a preoccupation with the shape and size of one's body. Like bulimics, anorexics have a distorted body image and perceive themselves to be heavier than they actually are. They are extremely fearful of gaining weight and obsessive in their efforts to avoid any weight gain. Anorexia nervosa is associated with serious medical complications primarily due to the near starvation of individuals who suffer from the disorder. Both of these disorders are strongly related to the development of a negative body image. Attie and Brooks-Gunn (1989) conducted an important two-year longitudinal study to assess the role of body image in the later development of eating problems. The results indicated that the best predictor of eating problems over time was negative body image during the pubertal years. They speculate that the normal increase in body fat during puberty is likely to trigger these concerns with body image. Research also continues to show an increase in the prevalence of eating disorders. This increase is unlikely to subside as long as the strong societal pressure to be thin remains.

Challenging Images, Changing Attitudes:
Helping Girls Accept Their Bodies

Research on body image suggests that programs designed to enhance girls' competence and self-esteem need to include content that can help them feel better about their bodies. This content includes: helping girls recognize the influence media has on their self-image and teaching them ways to challenge that influence, helping girls develop a daily awareness of how unrealistic models are, teaching the importance of shifting out of negative thoughts and substituting more positive self-accepting thoughts about their bodies, helping girls learn that attractiveness has more to do with behaviors than it does with physical characteristics, and teaching that the best reason to exercise is to be healthy and feel good about yourself—not to change your body.

When young girls reach puberty their bodies change and often they are not prepared for these changes. One important goal in the Go Grrrls curriculum is to help girls establish a positive body image. The challenge of helping young girls establish a positive body image is aptly described by one Go Grrrls participant:

> *I can't stand to even look at my body in the mirror—I just look fat and it's ugly, ugly, ugly. Just when I want boys to notice me I end up with this pudgy-pig look. I will not be happy with myself until I can lose weight and look decent.* (personal communication, 1999)

Not surprisingly, when girls do not accept their body image and become ashamed of how they look, their negative feelings about their physical appearance can lead to low self-esteem and symptoms of depression. To be successful, programs must include activities and discussion to help girls recognize how the media pressures them to desire unrealistic body types. With education and support, girls can understand and accept their changing bodies and learn to develop and maintain a positive body image.

Chapter 4

The Quest for a Positive Mindset: Girls and Low Self-Esteem

How could I possibly explain how awful I feel about myself; how I can't remember the last time I was actually proud of myself; how I can't stand any of the people I used to call my "friends"; how I feel guilty about every-thing I do; how I know you don't really care what's the matter with me. Nobody cares. Maybe that's why I'm crying. Would you understand this? NO, BECAUSE YOU'RE SELF-CONFIDENT, POPULAR, AND THIN! YOU HAVE NO IDEA WHAT IT FEELS LIKE TO BE SO INFERIOR TO EVERYONE AROUND YOU! SO SHUT THE F*** UP, WALK AWAY FROM ME, AND LET ME CRY IN PEACE!
—Marcie Wyrostek, 16-year-old, from: *Girl Power*, p. 53

The reason i named this zine 'I ♡ me' is because i do. I love myself, and i think it is important to love yourself; i feel like it is important to not only acknowledge who you are, but to accept it also. I know that i have felt like shit at times, we all do, but i am trying to work on loving myself: my ups and downs, my bitterness, my anxiety, my depression, my happiness; we all have flaws and i am not here to say that "no matter what, we are all loving and should love each other." I am saying that i, personally am trying to understand and like myself as well as love who i am and what actions i take every day. Loving myself is a personal revolution that is important to me as an individual.

—Val Taylor, 18-year-old, from *I ♡ Me* zine,
cited in Carlip (1995, p. 57)

During adolescence, girls begin a quest to discover who they are and what makes them different from others. For some girls, this adventure takes place in the bright context of self-acceptance and respect. For others, the journey is a shadowy struggle through self-hate. More frequently, girls experience some combination of these experiences. Harter (1990) describes the adolescent's search for self as "a major drama that unfolds on center stage with a complicated cast of characters who do not always speak with a single voice" (p. 353). It is difficult for adolescents struggling to create an identity from this "cast of characters" to develop and maintain a positive image of themselves. But creation of a positive self-image goes a long way toward improving a young person's day-to-day functioning.

Self-Esteem and Gender

Self-understanding refers to an adolescent's cognitive representation of the self—the substance and content of the adolescent's self-conceptions (Santrock, 1996). The process of developing self-understanding occurs in the broader context of living in a family, a neighborhood, a culture, and a society. Indeed, the way adolescents develop their cognitive capacities is closely tied to their sociocultural experience, which influences their self-understanding. One of the most important of these influences is gender.

The process of establishing a positive self-image appears to be more difficult for girls than boys. Early studies that examined self-esteem in national samples found females showed significantly lower self-esteem than males (Conger, Peng, & Dunteman, 1977; O'Malley & Bachman, 1979). One recent study (Rosner & Rierdan, 1994) shows clear differences in self-esteem between boys and girls at ages 8 to 9 and ages 16 to 17 (see figure 4.1). When self-esteem was assessed at ages 8 to 9, 60% of the girls reported positive feelings about

Figure 4.1
SELF-ESTEEM BY AGE AND GENDER

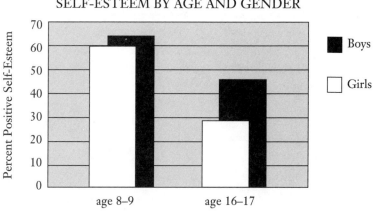

From Rosner and Rierdan (1994)

themselves, compared to 67% of the boys. However, by ages 16 to 17 only 29% of the girls felt positive about themselves, compared to 46% of the boys. A dramatic drop can be seen in girls' self-esteem over the eight years from ages 8 to 9 to ages 16 to 17, a drop that is significantly greater than what was observed for boys. Although Maccoby and Jacklin (1974) suggested that such overall self-image measures may have reflected reporting bias rather than genuine gender differences, that view is waning as new data reveal increased evidence of meaningful gender differences.

Given the unique sociocultural upbringing of American girls, their burgeoning self-understanding is subject to a number of powerful outside pressures. Evidence of these pressures clearly emerges in any analysis of the research on self-esteem. Several studies (Adams, 1977; Harter, 1989; Simmons & Blyth, 1987) found that perceived appearance is one of the strongest predictors of self-esteem in adolescence. For example, Harter (1989) found a strong relationship between perceived appearance and general self-worth. More recently, Lord and Eccles (1994) found that adolescents' self-concepts regarding physical attractiveness were the best predictor of their overall self-esteem, and we know that girls are more affected by their appearance than boys. Furthermore, the media and other sociocultural influences stress the importance of attractiveness to girls. In one study (Campbell, 1988), adolescent girls were found to be primarily concerned about their appearance, dating, and shopping, and rarely interested in a career or in school.

Factors That Influence Girls' Self-Esteem

In the 1960s, and again in the 1980s, Simmons and Blyth (1987) conducted research on adolescent girls' self-esteem. Across that span of years, they found no evidence that adolescent girls had developed a more positive self-image. Today, developing one's self-concept as a female does not appear to be any easier than it was 30 years ago. In this complicated process, girls appear to encounter several barriers: the poorly timed transition to middle school or junior high, the impact of puberty, and an expanding world of worry.

In their extensive analysis of self-image and adolescent development, Simmons and Blyth (1987) postulated that a primary task of early and middle adolescence is to achieve a positive sense of self in response to the changes that occur in adolescence. Their research is based on Murphy's (1947) notion of self-concept or self-image as "the individual known to the individual." Self-image is described as being composed of three dimensions: *self-esteem*, defined as the individual's global positive or negative attitude toward him- or herself; *self-consciousness*, the degree of uncomfortable self-awareness individuals report experiencing in social situations; and *self-stability*, an individual's certainty that they know what kind of person they are and how frequently they experience confusion about what they are really like. In this schema, negative changes in these measures should represent a disturbing outcome for the individual. For example, an unstable sense of self would be disturbing because people are motivated to maximize their level of self-esteem and establish stable self-images.

The results of research by Bush and Simmons (1988) show that across grade levels, girls' self-image is significantly lower than that of boys. More specifically, the findings show that males in K–8 schools and junior high schools experience an increase in self-esteem over time. Females in K–8 schools also experience a slight increase in self-esteem, but girls who make the transition to junior high school suffer a dramatic drop (see figure 4.2). A developmental readiness hypothesis is offered as the most feasible explanation for why girls experience this drop in self-esteem during the transition to middle school. Girls appear to be ill-prepared to adapt to the social and academic structure of a more bureaucratic and impersonal junior high school.

But what happens to these girls over a longer period of time? Does their self-esteem catch up to the K–8 group over time? Simmons and Blyth (1987)

FIGURE 4.2

ADJUSTED CHANGES IN SELF-ESTEEM BETWEEN SIXTH AND SEVENTH GRADE BY SEX AND SCHOOL TYPE

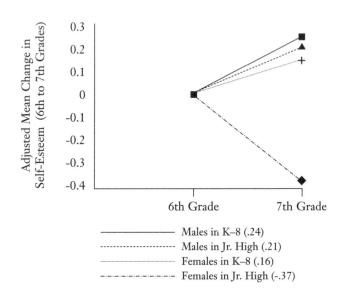

From Bush & Simmons (1988). Reprinted with permission of The Free Press, a Division of Simon & Schuster, Inc., from *Gender, Women and Stress* by Rosalind Barnett, Lois Biener, Grace Baruch. Copyright © 1987 by Rosalind Barnett, Lois Biener, Grace Baruch.

found that the answer is no, junior high school girls' self-esteem continues to measure well below that of the K–8 cohort. Their longitudinal analysis shows that the junior high transition has a lasting, detrimental effect on girls' self-esteem. These girls are at risk not only for *developing*, but also for *maintaining* low levels of self-esteem. Furthermore, in a well designed follow-up study, Simmons and Blyth found significant gender differences for all aspects of self-concept, self-esteem, self-consciousness and self-stability across 6th, 7th, 9th, and 10th grades.

Researchers have also examined the effect of puberty on self-esteem in females. One way of analyzing the effect of girls' changing bodies on their self-concept is to examine the research on early-maturing females. As noted in chapter 3, many studies support the finding that early-maturing girls are at significantly higher risk for both low self-esteem and behavior problems (Caspi, 1995; Petersen & Taylor, 1980). These girls also tend to be the most dissatisfied with their body image, which is a large factor in all girls' self-esteem. Additionally, because early-maturing girls tend to be heavier than their late-maturing peers, they are even more negatively impacted by the media's emphasis on thinness as the hallmark of female attractiveness (Petersen et al., 1993). Not surprisingly, males have been found to be responsive to the physical development of females (Caspi, 1995). As girls mature, therefore, they must also contend more directly with the social and sexual pressures placed on them by boys. Early-maturing girls must deal with this attention whether they are cognitively and emotionally ready or not.

Given these considerations, it is important to enhance the overall self-esteem of girls. Enhancement efforts must go beyond past attempts to boost children's self-esteem, however. For example, in some programs aimed at increasing self-esteem, children were encouraged to simply *feel* good about themselves. Seligman (1995, p. 27) claims that "by emphasizing what a child *feels*, at the expense of what the child *does*—mastery, persistence, overcoming frustration and boredom, and meeting the challenge—parents and teachers are making this generation of children more vulnerable to depression." Efforts to boost girls' self-esteem, then, should focus on areas of competence that are important to girls. Seligman has developed a program for the optimistic child that includes:

- changing children's automatic pessimism
- changing children's explanatory style
- teaching children the skills of disputing and decatastrophizing
- boosting children's social skills

The Go Grrrls program incorporates many of the key ideas presented in Seligman's work.

Expanding Worlds, Expanding Worries: The Influence of Negative Emotions

One aspect of low self-esteem and depressive affect is the manifestation of negative mood states. Larson and associates have studied the nature and impact of mood states in adolescence (Larson et al., 1980; Larson et al., 1990; Larson & Lampman-Petraitis, 1989). Expanding his earlier work with the "experience sampling" method (see Csikszentmihalyi & Larson, 1987), Larson randomly sampled over 400 fifth to ninth graders. From morning through evening the participants were randomly signaled to complete a self-report form that queried them about their thoughts, activities, and emotional states. An example of a participant's report of a worried mood state is as follows: *"a boy wants me to go to a party with him (he's a sophomore) but my mom probably won't let me go because I'm not old enough and I can't go on dates"* (Larson & Asmussen, 1991, p. 30). This research has fostered important understanding about the nature of adolescent emotions.

According to Larson, negative emotions reflect a schism or disjunction between what girls really want in life and how life is actually experienced. Negative emotions are experienced more frequently as young people move from pre-adolescence to adolescence, in part because of the increasing conflict between the ideal and the real and in part because of the cognitive development of adolescents, which makes their awareness of these differences possible. Larson and Asmussen (1991) speculate that this may also be a result of adolescents' expanded domain of "what matters." As young people's investment in the wider concerns of the world increases they are left more vulnerable to hurt, worry, and disappointment.

Results from one study (Larson & Asmussen, 1994) revealed that girls experience significantly more emotional states than boys. The domains of negative emotions for girls are presented in Table 4.1. School, non-school activities, friends, and family are domains experienced as negative emotions for a reasonable percentage of pre-adolescent and adolescent girls. (As we will discuss shortly, friends can be a significant source of positive emotion for girls, but they can also be a frequent source of anxiety and distress.) In the domains of "family" and "friends," girls experienced negative emotions more often than boys.

This research points to relationships as critical components of an adolescent girl's emotional world. Young people's cognitive development and expanding relationships in the world open up new potential for experiences of anxiety, anger, and hurt. One key aspect of the new, negative emotions experienced by adolescent girls involves their concern over the unfamiliar world of heterosexual encounters. Larson and Asmussen (1991) provide a clear example of this type of concern, citing one girl's feelings of disappointment: *"This guy Paul*

TABLE 4.1
DOMAINS OF NEGATIVE EMOTIONS FOR GIRLS

Domains	Preadolescent %	Adolescent %
Self	11.2	10.5
School	26.4	23.5
Activities (non-school)	17.2	9.4
Media	1.5	2.2
Material objects	2.8	2.4
Family	13.9	13.9
Friends	14.4	25.4
Others, unidentified	10.3	10.3

Adapted from Larson and Asmussen (1991)

asked me out but I don't know if he was joking or serious" (p. 33). As the researchers note, this girl must confront a confusing dilemma—if she decides this invitation was a joke but it turns out he was serious, she loses an opportunity; however, if she decides he is serious and it turns out he was joking, she will appear foolish. She is in a lose-lose situation, which fuels feelings of distress.

Larson and Asmussen's (1991) research found that the biggest domain of both positive and negative emotions for girls is romantic relationships, both real and fantasized. The socialization of girls in American society places romance at the center of their existence. Movies, TV, and books graphically describe the emotional impact of lost love: pain, anguish, and loss of meaning in life. Examination of the daily emotional life of adolescent girls led Larsen and Asmussen to conclude that "disappointments in love represent one of the major sources of distress, strain, and perhaps psychiatric disorder in adolescence" (p. 38).

Once again, American culture is not kind to the developing adolescent girl. Because of the emphasis on romantic love in our culture, young girls develop unrealistic expectations about love and relationships. When reality falls short of these expectations, girls experience pain and disappointment. Any attempt to help adolescent girls boost their self-image and cope with stress, then, must include instruction on ways to redefine love in a more realistic way. We must also help support adolescent girls when "Prince Charming" turns out to be a toad (Larson & Asmussen, 1991).

Female Connections: The Down Side

A major thesis of Gilligan (1982) is that adolescent girls place a strong emphasis on their relationships and connections with others. Their empathic connections, however, can lead to feelings of responsibility toward others, which place girls at higher risk for experiencing a sort of "chain reaction" stress. Kessler and McLead (1984) describe these phenomena as "network events," or events that have occurred exclusively to others but are experienced as stressful by the respondent. In their study they found that adult women experience more network stress than men. Furthermore, they reported a relationship between network stress and negative psychological symptoms. Like Gilligan, Kessler and McLeod conclude that women are more connected and emotionally involved than men. And although they experience greater social support the connections can also be stressful and lead to psychological symptoms.

Further support for this theory resulted from a study (Compass & Wagner, 1991) that examined the extent to which adolescents are affected by stressful events that occur in the lives of others in their social networks. The researchers had respondents complete an events scale that documented everyday and major stresses for three months. Stressful events were categorized as network, family, intimacy, peer, and academic. An event in the network category, for example, might be "something bad happens to a friend"; in the family category, "problems or arguments with parents, siblings or other family members"; in the intimacy category, "breaking up or being rejected by a boyfriend or girlfriend"; in the peer category, "friend moves away from you or you move away from friend"; and in the academic category, "doing poorly on an exam or paper." The results for junior high school males and females are presented in figure 4.3 below.

The results, as shown in this figure, represent significant gender differences in four stressful categories: network, family, intimacy, and peer events. These results confirm earlier findings that females experience greater interpersonal

FIGURE 4.3

MEAN NUMBER OF NEGATIVE EVENTS FOR MALES AND FEMALES IN JUNIOR HIGH SCHOOL

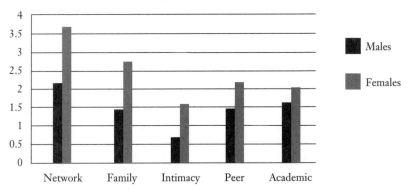

Adapted from Compass and Wagner (1991)

stress than males, validating Gilligan's contention that adolescent females are at risk because of their orientation to care for the needs of others. Compass and Wagner (1991) further note that: "adolescent females may be more dependent upon others for development of personal identity. Thus, stress within their social network is potentially a source of greater disruption to self-esteem" (p. 72).

The "I Should" Mantra: Unrealistic Expectations, Self-Criticism, and the Road to Depression

"I should not eat this food." "I should be able to make my best friend happy." "I should be able to get better grades." A lot of the self-criticism that girls engage in comes from unrealistic self-demands—the "I should" mantra. Because self-criticism is so predominant, many girls develop a punitive perspective about themselves, establishing a damaging inner dialog. This type of self-criticism can set off a downward spiral of increasingly self-critical thoughts that can lead to feelings of inadequacy and guilt. These self-critical demands represent a cognitive perspective that can drag girls into a miasma of self-discouragement. Changing "I should" statements into more realistic, "I would like to" statements is a beginning step toward helping girls set realistic standards and change the way they talk to themselves.

Regardless of their source—network events or self-criticism—problems in low self-esteem and negative mood states can become serious. In fact, low self-esteem has been implicated in depression, suicide, anorexia nervosa, delinquency, and other behavioral problems. When problems of low self-esteem are coupled with other life difficulties such as divorce in the family, social isolation, or aggressiveness, the impact is magnified (Rutter & Garmezy, 1983).

Defining Depression

It is difficult to believe that at one time mental health professionals did not think depression was possible in adolescence. That notion has changed rapidly as we confront the existence of depressed moods, excessive worry, and clinical depression in many young people. For reasons that will be explored shortly, depression is especially common among girls.

Some important distinctions must be made if one is to understand depressions (Petersen, Compas, Brooks-Gunn, Stemmler, Ey, & Grant, 1993). Many adolescents experience a *depressed mood*, defined as a period of sadness that can last a brief or extended period of time. This type of depression is likely to result from events, such as loss of a friendship or failure at a task. *Depressive syndromes* are a cluster of behaviors and emotions that include loneliness, crying, fear of performing badly, feeling the need to be perfect, and feeling unloved, worthless, guilty, sad, and worried. Lastly, *clinical depression* occurs when a young person is diagnosed as having a major depressive disorder or dysthymic disorder. Serious concern emerges when a major depressive disorder or dysthymic disorder is present. A major depressive disorder is evident when an individual experiences the following symptoms for a least a 2-week period (American Psychiatric Association, 2000):

- depressed mood or irritability most of the day
- decreased interest in pleasurable activities
- changes in weight or failure to make necessary weight gains in adolescence
- sleep problems
- psychomotor agitation or retardation
- fatigue or loss of energy
- feelings of worthlessness or excessive feelings of guilt
- reduced concentration and decision making ability
- repeated suicidal ideation, attempts, or planned attempts

A dysthymic disorder occurs when adolescents experience a period of at least 1 year in which they have been depressed or in an irritable mood every day, without more than 2 months in which they did not experience any symptoms. Individuals experiencing dysthymic disorder also have two of the following symptoms:

- eating problems
- sleeping problems
- lack of energy
- low self-esteem
- reduced concentration or decision making
- feelings of hopelessness

Surprisingly, there are no clear studies that document the incidence of depression in adolescents. When examining depressive syndrome studies (Achenbach, 1991) researchers have found that 5% of the adolescent population is afflicted. Clinical depression has been reported to affect approximately 7% of the general adolescent population (Petersen et al., 1993). Lewinsohn and colleagues (1988) found that up to 20% of all 18-year-olds have had at least one episode of clinical depression. Studies that have examined groups of adolescents receiving mental health services report that depression can be as high as 57% (Kovacs, Feiberg, Crouse-Novak, Paulauskas, Pollack, & Finkelstein, 1984). Compas and colleagues (1997) report findings that document gender differences in depression for clinically referred youth but not nonreferred adolescents.

There are important developmental implications in depression. Overall, adolescent depression shows a fourfold increase over childhood depression (Kashani et al., 1989). One study (Radloff, 1991) found pronounced increases in depressed moods in adolescents between the ages of 13 and 15, a peak at approximately 17–18, and then a decline during adulthood. One conclusion is clear: Depression is the most frequently reported mental health problem among adolescents.

Blue is for Girls: Gender and Depression

Rates of depressive disorders are greater for girls than for boys and this is considered a true gender difference, not merely a difference in reporting rates (Petersen, Kennedy, & Sullivan, 1991). In one study, girls were found to be twice as likely as boys to become depressed (Nolen-Hoeksema, 1990). Most studies have examined depressed mood and found parents rated 10–20% of their boys and 15–20% of their girls as depressed (Achenbach, 1991). However, when adolescent self-reports rather than parental ratings were used, the incidence of depression rose to 20–30% for boys and 25–40% for girls.

The explanation for the gender difference is probably related to several factors. While boys are more likely to distract themselves, girls tend to ruminate on their mood. This rumination is believed to amplify negative emotions and reinforce their negative self-evaluations (Nolen-Hoeksema, 1991). Another possible explanation for girls' greater incidence of depression is that girls are more likely than boys to attribute negative events internally, leading to a more negative mood state. This internal attributional style can also lead to increased feelings of helplessness (Compas, Orosan, & Grant, 1993).

There are other possible explanations. As we have reviewed elsewhere, during adolescence girls develop a more negative body image, which tends to be associated with increased feelings of depression. Additionally, girls are thought to experience more challenges during early adolescence than boys (Petersen, Sarigiani, & Kennedy, 1991). For example, girls are more likely than boys to go through puberty before or during the transition to secondary school. The complexity of these multilayered challenges may be overwhelming, and the resulting sense of inefficacy may lead to depression. Finally, the physical transformation that girls experience at this time includes hormonal changes that may trigger depression. Processes that lead to depression, then, include the biological, psychological, and social (Compas & Hammen, 1996). With so many potential causes for depression, perhaps we should be surprised that so many girls live through their teen years *without* being depressed.

Depression and Diversity

Most of the research on self-esteem and ethnic minorities has been conducted with African American adolescents. But surprisingly little research has been conducted in this area in spite of the fact that adolescence is a special juncture for ethnic minority individuals (Dreyer et al., 1994; Fraser, 1987; Phinney et al., 1994; Spencer & Dornbush, 1990). Although younger children are aware of cultural and ethnic differences, it is during adolescence that they consciously confront ethnicity for the first time (Santrock, 1996). How does this awareness impact ethnic minorities' self-esteem? For a long time many people assumed that members of minority groups would have lower self-esteem than Whites. As Gibbs (1990) points out, however, we must be careful not to overpathologize and stereotype minorities as victims of their racial identity or social class status. Several studies (Gibbs, 1985; Gordon, 1978; Rosenberg & Simmons, 1971) have found no differences in self-esteem between nonclinical samples of African American youth and White youth. It appears that the majority of African American youth cope effectively with their ethnicity and social class status. When we look beyond self-esteem to depression, studies report contradictory findings (Petersen et al., 1993). When differences do emerge, most researchers are making ethnic group comparisons across samples of boys and girls. One exception to these barriers in understanding the impact of being a minority adolescent *and* a female is a study by the Commonwealth Fund (Phillips, 1998, p. 24). In this study, researchers found depressive symptoms in 30% of Asian girls, 27% of Hispanic, 22% of White, and 17% of African American girls surveyed.

Gay, lesbian, bisexual, transgendered, and questioning adolescents face high rates of both depression and suicide in comparison with their heterosexual peers (Savin-Williams, 1994). The Center of Population Options (1992) states the issue clearly: "Lesbian, gay and bi-sexual adolescents face tremendous challenges to growing up physically and mentally healthy in a culture that is almost uniformly anti-homosexual" (p. 1). As one study found (Rosesler & Deisher, 1972) gay, lesbian, and bisexual youth identified their major problem as needing to keep their homosexuality a secret because of their belief that they could be rejected by mainstream society.

Strong feelings of alienation often lead to the risk of suicide. Studies suggest these youth are 2 to 3 times more likely to attempt suicide than other youth according to the Report of the Secretary's Task Force on Youth Suicide (Gibson, 1989). This makes suicide the leading cause of death among lesbian, gay, and bisexual youth; in fact, 30% of all suicides are related to sexual identity. One study (Posner, LaHaye, and Cheifetz, 1989) examined suicide notes and found themes of "inner badness." Society's rejection, violence, and harassment toward lesbian, gay, and bisexual adolescents create extremely difficult living conditions (Gustavsson & MacEachron, 1998). Hetrick and Martin (1987) believe that a primary developmental task for homosexual adolescents is adjusting to a socially stigmatized role.

Outward Changes, Inward Changes

Adolescent girls' negative self-image, self-deprecation, and depression have many causes. While it is important to help girls learn skills that may "innoculate" them against depression, it is equally important to analyze culture and institutions that may exacerbate the problem. For example, given the evidence that the middle school transition appears to be particularly traumatic for many girls, we must reevaluate the structure of our schools. We must de-emphasize the notion that attaining romantic love is the pinnacle of success for girls. And while we reconsider societal and institutional changes, we must teach girls how to use their inner voices for self-encouragement rather than self-disparagement.

Chapter 5

Making and Keeping Friends: Peer Pressure, Intimacy, Popularity, and Friendship Friction

I have always been proud of my relationship with my friends. Our friendship is a bond stronger than steel because it is bound with the flesh of seven extraordinary beings, with the will to survive in a small town buried in a small valley in rocky mountain society. Although we no doubt have our conflicts, we are tight. We understand one another's yearnings, our burning desire to shine, to stay afloat above the surface of a tide pool. Society. Our peers, our families, everyone desperately pulls at our essence. We have each other, and that is all.

—Haley Eager Thompson, 15-year-old, from
Ophelia Speaks by Sara Shandler (1994, p. 142)

My friends are the people I am most happiest with. As well as having good times with them they can also be very sympathetic and helpful with any problems. Maybe because we all have the same problems at this age, school, parents, and boyfriend. I also feel a lot easier in having a joke and enjoying myself with them.

—Adolescent girl from *I like to say . . . what I think*
by Simmons and Wade (1984, p. 74)

What is the value of friendship to adolescent girls? At a recent Go Grrrls meeting, a first-year middle schooler shared her thoughts about the importance of having friends:

It's scary out there without your friends, you know? I mean, it seemed like I didn't know anybody when I got here, and I was just looking at the ground when I walked down the halls. It's not like grade school where everybody knows who you are, and even your teacher just knows stuff like when your birthday is.

It's all different. And the older, popular kids are all looking at you like you're a space alien or something. (Personal communication, 1999)

Most adult women can probably recall the importance of friendship and the complex structure of the popularity pecking order during the middle school years. Given the intensity of these experiences, it is surprising that adolescent girls' friendships have not merited earlier or greater study.

Henry Stack Sullivan's early work on adolescent friendships, for example, has only recently received the attention that it deserves. As a psychiatrist who observed many troubled youth and a keen observer of interpersonal interactions, Sullivan developed a theory about the importance of peer relationships and subsequent adult development. Perhaps more than anyone else, Sullivan (1953) saw the potential benefits of friends to one's psychosocial development. He proposed that friends help build self-esteem, provide emotional support, share information and advice, and offer help to one another. Friends serve as an interpersonal bridge to the world and contribute to one's evolving identity. A person simply cannot get along well in the world without friends.

Sullivan believed that friendships are critical to children's social development in two fundamental ways. First, friendships serve to broaden the way children experience their social world, opening up new possibilities for social exchange. Families provide children with a rich social environment, but this environment is, naturally, narrow in scope. One's family represents a small part of the complex social world a child must eventually enter, and without the influence of friendship, a child would develop an extremely parochial view of reality. Peer relationships, and friendships in particular, provide corrective experiences to these limited perspectives.

Secondly, Sullivan surmised that friendships are critical to healthy development because social exchanges with friends are open, reciprocal exchanges. Each friend must share her reality and neither has an absolute say in what that reality is. The process of reciprocal exchange, which includes argument, discussion, and compromise, eventually leads to the ability to collaborate. Collaboration often results in new, expanded perspectives that would not have materialized without interpersonal interaction.

The process of sharing and mutual understanding in friendship helps children develop a sense of uniqueness, but it also leads to a strong sense of commonality—a shared experience. Sullivan recognized that this type of commonality is not possible with parents, who are authority figures. Sullivan (1953) describes the process:

> I would hope that preadolescent relationships were intense enough for
> each of the two chums to get to know practically everything about the

other one that could possibly be exposed in an intimate relationship, because that remedies a good deal of the often illusory, usually morbid, feeling of being different, which is such a striking part of rationalizations of insecurity in later life. (p. 256)

Because of Sullivan's early work, there is now widespread appreciation for the importance and value of friendships in healthy development. Recent work has recognized the particular significance of friendships in adolescent development. Developmental psychologists Newman and Newman (1995) suggest that the central task of early adolescence is locating a peer group that is accepting, supportive, and compatible with one's interests. Peer groups are of critical importance during early adolescence and their influence begins to decline as adolescents get older (Brown et al., 1986). Membership in a peer group enhances adolescents' psychological well-being and ability to cope with stress (Hanswell, 1985).

Social conditions in the United States have caused parents and professionals who deal with youth to refocus attention on the role of peer relations in a young person's development (Pipher, 1995; Youniss, 1980). A major thesis in *Reviving Ophelia*, for example, is that our culture does not provide a stable context for the developing adolescent girl; that the culture is, in fact, toxic. In concert with this lack of cultural stability there is a shift away from full-time parental involvement in children's lives and movement toward greater "age-mate rearing." Much has been written on the social changes that have moved children further from parental monitoring and instruction. Fathers and mothers work more, single parent families are growing in number, and time students spend in school is increasing—all changes that place peers in the forefront of a child's socialization. Indeed, researchers have discovered that American teenagers spend approximately 20 hours per week of nonclassroom time with peers, while teenagers in Japan and the Soviet Union spend only 2 or 3 hours per week of nonclassroom time with peers (Csikszentmihalyi & Larson, 1984).

Peer groups play critical roles in the positive development of the adolescent. In such nonthreatening peer groups or friendship environments adolescents are free to truly explore their feelings. In the context of friendship teenagers reach for words that match their new life experiences. They are free to share deep feelings of excitement, fear, anxiety, and hurt. As they engage in the intense interactions that take place before, during, and after school (not to mention the myriad of late-night phone calls), they learn to share of themselves in an intimate manner. This process of verbalizing feelings and sharing with and trusting others sets the foundation for an adolescent's ability to experience affection and love in adulthood.

Developmental Issues

Sullivan set the stage for understanding the value of friendship. But from a developmental perspective why is friendship important? Gottman and Parker (1987) have identified six functions of adolescent friendships, which are presented in the following list:

1. Companionship: Friendship provides adolescents with a partner, someone to spend time with and join them in collaborative activities.

2. Stimulation: Friendship provides adolescents with interesting information, excitement, and amusement.

3. Physical support: Friendship provides the expectation of support, encouragement, and feedback that helps adolescents maintain an impression of themselves as competent, attractive, and worthwhile people.

4. Ego support: Friendship provides the expectation of support and encouragement. This helps adolescents see themselves as competent and worthwhile individuals.

5. Social comparison: Friendship provides information about where adolescents stand relative to others and helps them assess themselves.

6. Intimacy/affection: Friendship provides adolescents with a warm, close, trusting relationship with another individual, a relationship that involves self-disclosure.

Hartup (1983) has summarized the importance of peer relations in child development:

- Poor peer relations are associated with discomfort, anxiety, and a general unwillingness to engage the environment.

- Children master their aggressive impulses within the context of peer relations.

- Sexual socialization cannot take place in the absence of peer interaction.

- Peer relations are related to role-taking ability, empathy, and moral reasoning.

- Children who are rejected by their peers are at greater risk for delinquency, school dropout, and mental health problems.

Children offer each other important knowledge and skills that are often unavailable in interactions with adults. Friendships are critical because they provide unique opportunities for learning social skills and because they help develop a sense of group belonging.

It's a Girl Thing: Girls and Friendships

Much has been written about gender differences in peer groups and friendships. Research has documented the tendency for boys to prefer larger peer groups and girls to prefer friendships in pairs. The distinctions are even characterized by colorful phrases: boys are referred to as the "band of rebels" and girls as "intimate confidantes" (Rubin, 1980). Boys' friendships are distinguished by sharing actions and deeds whereas girls' friendships are based more on sharing thoughts and feelings (Furman & Buhrmester, 1985; Youniss, 1980). Belle (1988) asserts that girls seek more help and support from peers than boys do, and the support tends to be more emotionally focused than the support boys gain from their friends.

The importance of girls' friendships gains significance in early childhood and continues throughout the life course. Studies have found that girls are most comfortable when they are engaged with a single best friend (Lever, 1976). Girls are often observed to be physically affectionate, holding hands, and reaffirming in their special significance to each other. One 12-year-old beautifully describes this bond:

> Naomi had a (sleepover) party on Saturday. We had true confessing and every-one told their secrets. Then we felt so close! We hugged each other and said we loved each other. Some people cried. (personal communication, 1999)

Clearly, intimacy is a critical element in girls' friendships. Studies have found marked differences in the self-reported friendship intimacy of girls compared to boys (Buhrmester & Furman, 1987). These researchers conclude that "it appears that male-male friendships never achieve the same level of intimate disclosure as female-female friendships" (Buhrmester & Furman, 1987, p. 51). Ask most adolescent girls what they want in a friend and they will tell you, "someone to share problems with" and "someone who will listen to me when I need to talk." Gilligan and associates (Brown & Gilligan, 1990; Gilligan, Brown, & Rogers, 1990) have studied girls' relational worlds and found that girls are indeed sensitive to rhythms in relationships and are more attendant to feelings than boys. Girls have a strong desire to develop connections with others. Thus, intimate friendships are particularly important in the development of female adolescents.

Girls show more concern for how friendships may be threatened by others. Because girls are so focused on their intimate relationships it is not surprising that feelings such as jealousy are more likely to be a concern among girls than boys. Another important difference between male and female friendships is that males are more willing and likely to make new friends than girls, who rely upon more exclusive friendships (Berndt, 1995). The need for basic friendship skills—how to strike up a conversation with someone new, for example—becomes critical as girls move to new environments where they do not have an existing set of friends. Furthermore, since girls are more concerned about establishing friendships, friendship skills are more critical for them to learn. In one study, the majority of girls (85%), reported that they "very much" want to have friends they can count on (Stromme & Stromme, 1993).

In another study, adolescent girls were asked to respond to the statement "the sort of person I would most like to be is." Table 5.1 shows the characteristics that girls endorsed.

TABLE 5.1
GIRLS' MOST DESIRED CHARACTERISTICS

Characteristics	Percent endorsing
Physical appearance and popularity	51
Friendly (e.g., courteous, good humored)	22
Material (e.g., money, possessions, clothes)	11
Honest and reliable	8
Cooperative and helpful	4
Self-sacrifice (e.g., for social justice)	4

Adapted from Simmons and Wade (1984)

This rank shows the emphasis girls place on friendship, physical appearance, and popularity. Unfortunately, the study grouped physical appearance and popularity together—something that girls need to understand are separate concepts. Being friendly is one of the two top values the girls endorsed (Simmons & Wade, 1984).

The researchers also had the girls respond to a serious of open-ended statements. Typical responses to the statement "the sort of person I would most like to be like" included: "Someone who is well liked by everybody" "Someone who can get on well with people (isn't shy)" and "Someone who has a good sense of humor" (Simmons & Wade, 1984, p. 47). These studies confirm that friendship plays a significant role in the psychosocial development of girls. Because girls care about friendships, they are susceptible to both positive and negative friend-ship influences.

Peer Pressure: The Good, the Bad, and the Subtle

Peer pressure. The very phrase elicits groans from adolescents who have been drilled on the dangers of succumbing to this allegedly dark force. We have all heard some variation on the age-old parents' question, "If all of your friends jumped off a bridge, would you do that, too?" So what is peer pressure? Peer pressure, or influence, is a multidimensional force that has been described as exerting itself in one of two ways: as informational influence or as normative influence. Informational influence is described as the pressure to accept infor-mation from others as evidence of reality (Deutsch & Gerard, 1955). Norma-tive influence, the most commonly discussed form of peer influence, is defined as the pressure to conform to the expectations of others. Peer groups' norma-tive influence is stronger among those motivated to be part of the group (Brown, 1990). Berndt (1995) claims that too much emphasis has been placed on normative influence when the stronger source of influence is *interactional*—having to do with interactions with friends who provide support and avoid con-flicts.

As exemplified in the classic "jump off a bridge" example, friendship influ-ences are most frequently discussed in terms of negative impact. But peer pres-sure can exert a positive influence on behavior as well. One study documented the positive power of peer influence by examining what happened when low-scoring students had friends who were high-scoring students: The low-scoring students increased their academic performance (Epstein, 1983). Indeed, having a good friend can help a young person ward off the pressure to conform to a broader peer group. An adolescent who has the approval of a good friend she cares about is less likely to need approval from her peer group. Clasen and Brown (1987) note that adolescents perceive more pressure toward self-enhancing activities from their peers than toward antisocial or destructive activ-ities. Some researchers have even found that members of peer groups can predict one another's future behavior and future occupational desires (Johnson, 1987). All of this research points to the potential advantages of helping adoles-cents build friendships and peer support groups to cope with shifting demands. In this way, friendship provides an island of security that can bolster a young person's independence.

Peer influence is generally not accomplished through direct instruction. Rather, we are learning that peer influence is a subtle and multidimensional process (Brown, 1990). Too often prevention efforts are based on the mistaken notion that peer influence is direct. The "Just Say No" campaign, for example, has falsely suggested that resistance to peer pressure is the key factor in stopping risky adolescent behaviors such as involvement with drugs and sex. When adolescents are asked about pressure to use drugs they will often say there is none: "It's there if you want it but nobody gives you a hard time if you don't" (Brown, 1990, p. 190).

Not surprisingly, peer influence is likely to be strongest in early adolescence. Several studies have found peer influence peaks during the early-adolescent years (Berndt, 1979; Blyth, Hill, & Thiel, 1982; Collins & Thomas, 1972). A series of studies established that youths' fear of rejection from the peer group increases after the age of 13. One classic study specifically examined the relationship between age and anxiety about peer associations. Results indicated that peer anxiety begins at age 13 and peaks by the middle adolescent years (Powell, 1955).

Adolescents' increasing anxiety over peer associations can lead to high degrees of conformity with their peers. Important research done by Costanzo and Shaw (1970) found that conformity was related to age level, with the 11- to 13-year-old group showing the highest degree of conformity. Peer groups can be a place where conformity becomes a central concern. Girls may go to great lengths to conform to the norms of a peer group they wish to belong to. A 12-year-old seeking help from a teacher explains the pressure to conform this way:

> *I was wondering if either of you could tell me about Marcy and her group, what they like and what they don't because I think they're my type more so than Mary Beth or Stephanie, etc. And I would like to know what they're interested in so in talking to them I know what they hate. The reason for this is because I might say something that might turn them off so every time I see them they won't say "There goes the fag that said so & so."* (Rubin, 1980, p. 100)

Friendships can have a powerful influence on adolescents, especially during the early-adolescent years. During this early stage, anxiety about friendships and peer groups may lead to pressure to conform. Helping young people recognize and resolve their anxiety and insecurity about peer interactions is a first step in helping them benefit from the value of friendships. As they feel more comfortable about who they are as friends to others, young people feel less pressure to conform to others' norms.

The Middle School Transition

Imagine what it must be like for a young adolescent girl who is facing a new middle school environment with no friends. Picture a crowded hallway just as the bell rings, with girls and boys rushing about and calling out to each other.

For a newcomer, it can be an excruciating experience to stand alone, looking awkward, without the slightest idea of how to enter a peer group. Certainly, finding a niche in a supportive, familiar peer group can greatly help girls cope with the newly encountered bureaucratic structure of middle school. As Brown (1990) notes, "The depersonalized and complex routine of secondary school increases the young teenager's need for sources of social support and informal exchanges."

Part of the difficulty girls face in their transition from elementary school to middle school is related to how school structural changes impact relationships and friendships. In elementary school, relationships are more easily maintained because girls have contact with the same individuals throughout the school day. But in middle school they face a constantly changing environment as they migrate to different classes with different teachers and changing classmates several times a day. It becomes more difficult to know all of one's classmates and harder to maintain old friendships due to schedule conflicts. A girl's best friend, for example, may not be in any of the same classes she is in. Where in elementary school a girl may have developed a satisfying relationship with a teacher, there is now a plethora of teachers who spend less time with each student, making meaningful teacher/student relationships difficult to develop.

Early-adolescent girls not only face the challenge of adapting to a shifting social terrain, but they must also begin to develop new skills to deal with their increasing interest in the opposite sex. As they move into puberty, young people become more interested in the opposite sex and must adapt to a new set of social roles and expectations. In elementary school they previously concerned themselves almost exclusively with same sex interactions, in middle school girls must learn a new set of behaviors for heterosexual encounters. For early-maturing girls, these new interactions can be particularly difficult. Early maturers, whose physical appearance frequently attracts the attention of older girls and boys, may be drawn into interactions with boys before they are socially and psychologically ready. This may be when early-maturing girls have more frequent encounters with delinquency, drugs, and other risky behaviors than do normal or late-maturing girls (Magnusson, 1988).

In addition to the challenge of adjusting to a new school environment and learning new interactional styles to use with the opposite sex, girls also experience an increasing need for independence from their parents. The onset of puberty is a time when adolescents begin to rely less on their parents and more on friends and peer groups for emotional support. If youngsters do not develop close friendships in which to share the new experiences of middle school life, and to supplement their earlier, larger connection with parents, they may feel emotionally isolated. Not surprisingly, adolescents may need help with learning and implementing the many skills it takes to effectively navigate changing school structures, new heterosexual interactions, changing expectations of friendships, and increased independence from parents. For girls, friendships offer a natural support system that can strengthen their ability to face the many challenges yet to come in their changing lives.

Friendship Friction

I have a serious problem between five extremely close friends of mine. Last year, in sixth grade, we were the closest group a person could imagine. We share so many memories of sleepovers, secrets, fights, and mischief. This year, in seventh grade, things have drastically changed. Two of my friends have left me and the others behind. What I mean is, they have found other friends to hang around with who are more interesting and popular, or something. It's like they don't even notice me anymore. What hurts the most is when I see them walking down the hall or making plans after school with their new best friends. (Backstrand, 1997)

Good friendships must survive friendship friction—problems that are likely to arise between friends. In order to learn how to maintain friendships, girls must learn to express their own viewpoints and assert their feelings clearly in a manner that shows sensitivity and respect for the other person. Learning how to negotiate and compromise are skills critical to the process of successfully maintaining friendships. Being sensitive to the feelings of others can require advanced social skills and tact.

Girls' desire to be popular is often the source of friendship friction during adolescence. Using participant observation of a junior high school, one researcher found that conflicts and tensions in friendships were most often observed to emerge from the rivalry created between girls in their desire to obtain high social status (Eder, 1985).

Friendships are considered more satisfactory when they are stable over time. But what makes a friendship stable over time? The overall quality of the relationship is considered critical. A study that examined friendships over time investigated factors that caused satisfaction with friendships to decrease (Shaver, Furman, & Buhrmester, 1985). Friendship failures were attributed to poor communication and low self-disclosure among friends. The implications of this research are clear; to maintain stable and satisfactory friendships one needs a complement of social skills. It is necessary to learn how to approach initial interactions, use self-disclosure, provide support, and solve friendship problems.

Friendship and Psychopathology

Young people who do not have close friendships or report only superficial friendships are more likely to be depressed and anxious and have lower self-esteem than young people with intimate friendships (Buhrmester, 1990). The isolation that follows from lack of friendship support is apparent in these words:

> *For the past two years, I know I just haven't been myself. I've become very reserved and sometimes I even feel uncomfortable around my best friends. I'm very lonely, and I always feel like people are judging and watching me. Sometimes I think I am depressed. I really want to talk to someone about this, but I'm very shy and don't like people feeling sorry for me. My friends are okay, but they like treating me like I'm inferior and teasing me. My parents would not understand and listen to me. I usually try to deny how I feel, but my deepest wish is to be and feel normal like I once was.* (M.F., from *New Moon*, 1997)

Friendships can be seen as a protective factor, providing youth with a gateway to the positive interactions that are necessary for successful adult functioning.

The ability to get along with one's peers is one of the best diagnostic indicators of a child's future adjustment. In a well-known study, Roff (1961) found that failure to engage in the activities of the peer culture and occupy a comfortable place within it is a precursor to later adjustment problems. His research, limited to men, examined the records of individuals who had been discharged from the military because of conduct problems. When he went back to examine the quality of their childhood peer relationships he found records documenting a history of problems with peer interactions. These findings were not present in a comparison group of men who were selected based on similar background.

Perhaps even more convincing is the research of Cowen (1973), who "red tagged" children having poor peer relations in the first grade. When he went back to study their adjustment 13 years later he found that they did, in fact, appear in psychiatric facilities with a disproportionally high frequency. Perhaps the best-known facet of this study is the fact that assessments by one's own peers were shown to be more powerful predictors of later adjustment problems and the need for psychiatric treatment than the views of parents, teachers, or mental health clinicians.

Over the last 25 years we have learned that friendships are central to positive mental health. One thing is clear—peer friendship is an important part of a child's development. People have an innate desire for human companionship, and peer friendship is critical if we are to feel connected and socially involved with one another. The noticeable, detrimental effects of the absence of peer friendship underscores the fact that they are an essential component in healthy development.

Friendship Power: The Benefits of Buddies

As noted earlier, Sullivan (1953) was the first major theorist to suggest that friendships were important to healthy development. Later, Rubin's (1980) book *Children's Friendships* eloquently described how close friends can promote the learning of social skills, encourage self-understanding, and foster a sense of belonging. Studies have found that close friendships are related to positive self-esteem, empathy, and decreased loneliness (McGuire & Weisz, 1982; Mannarino, 1980). Having at least one close friend can protect even unpopular children from feelings of loneliness and conversely, early adolescents who do not have a close friend are considered at risk for loneliness (Bukowski et al., 1993).

Relationships between friendship and positive adjustment have held up in studies of diverse groups (Cauce, 1986). For example, one study (Cauce, 1986) conducted with lower-income African American seventh graders found that those who perceived their friends as supportive had more reciprocated friendships, were perceived as more popular by classmates, and were more often nominated by peers as leaders. Studies of gay and lesbian youth document the importance of friendships for "coming out" and the enhancement of self-esteem (Savin-Williams, 1994). These studies suggest that adolescents who have satisfying friendships are more likely to be popular with their classmates and to have more advanced social skills. Adolescents with at least one close friend have more positive personal adjustment than adolescents lacking such friendships.

It is no surprise to find that young adolescents express a desire to learn about friendship. In fact, when asked about their interest in learning how to make friends and be a friend, 69% of the girls in a parent-adolescent survey said they "very much" wanted help in doing this (Stromme & Stromme, 1993). The timing of teaching friendships skills is critical to young people's healthy development. As they are learning to share and express their concerns they are also beginning to experiment with new behaviors and develop new feelings. As their concerns grow larger they learn how their friends can help them. This may partially explain the percentage of girls who "very much" desire to learn friendships skills as they get older.

In a famous study, Gottman and colleagues (1979) were interested in learning if children that had social knowledge of friendship were more likely to be popular. They devised a task to assess children's knowledge of friendship-making tactics. They classified the friendship tactics used by third and fourth graders in the study as: offering greetings "Hi, Caitlin," offering information "I like to play soccer," requesting information "Do you have a sister?" and extending invitations "Can you come over to my house after school?" The results showed that indeed, children who were popular knew more about how to make friends than unpopular children.

Studies have found critical differences between adolescents engaged in friendships and those who are not. These benefits of friendships are summarized in Table 5.2.

TABLE 5.2

STUDIES THAT HAVE FOUND BENEFITS TO FRIENDSHIPS

Adolescents with friends have:	Friendships promote:
• greater sense of altruism	• establishment of egalitarian relationships
• greater perspective taking abilities	• a sense of identity
• greater intelligence	• reduced symptoms of depression
• positive peer status	• positive involvement in school
• more academic success	• positive self-concept
• motivation to do well	• enhanced personal adjustment
• higher mental health and competence	• decreased feelings of loneliness

(Sources: Berndt & Das, 1986; Berndt & Keefe, 1995; Brown et al., 1986; Clark & Ayers, 1988; McGuire & Weisz, 1982; Reisman, 1985; Sarason et al., 1993; Slavin & Rainer, 1990; Youniss, 1980)

As noted earlier, however, friendships can be *both* positive and negative. As Mechanic (1983) claims, intimate friendships that revolve around worries, personal problems, and intense introspection of feelings may increase one's sense of stress and anxiety. It is important to teach young people that friendship is about sharing problems *and* finding solutions about supporting each other emotionally *and* about celebrating successes.

Starting friendships and maintaining friendships are altogether different processes, but both require social skills. Because friendships can exert a strong influence on adolescents, it is important to teach girls friendship skills. Mastering these skills helps girls avoid some of the problems associated with the absence of friends and tap into the potential benefits that friendship has to offer. This is particularly true in early adolescence, when insecurity and anxiety about friends is greatest. Friendships and peer groups become even more important for youth who are adapting to transitions such as changing schools. The exchange of thoughts, feelings, and ideas can have long-lasting impact as adolescents obtain the support needed to cope with the challenging world ahead.

Chapter 6

Establishing Independence:
Learning Survival Skills

I believe in speaking my mind and telling people what I feel and what I think and not to bite my tongue. What I mean is if someone is doing something to you, you should let them know about it before it gets worse. So always speak your mind and that's when you're powerful. And never let any man or woman take advantage of you.

—Shakoiya, 11-year-old, from *Girls Speak Out:*
Finding Your True Self by Andrea Johnston (1997, p. 154)

Today, i am strong. I almost feel like I could take on the world. I strive on strength. But also caring and love. It just occurred to me that I am actually a strong woman. Yes, I do feel I am a woman now though I haven't gotten my period yet.

—Elizabeth, 12-year-old, from *Girls Speak Out*, p. 160

Leticia's newest seventh-grade friend, Sarah, just invited her to visit her house after school. She wants to go, but she knows that Sarah's parents both work and that she invited a couple of guys over, too. Leticia thinks there will probably be some beer around. What should she do? Taylor met an older boy at the local mall. He's 17, has a driver's license, and wants her to meet him in the parking lot this weekend. She likes him a lot but feels nervous about going. What should she do? Nancy has been feeling lonely. She has few friends and frequently spends schooltime alone. She cries often and doesn't feel happy with her life. Audrey was suspended from school because she and her friends were caught drinking alcohol on the school grounds. Her parents are concerned about her alcohol use and she has been caught coming home intoxicated on numerous occasions.

All of these girls lack certain social or life skills. With a little work, these young people could lead more satisfying interpersonal lives. Leticia and Sarah would benefit from problem solving skills, including learning how to think about consequences and how to generate different alternatives for difficult situations. Friendship skills could help Nancy address her feelings of loneliness. She could also be taught coping skills to deal with her negative and depressing thoughts. Audrey could be helped by learning about the consequences of drug use and the skills needed to resist peer pressure. All of these girls are facing problems common to today's early adolescents. If they are to resolve their problems successfully, these girls will need to adapt to complex social changes and employ several new life skills. But no one has ever really, specifically taught them how to solve problems or speak up for themselves.

An approach referred to as social skills training implements methods of helping young people solve problems and assert themselves. This approach views problem behavior in young people as indicative of a lack in the skills needed to cope with various situational demands. The emphasis is on social skills: skills that are maximally effective in resolving the demands of problem situations while minimizing the likelihood of future problems. Teaching social skills to young people is an effective strategy for helping them confront stressful or problematic situations. Young people need to acquire numerous social skills because during adolescence they develop new patterns of interpersonal relationships, confront new social situations, and learn new behavioral responses (Jessor, 1982). Without sufficient social skills, these experiences can become avenues to pregnancy, delinquency, drug abuse, and social isolation. One reason the acquisition of life skills such as problem solving is considered critical is because it is during early adolescence that young people begin making life-altering decisions about, among other things, education, drugs, weapons, and sex.

The Only Constant is Change: The Need for Teaching Basic Life Skills

The world of young people is perhaps best characterized by the word "change." To adapt to their new, increasingly independent roles, young people must confront and resolve problems for which they have little past experience. Furthermore, today's early adolescents encounter a sort of "change within change" in that their personal roles change and challenges occur within the context of rapidly shifting social conditions.

Young people's risk-taking behavior is a serious national problem. Confronting the pressures of sex, alcohol, and drugs is now a normal part of the process of growing up in American society (Jessor, 1992). Jackson and Hornbeck

(1989) state emphatically, "in our society, peer pressure to engage in early sexual activity and the availability of alcohol, drugs, and cigarettes virtually guarantee that every American young adolescent will be confronted with decisions about whether to engage in behaviors that could have life-long, if not lethal, consequences" (p. 833).

Many people wonder how we can help children adapt to these personal and environmental changes. The Carnegie Council on Adolescent Development (1995) suggests that "if adolescents are to solve problems of human relations, develop healthy lifestyles, access social systems, cultivate intellectual curiosity, and meet the demands of the workplace, they must learn basic life skills" (p. 55). Among the skills often listed as critical to the healthy development of children are those that enable children to make responsible decisions and resolve simple as well as complex problems. For girls, the adaptations may be more dramatic due to the timing of physiological changes and cultural pressures to remain passive. Learning how to express one's own opinions, understanding and respecting the opinions of others, and learning problem solving methods when one's own needs or interests conflict with others are critical facets of healthy development. In the face of a culture that offers little support for girls' healthy development, such skills are essential for survival.

That Can't Happen to Me: Egocentrism, Invulnerability, and Risk-Taking Behaviors

Adolescent egocentrism can help explain adolescent risk-taking behavior. Egocentrism in early adolescence is grounded in the young person's ability to take the perspective of another person (Elkind, 1978). The process begins when young people recognize that they may be the potential focus of another person's attention. The difficulty is that they overgeneralize this awareness and assume themselves to be the focus of most other people's attention most of the time. The result is heightened self-consciousness. In addition to giving teenagers the false notion that they inhabit the center of the universe, adolescent egocentrism fosters an adolescent's sense of personal uniqueness. Intense inward focus may make a young teenager feel that no one understands how she feels.

Egocentrism also manifests in an adolescent's sense of being invincible and invulnerable to consequences in the outside world. "Disasters happen to other people, not me" is a common egocentric idea. Because adolescents feel immune to laws that apply to others, they are more likely to engage in high-risk behavior (Arnett, 1992). For example, one study (Arnett, 1995) found that reckless sexual behavior was related to egocentrism.

In order to help young girls resist social pressures to engage in risky behaviors and to help them break free from the illusion of egocentrism, it is necessary to teach life skills. This type of training becomes possible in early adolescence because of youths' cognitive development. The increase in cognitive and decision making abilities that accompanies formal operational thought should make it possible to reduce adolescent risk taking (Keating, 1990). As adolescents' decision making ability increases, they become more aware of potential risks, can reflect upon their behavior, and consider its consequences, and are more likely to consult with others, all of which facilitate a healthier lifestyle.

Thinking about Thinking: Cognitive Development in Early Adolescence

The cognitive developmental advances that adolescents experience have important implications for addressing adolescent risk-taking behavior (Crockett & Peteresen, 1993). In early adolescence girls begin to think about the world in a different manner. Overall, development throughout adolescence coincides with the growing capacity for abstract thinking (Keating, 1990). Therefore, interventions offered to early adolescents are ideal because they capitalize on young people's emerging cognitive capacities as they move from concrete to more complex thinking abilities (Carnegie Council on Adolescent Development, 1995). A humorous example of this new ability is represented in one young person's statement: *"I began thinking about why I was thinking what I was. Then I began thinking about why I was thinking about why I was thinking about what I was"* (Santrock, 1996).

As thinking becomes more reflective, adolescents also develop what is referred to as social cognitive monitoring. Social cognitive monitoring is a person's ability to monitor and make sense of his or her thoughts: "I don't think I am easily influenced by others" or "I'm going to have a difficult time telling this person 'no.'" These kinds of thoughts exemplify how adolescents monitor their social world. Psychologists often refer to the thinking processes of adolescents as "formal operational thought" (Piaget, 1970).

Formal operational thinking involves the development of six conceptual skills (Neimark, 1982):

- The ability to mentally manipulate more than two categories of variables simultaneously
- The ability to think about changes that come over time
- The ability to hypothesize logical sequences of events
- The ability to anticipate consequences of behaviors
- The ability to examine statements and conclusions logically
- The ability to think in relativistic ways about the self, others, and the world

These skills are directly related to potential risk-taking behavior because they influence how adolescents negotiate interpersonal relationships, set goals, and make personal plans. Of course, these conceptual skills reflect what is *possible* for adolescents, not what is necessarily typical (Newman & Newman, 1997). Prevention efforts need to carefully consider individual developmental differences present in young people. Depending on their age and personal developmental level, adolescents may need more concrete or more abstract approaches (Crockett & Petersen, 1993). In general, these conceptual skills lead to a more flexible, abstract, and reflective view of the world. Furthermore, the ability to conceptualize change, think logically, and anticipate consequences of behavior promotes a more realistic view of the future. In short, new cognitive abilities allow young people to learn critical social skills.

Social Skills Training

Social skills refer to the verbal and nonverbal abilities needed to cope with and master an increasingly complex set of life tasks. In early adolescence skills are especially needed for addressing new life concerns such as love, sex, and peer relations. Young people can benefit from learning specific skills such as negotiating a relationship (starting a conversation, establishing parameters), expressing feelings (responding to a stressful conversation, being empathic, communicating directly), and resisting peer pressure (saying "no" quickly, being persistent, leaving the situation)—all critical skills in early adolescence. Social skills training strategies are widely used in both prevention and intervention programs for adolescents (LeCroy, 1994).

Several authors endorse the need for social skills training. Dryfoos (1990) identifies strategies for the prevention of high-risk behavior, noting that "children can learn how to resist influences of their peers through *social skills training*. These curricula have demonstrated improvements in social competency and decision making" (p. 248). In a discussion about schools at the turn of the millennium, LeCroy and colleagues (1999) argue that "our schools must begin to acknowledge the importance of instructing students in a new set of basics: social skills" (p. 376). About the future of adolescent health promotion, Hamburg and colleagues (1993) state that "health promotion efforts that foster adolescent mental health achieve change by helping adolescents develop skills for coping with stress, by involving them in personally meaningful activities, by promoting the development of healthy social environments, and by promoting positive mental health through public policy" (p. 380). They further state that "examples of programs that promote positive mental health are skill building activities that teach coping and problem solving skills." The Carnegie report on preparing adolescents for the new century also emphasizes the need for life skills training.

Successful evaluations have continued to support the social skills or social competence model. Social skills training has been associated with various positive outcomes such as enhanced self-esteem (Stake, DeVille, & Pennell, 1983), drug resistance (Botvin, 1996), pregnancy prevention (Barth, 1996; Schinke, Blyth & Gilchrist, 1981), and reduced aggressive behavior (Bierman & Greenberb, 1996). More recently, evaluations have documented impact across a wider range of populations. For example, while social skills training has been found effective for general pregnancy prevention (Barth, 1996) a more recent evaluation (Hovell et al., 1998) revealed successful pregnancy and AIDS prevention in Anglo and Latino youth. Botvin's life skills training study was primarily based on White Midwestern youth but recent studies of Hispanic and African American populations have proven the success of social skills training in those populations as well (Botvin et al., 1989; Botvin et al., 1992). Other studies (Caplan et al., 1992) document the success of social skills training for both suburban and inner city youth. And many studies have been directed specifically at young adolescents (Caplan et al., 1992; LeCroy, 1994; Thompson, Bundy, & Wolfe, 1996). Problem solving and social skills models can be very effective when applied to gender-specific interventions like the Go Grrrls program.

In their social decision making and problem solving approach, Elias and Clabby (1992, p. 17) describe three essential components: self-control skills, social awareness/group participation skills, and social decision making/problem solving skills:

Self-control skills:	These skills are necessary to accurately process social information, delay behavior long enough to thoughtfully access one's social decision making abilities, and approach others in a way that avoids provoking their anger or annoyance.
Social awareness/ group participation skills:	These are skills that underlie the exercise of social responsibility and positive interaction in groups. They include learning how to recognize and elicit trust, help, and praise from others; recognize others' perspectives; choose friends; and share, wait, and participate in groups.
Social decision making/problem solving skills:	These skills are incorporated into a sequential strategy that is used to understand, analyze, and react to stressful and problematic situations and situations that involve meaningful choices or decisions.

All three of these components are a focus of the Go Grrrls program. In this chapter, attention to problem solving skills is emphasized.

The Problem Solving Process

Teaching problem solving skills has become a central focus in many prevention strategies. These skills are believed by many to be among the most important keys to adapting to difficult social situations. In *Great Transitions: Preparing Adolescents for the Century*, decision making training is recommended for all schools: "Life skills training should become a vital part of education in all relevant institutions, including most especially the family, schools, and community-based organizations, so that adolescents learn to make informed, deliberate, and constructive decisions" (Carnegie Council on Adolescent Development, 1995, p. 55). In many respects problem solving skills represent a learning orientation different from what young people are likely to have received in school. Often, learning in school is focused on recalling known solutions and developing rote knowledge. A problem solving model, however, attempts to set up a habit of searching, developing hypotheses, and inventing new approaches to problems. It encourages divergent thinking as opposed to the more common convergent thinking. In its best form it represents a discovery process whereby there is a synthesis of ideas.

By learning how to face new situations, define problems in specific terms, and generate alternative solutions, one engages in the problem solving process. Problem solving requires that a person create novel solutions instead of falling back on previous responses. Problem solving is a complex skill for young people to learn because it requires the ability to tolerate ambiguity and develop patience for trial and error searching. It requires making decisions based on knowledge of consequences and developing the tenacity to follow through on alternative solutions. These skills and abilities can be learned through exposure to problem situations and guided practice.

Some key problem solving abilities include:

- Using a sequence of goal-directed actions
- Using consequential thinking
- Anticipating potential obstacles
- Expressing a positive sense of efficacy about problem solving
- Thinking of several ways to reach one goal

In the Elias and Clabby model (1992, p.18), the problem solving process is comprised of eight essential steps:

1. Look for signs of different feelings.
2. Tell yourself what the problem is.
3. Decide on your goal.
4. Stop and think of as many solutions to the problem as you can.
5. For each solution, think of all the things that might happen next.

6. Choose your best solution.

7. Plan it and make a final check.

8. Try it and rethink it.

In the Go Grrrls problem solving model, these essential steps have been condensed for easier recall.

While it is important to understand the rationale, skills, and stages involved in problem solving, the techniques are best learned not through routine lessons but rather in working through sample problem situations that have meaning and importance to the young people involved. When they face problems that they really want to solve, young people are more motivated to learn the basic problem solving steps that can ultimately be generalized across situations. Role-playing provides the mechanism for exploring alternative actions in situations that approximate reality. Using the role-playing process means that the teaching of problem solving takes place in a unique group context where learning is a dynamic experience. In that group context, young people are encouraged to confront, define, and respond to problem situations at the action level.

Health promotion efforts are specifically calling for an emphasis on teaching decision making skills, especially for younger adolescents (Crockett & Petersen, 1993). Learning specific problem solving skills is likely to be most beneficial. Furthermore, it has been hypothesized that when young people encounter particularly emotionally arousing topics such as substance use or sexual behavior they are more likely to use immature thinking and reasoning. Efforts to teach problem solving and decision making skills should, therefore, include sample situations involving substance use and sexual decision making. Lastly, it should be noted that even with role-play and practice, the ability to make decisions does not always generalize to use in real life, where experience and practice are needed. Combining problem solving thinking with continuing encouragement to use these skills is probably the most effective strategy. When young people are given problems solving skills, they can build a foundation of general competence and meet life's challenges with greater success.

Get Up, Stand Up: Assertiveness Skills Training

Even if a girl has repeatedly practiced a problem solving process, this knowledge will not help her if she does not feel comfortable speaking up for herself. Along with acquiring decision making skills, then, young people must develop their personal assertiveness. In conjunction with good decision making, assertiveness allows girls to resist peer pressure to use drugs or become involved in sex when they don't truly desire to do so. This skill is difficult for an early-adolescent to employ because of the desire to conform to peer norms and expectations. The key to helping students use this skill is to teach them to be assertive in a way that allows them to maintain a positive peer relationship while exercising autonomous behavior.

Assertiveness instruction is a key component of social skills programs. Early smoking prevention programs sought to increase assertive behavior to prevent the onset of smoking (Rhodes & Jason, 1988). Resistance training was also a key component of the Student Taught Awareness and Resistance (STAR) skills approach for substance use prevention (Pentz et al., 1989). Similarly, pregnancy prevention programs have emphasized assertiveness skills along with problem solving, self-control, and coping strategies (Gilchrist & Schnike, 1985). More recent programs (Caplan et al., 1992; Fodor, 1992; LeCroy, 1994; Thompson, Bundy, & Wolfe, 1996; Wise et al., 1991) continue to emphasize assertiveness as a primary program component.

Assertiveness is a particularly critical skill for early-adolescent girls, as mentioned in chapter 2, girls are frequently encouraged to behave passively. Assertiveness is a key survival skill for girls who grow up with cultural pressure to be passive and compliant while boys learn to be active and assertive. Girls are even encouraged to cooperate with their own oppression (Leonard, 1995). One author describes the process of cooperating with this oppression as follows: "I acknowledged the work ahead: The girl I'd invented, who had become me, who was so full of words waiting to be spoken and skills to be mastered, she had to be pushed down like an ugly jack-in-the-box, the lid sat on" (Friday, 1999, p. 289). Assertiveness training can help girls replace this harmful mission of self-suppression with a goal of self-expression. While few studies have been directed specifically at girls, one study (Wise, Bundy, & Wise, 1991) found that girls benefitted more from assertiveness training than boys did.

As with problem solving techniques, assertiveness is best taught in an active group setting. But because girls are usually unfamiliar with the word, let alone the concept of assertiveness, it is important to begin by defining terms. The process of definition, modeling, performance, and feedback helps girls personalize and use assertiveness skills.

Social Skills Training and the Media

Young people in our society experience massive exposure to TV, radio, the Internet, and computer games, all of which shape their thought processes and images of life. Indeed, some have argued that children identify more with images than with real adult figures. Increasingly, people are questioning the impact of computer games, for example, because they may influence young people to see themselves as merely playing a role in a game-focused existence rather than assuming responsibility for their decisions and actions. Perry (1991) suggests that the media has created a life for young people that is a succession of images that are bought, sold, and copied. Images of consumption, physical attractiveness, and power dominate the TV, radio, and Internet.

What is the impact of the over 20,000 TV advertisements that the average adolescent is exposed to? In many ways these ads are intended to *overcome* young people's rational decision making processes (Keating, 1990). Social skills training programs may prove to be an essential counterbalance to these misleading experiences and images of illusory reality. Young girls who are equipped with the problem solving and assertiveness skills they need to find and express their sound decisions and opinions will be more likely to resist the shallow, consumer-oriented images they encounter every day.

Chapter 7

Let's Talk About Sex:
Sexual Health, Sexual Risk

I'm 15 years old, and I had sex for the first time recently. I had all of these expectations about how great it was going to be. He didn't have much experience either, we were both pretty scared about the whole thing. It was all over in a hurry. My first thought was, "Is that all there is ?" It was a very disappointing experience.

—Claire T., 15-year-old, from *Adolescence* by Jon Santrock (1996, p. 384)

The first time I was with this boy, we were at a party together, and we started making out. And then, all of a sudden, there were his hands on my chest. I felt really funny about it, because it wasn't my idea, it was his idea, and he sort of rushed into it. Since it was the first time we were ever together, I felt like it was too fast, but I let him do it because I didn't exactly know how to tell him not to.

—Elsa, 14-year-old, from *Changing Bodies, Changing Lives* by Ruth Bell (1998)

A century ago, there was a 7-year gap between the time a girl reached puberty and the time she was married. In 1988, that gap extended to 12 years (Alan Guttmacher Institute, 1994). The earlier onset of menarche combined with increasing societal demands to delay marriage until the mid- to late twenties have created this prolonged hiatus between physical maturity and marriage. It is unreasonable to suppose that adolescents experiencing the rush of hormones and desire for intimacy that occur during this time will remain asexual. Adolescents *will* explore sexuality. And because preteens and teenagers will explore sexuality, adults need to communicate with them about sex.

The simple need to communicate with girls about sex is complicated by the emotionally charged nature of sexuality in our culture. The topic of sex intersects peoples' personal, spiritual, and moral belief systems. Parents have widely divergent notions about what their children should know about sex. Some parents insist that sexuality is a topic best left entirely in the home. Other parents practically beg health and school professionals to teach their children about sex so that they can be spared the embarrassment of "the talk." Indeed, mention of the words "healthy" and "sexuality" in the same breath sounds scandalous to some. Adding the word "girl" to the phrase creates even more friction, as girls are still frequently regarded as this culture's "sexual gatekeepers," responsible for controlling their own and males' sexual behaviors (Tolman & Higgins, 1996).

Lack of Knowledge is Lack of Power

Despite widespread discomfort with the topic of girls' sexuality, we must inevitably return to the fact that girls will engage in sexual behaviors. Several messages need to be conveyed: that girls have the right to be healthy, sexual beings to set sexual limits for themselves that are respected by partners, and to make informed decisions. In order for this to happen, we must begin to equip girls with knowledge about sex, help them explore their own attitudes and values, and teach them the behavioral skills they need to protect themselves. Statistics describing teen pregnancy and STD rates serve as dramatic, numerical evidence of our national failure to adequately address teens' need for sexuality information and discussion. Roughly 10 percent of all U.S. girls between the ages of 15 and 19 became pregnant in 1990 (Centers for Disease Control and Prevention, 1995). Approximately 3,000 preadolescent and adolescent females become pregnant each day (Dryfoos, 1990). According to a 1994 report from the National Commission on AIDS (in Wallace & Williams, 1997), three million (1 of every 8) teenagers are infected with a sexually transmitted disease each year.

The numbers relating specifically to early-adolescents' risky sexual behavior are similarly disturbing. In 1989, 11,820 new cases of gonorrhea were detected among adolescents aged 10 to 14 (Wallace & Williams, 1997). Five percent of U.S. female students reported having had intercourse prior to age 13 (Center for Disease Control and Prevention, 1996). Furthermore, in 1992, 25% of Hispanic American girls, 39% of African American girls and 26% of Caucasian girls reported having had intercourse prior to age 15 (Center for Disease Control and Prevention, 1995). Given that early adolescents are notoriously unreliable users of contraceptives/protection, these percentages are unsettling. And given the large numbers of young teens engaging in intercourse, it seems clear that effective prevention programs must be implemented during the very earliest period of adolescence.

What factors contribute to the high U.S. rate of early sexual activity, pregnancy, and incidence of STDs? One factor may be a lack of education about basic reproductive facts. Knowledge of reproductive biology is a necessary prerequisite to protecting oneself from unwanted pregnancy and STDs. But early adolescents do not demonstrate a comprehensive understanding of these mechanics.

Thornburg (1981) found that 51.4% of all sexual information was acquired at the age of 12–13 years. Girls in this study indicated that their primary sources of sex information were first their peers, then literature, and third, their mothers. Other studies confirm that friends are cited as the most common source for sexual information (Handelsman, Cabral, & Weisfeld, 1987; Sanders & Mullis, 1988). But peers are an extremely unreliable source of sexual information. In one study (Phelps et al., 1992) half of 12- to 13-year-old American teenagers indicated that they thought a girl could not get pregnant the first time she had intercourse. Mellanby and colleagues (1991) surveyed 15- to 16-year-olds, one fifth of whom believed that midcycle is the "safest" time to have intercourse without causing pregnancy.

Quality education and information about sexual development and mechanics are necessary features in any program designed to decrease early sexual activity and teen pregnancy and disease. But education about the facts of reproduction alone appears to be an inadequate measure to prevent young people from engaging in early or unprotected sexual intercourse. While lack of knowledge is lack of power, sexual knowledge does not necessarily translate into safe sex practices (Zabin, 1993).

Shaping Values about Sex

Neither knowledge nor protective attitudes or beliefs are likely to prevent all teens from engaging in early sexual activity, but both factors play a part in decisions teens make about their behavior. Adolescents' attitudes about sex are shaped by peers, family, and the culture at large. Media messages, for example, may play a part in establishing teens' attitudes about intercourse.

Hall (1992) notes that media reports frequently overemphasize stories about teens who have sex prior to age 16, when in fact most teens do not. Mellanby and colleagues (1992) suggest that "incorrect statistics about teenagers may leave those under 16 who are not sexually active considering that they are 'abnormal' " (p. 455). A young person who believes that "everybody's doing it" and that they are abnormal if they do not may be more likely to engage in intercourse than a peer who has been taught that most teens their age have not yet had intercourse.

Many prevention programs target students' reported attitudes about sexual activity. But despite the logical assumption that attitudes about sexual activity should influence behaviors, programs that attempt to change teens' knowledge and attitudes about engaging in premarital sex have been unable to demonstrate measurable changes in actual behavior (Mellanby et al., 1992; Zabin et al., 1993). In fact, a recent meta-analysis (Franklin et al., 1997) found that most adolescent pregnancy prevention programs have had little effect on the sexual activity of adolescents.

Although outcome studies are limited, evidence suggests that a skill-building approach is a key component of any successful sexuality education program (Barth et al., 1992; Quinn, 1986). Any program that purports to change behavior (not just knowledge base or attitudes) must offer participants the opportunity to learn and practice skills. Social skills training approaches have been found to be effective in programs designed to prevent as well as remediate problems in living for adolescents (Botvin, 1989; LeCroy, 1982). Many teen pregnancy prevention programs incorporate training in assertiveness, refusal skills, and problem solving methods. Practice using such skills may result in a decreased incidence of teens engaging in unwanted sex, but even skill-based programs have achieved limited outcomes. One reason for this lack of effectiveness may be that most skill-based programs tend to be myopic; they are built around a narrow and inadequate concept of the factors that place adolescents at risk for early sexual activity. A more balanced, comprehensive approach seems to be warranted.

Multifaceted Problem, Multifaceted Solution: There is No Magic Wand

An effective pregnancy prevention program can be developed only after careful consideration of the factors that place adolescents at risk for early sexual activity. Why do girls have sex? A review of the literature reveals a plethora of reasons and risk factors, manifesting in several realms. The following list (adapted from Jorgensen & Alexander, 1983) illustrates some of the variables related to adolescent pregnancy risk.

Psychological
- External locus of control
- Permissive sexual norms
- Low self-esteem
- Intimacy-need deficits in family during childhood and early adolescence

Interpersonal
- Perceived love in the relationship
- Traditional gender role structure (male dominant/female submissive)
- Precocious (early) dating and emotional involvement

Social Network
- Sexually permissive peers (norms and behavior)
- Peer rather than family orientation
- Freedom from parental controls in dating relationships

Societal
- Increasingly permissive sexual norms in adult society
- Mass media display of sexual messages (advertising, books, film, television, etc.)
- Earlier puberty among early adolescents today compared to past decades

Additional risk factors frequently cited include: low educational investment, poor decision making skills, nonparticipation in after-school activities, and loneliness. Adolescents exposed to multiple risk factors are at a heightened disadvantage for engaging in early sexual activity (and other risky behaviors).

Girls in urban settings may be exposed to earlier and stronger pressures to become sexually active at an early age. Vera and colleagues (1996) conducted focus groups with at-risk 4th and 5th graders and their parents from urban Chicago. Parents offered several factors they believed contributed to their children's early experimentation with sex: children witnessing intercourse in public places, lack of proper information about sex, low self-esteem, use of sex to get gang protection, and coercion.

Because funding for prevention programs is often problem-directed—drug abuse prevention, pregnancy prevention, school dropout prevention—practitioners and administrators frequently develop the illusion that there is a specific causation for each problem. But adolescents involved in one risky behavior are likely to be involved in others (Brooks-Gunn & Paikoff, 1997; Gottfredson & Hirschi, 1996). A girl who is involved in drug abuse, for example, is more likely to be involved in other problem behaviors (such as early sexual activity) as well. It is naive to expect to ameliorate any one of these problems using a single, problem-specific approach. Brooks-Gunn and Paikoff (1997) note that there is a "confluence of a series of behaviors such as sexual intercourse, smoking, drinking, and illegal drug use, [that], especially if occurring in the first half of the adolescent years, has been shown to place youth on a precarious developmental trajectory" (p. 211). Because there are common elements to adolescent problem behavior it makes sense to design a prevention program around risk factors that comprise these common elements.

Sex: Not Just Intercourse

While the focus of this chapter thus far has been on the incidence and prevention of early intercourse, it is important to acknowledge that sexual behaviors encompass a wide range of activities, from hand-holding to coitus. This is hardly a radical statement, yet a review of the existing literature on girls' sexuality seems to suggest that intercourse is the sole measure of an adolescent's sexual activity. Brooks-Gunn and Paikoff (1997) note the lack of studies of "normal" adolescent sexual development, with most research on teen sexuality focusing on the age and circumstances surrounding the onset of coitus, which is generally seen as a negative event. These authors challenge us to consider the topic of adolescent sexuality in a broader context: to pay attention to sexual behaviors other than intercourse, to explore the meanings adolescents themselves attach to sexual acts, and to study the decision making process adolescents use before choosing to engage in sexual experiences.

A report issued by the National Council for Research on Women (Philips, 1998, p. 34) echoes these recommendations and suggests that using sexual intercourse as the sole definition of girls' sexuality is problematic because this focus may:

- frame sexuality as an event, rather than as a fluid and multidimensional part of girls' identities
- dichotomize "sexual activity" and "virginity," suggesting that girls not engaged in heterosexual intercourse are asexual
- reproduce sexist and heterosexist notions that girls' and women's sexual lives do not begin until the moment of vaginal/penile penetration
- marginalize lesbian and bisexual girls and overlook autoeroticism by equating sexuality with heterosexuality and sexual activity with male/female intercourse
- discourage adolescents from practicing safer sex through masturbation and non-intercourse sexuality with partners because these are not thought to count as "real sex"

So what kind of sexual experiences are young adolescent girls having? One unusual study (Coles & Stokes, 1985), focusing on teen sexual activity other than intercourse reported that 31% of girls and 54% of boys had participated in breast touching by age 14. The same study reported that 13% of girls and 23% of boys had participated in vaginal play by age 13. Additional studies are needed if we are to develop a true understanding of teen sexual behaviors. In the meantime, listening to girls' voices may provide us with a more realistic perspective on the range of adolescents' sexual experiences. For example, compare the tales of Annie and Andrea, both 14-year-old girls:

The first time I kissed my boyfriend, we didn't have to say anything to each other, we just felt this thrill run through us. Just being so close to him, holding him, it was like we were part of each other. (Bell, 1998, p. 114)

I rinsed my mouth out the first time somebody French-kissed me. I was kissing this guy goodnight after our date, and he just stuck his tongue in my mouth. Just like that. It took me totally by surprise, and I didn't like it one bit. I never went out with that guy again! (Bell, 1998, p. 115)

Another 14-year-old describes "making out":

When I was with my boyfriend and we were all alone for the first time, we were making out. We were out in a park where it was real private behind a bunch of trees, and I was feeling so close to him. We were French-kissing real long kisses, so sometimes I had to pull away to catch my breath. He was rubbing my back and I was rubbing his. We must have stayed there for an hour, just hugging and kissing and rolling around, but then I had to get home, so we had to stop. When I got to my house, my lips were all red and swollen from so much kissing, so I went in and washed my face with cold water. I don't think my mother noticed, because she didn't say anything. (Bell, 1998, p. 115)

Although healthy adolescent sexuality is a largely unmapped area of research, we must acknowledge teen girls' range of sexual feelings and behaviors and their desire for relationships if we are to truly engage them in discussions about sex. They are eager to talk.

Double Standard, Double Bind

As mentioned previously in this chapter, girls are still frequently regarded as this culture's "sexual gatekeepers," responsible for controlling their own and males' sexual behaviors (Tolman & Higgins, 1996). The fact that girls continue to be held responsible for controlling male sexual behavior is an indicator that the double standard is alive and well at the turn of the millennium. Boys are often given the message that sexual conquest is an indicator of manliness. Girls, on the other hand, are given the message that "good girls don't." Diana, a 16-year-old, demonstrates an understanding of the unfairness of this double standard:

You know how it's okay for a guy to go around telling everybody about how horny he is and bragging about how he's going to get some this weekend? Well if a girl ever said those things, everybody would call her a slut. (Bell, 1998, p. 105)

Natasha, age 16, notices that:

Girls who are sexually active, especially if they don't hide it, they're seen as cheap or easy. Guys be like, you know, "I'm gonna see what I can get. You done

her? Yeah, I done her, too." And adults look down on you when you're a sexually active teen, like they never did it when they were young too, right?
(Phillips, 1998, p. 34)

The double standard sets girls up for a role that they are ill-prepared to play. While they are expected to be the sexual "resisters," other cultural beliefs about girls' approved behavior and demeanor conflict with this expectation.

Girls are, for example, frequently socialized to be passive rather than assertive. This "double bind"—to be simultaneously passive and actively resistant—can lead to confusion and guilt. Several studies indicate that both female and male adolescents who adhere to the belief that males should be dominant and assertive while females should be submissive and passive are more likely to be involved in sexual activity and less likely to use effective contraception than teens with a more flexible concept of gender role (Foshee & Bauman, 1992; Jorgensen & Alexander, 1983; Resnick & Blum, 1985). Lloyd (1991) "proposes that these gender-related 'themes' result in the greater potential for aggressive and exploitive behavior in male-female relationships" (p. 944).

Again, if we listen to girls' voices, this exploitation is in evidence. While they are expected to stop boys' sexual advances, many girls feel that they should not or cannot do this. A reprise of "Elsa's" quote from the introduction of this chapter will serve as an illustration:

> *The first time I was with this boy, we were at a party together, and we started making out. And then, all of a sudden, there were his hands on my chest. I felt really funny about it, because it wasn't my idea, it was his idea, and he sort of rushed into it. Since it was the first time we were ever together, I felt like it was too fast, but I let him do it because I didn't exactly know how to tell him not to.*
> (Bell, 1998, p. 110)

In a qualitative study of adolescent sexuality, Karen Martin interviewed teenagers to elicit firsthand information about teens' sexual decision making. The participants' responses confirm that girls frequently engaged in intercourse as passive recipients rather than empowered agents of their own behavior. Consider this typical response to the question, "How did you decide to have sex?":

> *It just happened really. I mean, I didn't want to cause I couldn't ever picture myself having sex, but umm, all my friends did, and umm, so it just happened and he was my first so. . . .* (Martin, 1996, p. 72)

There are, of course, many reasons why girls have sex: to feel close to someone, to keep a boyfriend, to gain gang protection or drugs, because they are coerced by an older partner, because they are raped, because they are passive and don't know how to say no, because they are curious, because their hormones have kicked in and they want to—the list goes on. But for early adolescents in particular, unwanted sexual activity is a serious problem.

Special Risks for Younger Girls

While it is important not to fall into the trap of defining girls as sexual gatekeepers, it is equally important to equip them with adequate confidence and skills to recognize the risk for unwanted sexual activity and to refuse unwanted advances when possible. Small and colleagues (1993) found that 20% of a sample of 1,149 adolescent females reported some type of unwanted sexual contact in the past year. Over one third of this 20% reported they had been forced to have intercourse. Young adolescent girls are at the highest risk. The Alan Guttmacher Institute (1994) reports that "some 74% of women who had intercourse before age 14 and 60% of those who had sex before age 15 report having had sex involuntarily" (p. 22). This disturbing statistic demonstrates the importance of initiating prevention programs early enough to alert girls to the potential for harm and of emphasizing during the program that girls who have been forced to have sex should not feel ashamed of themselves. Sexual assault must be presented and defined as the act of violence and power that it is, and girls need to be supplied with helpful resources and encouragement to seek help if they have experienced or ever experience this type of violence.

It is also imperative to help girls understand that unwanted sexual activity is related to the use and abuse of alcohol and other substances. Girls who have little experience with alcohol or other drugs may be even less able to regulate intake of these substances than more experienced users, leaving them, at best, less inhibited than they would normally be and, at worst, vulnerable to predators.

Another factor involved in the discussion of unwanted sex is coercion by an older male. According to AGI tabulations of the 1988 National Maternal and Infant Health Survey, women who give birth at a younger age are more likely to have become pregnant by a considerably older man (6 or more years older). The reports indicate that 30% of the 15-year-olds who gave birth in 1988 had partners at least 6 years older than they were. The power differential between a 21-year-old man and a 15-year-old girl is not difficult to imagine. And girls in these relationships tend to be among the least reliable users of contraceptives (Phillips, 1998).

The special risks that early-developing girls face have been documented in other chapters. They also tend to become involved in sexual activity at younger ages than their average- or late-developing peers.

Layers of Complexity

Sexuality is a normal, healthy part of adolescence. Choices that teens make about their sexuality can have far-reaching impact on every facet of their lives. In order to help young adolescents negotiate the complex route to emotional and physical sexual maturity, we must provide them with basic facts about sex, reproduction, and sexually transmitted diseases. Teens also need a forum to explore their attitudes and beliefs about sexuality. They need to be taught specific methods to resist unwanted sexual advances and they need an opportunity to practice these skills in an unthreatening situation.

Because a small but significant percentage of early-adolescent girls have sexual intercourse, it is imperative that we provide teens with access to birth control information and supplies. However, in addition to promoting sexual knowledge, exploration of attitudes, practice with refusal skills, and access to birth control, it is necessary to provide adolescents with opportunities to succeed, neighborhoods where they don't witness public acts of intercourse, and families where they are able to talk about their concerns. As is true of other risky behaviors, the causes for early sexual activity are complex. So are the solutions.

Chapter 8

When It All Seems Like Too Much: Seeking Help, Locating Resources

We could have a class where we talk girl talk about stuff you worry about. Right now, I'm on the phone with my friends, but they don't have all the answers. What do they know that I don't about boys or how to handle your parents? Someone who knows what it's really like could give us tips, like what to do when a boy is after you to go with him and you want to say, "Get out of here, you nerd," but in a nice voice, so you don't hurt his feelings.

—14-year-old girl, from *A Matter of Time* by Carnegie Council on Adolescent Development (1992, p. 30)

The greatest problem is that nobody understands. . . . They only know what's in the books. They don't know life. What I did just isn't in the books! I stayed out at night, stole cars, robbed stores, and we were a whole gang. The boy I went with isn't a bad boy. People don't understand that either. I think we just get into an age where many of us get into trouble. Most of us have nobody to sit down with and just talk, and it seems that we can never talk with our parents.

—From *The Adolescent Girl in Conflict* by Gislea Konopka (1966, p. 58)

Many—even most—young people traverse adolescence without serious problems. Dryfoos (1998) estimates that 40% of the total 3.6 million 14-year-olds in the United States are at little or no risk for experiencing serious problems. They cope successfully with the demands placed upon them by family, friends, schools, and the community. But adolescence is the period during which many serious problems emerge in young people's lives. A full third (approximately 1.2 million) of our 14-year-olds are estimated to be at high to very high risk (Dryfoos, 1998). As the noted child psychiatrist Michael Rutter states, "paradoxically, just as it was being appreciated that most adolescents did not manifest psychosocial disorders, the evidence began to accumulate that, since the Second World War, there has been a marked rise in psychosocial problems of young people" (1995, p. ix).

Consider the broad range of risky behaviors and pitfalls that await vulnerable adolescents. We know, for example, that delinquency—both major and minor—begins for most youth in early adolescence and reaches its height during later adolescence. Experimentation with alcohol, tobacco, and other drugs also begins for most children during adolescence, and it is during this time that they may establish critical use patterns that reach into adulthood. Exploration of one's sexuality begins in early adolescence and for many girls this experimentation leads to sexual intercourse, unwanted pregnancy, or sexually transmitted diseases. In addition to these problems, many adolescents begin to lose interest in school. This lack of scholastic interest can lead to an academic downward spiral: Falling grades lead to a lack of motivation to learn, which leads to school failure and school dropout. All of these social problems can substantially alter an adolescent's life course and have a lasting, detrimental impact.

Societal Context: The Big Picture

The problems described above do not emerge in a vacuum. They occur in the context of economic, cultural, and gender circumstances. Of particular importance are the settings in which many of our adolescents are growing up. Today, many of our neighborhoods are disorganized, seriously impoverished, drug-ridden, and simply unsafe. Young people who live in such environments face poverty and discrimination. Their day-to-day lives are devoid of the resources, support, and opportunities necessary for healthy development and preparation for adulthood.

These environmental factors limit adolescents' ability to reach their full potential. Society has created a context in which the health of our youth all too often is compromised, their self-confidence and self-image demeaned, and their opportunities for a safe, secure, satisfying life limited. Most adolescents, especially girls, do not have access to the resources and support structure they need. There are few portals of entry into opportunities that can facilitate healthy development and proper preparation for adulthood.

While environmental deficits certainly limit many youth, it is important to remind ourselves that not all young people who reside in impoverished neighborhoods are troubled and in need of help. But research has shown that adolescents from economically disadvantaged households are at higher risk than more economically privileged adolescents (National Research Council, 1993).

Indeed, adolescents that grow up in poverty tend not to see a positive future, cannot envision a role for themselves in society, and are not motivated to take steps in securing a healthy lifestyle.

We have learned a lot from the young people who survive adversity. They are important reminders of how critical it is to reach out to all young people. Many young people who face lives filled with vulnerability seize opportunities to transcend their adversity. Dryfoos's (1998, pp. 37–40) description of common characteristics of high-risk, resilient, and low-risk youth provides further insight into the complex personal and environmental factors affecting adolescents' behavior:

High-Risk Youth
- Early "acting out"
- Absence of nurturing parents
- Evidence of child abuse
- Disengagement from school
- Easily influenced by peers
- Depression
- Residence in disadvantaged neighborhoods
- Nonexposure to the world of work

Resilient Youth
- Attachment to a caring adult
- Independence and competence
- High aspirations
- Effective schools

Low-Risk Youth
- Strong supportive families
- Effective schools
- Safe neighborhoods
- More likely to be White non-Hispanics
- Reside in suburban areas with many social resources

Adolescents Facing Multiple Risks

Regardless of the assessed level of risk that any given teenager faces, there are far too many opportunities for all young people to wander off the path to health, success, and maturity. Millions of adolescents are growing up in a society that does not provide the support they need to experience healthy, optimal development. Table 8.2 presents the risks of adolescence according to social problem areas. A brief examination of this table leads to the conclusion that there are a plethora of serious risks facing young people today. Almost all adolescent experts agree that the demands and risks facing today's adolescents are more numerous and complex than they were a generation ago. In a *Newsweek* article, David Gelman (1990) calls modern adolescence a "much riskier passage" for today's youth than it was for past generations. Much of this increased risk can be attributed to the earlier age at which young people are exposed to risk.

As Table 8.1 reveals, a large percentage of young people face pressures to use alcohol, tobacco, and other drugs; to engage in sexual intercourse at earlier ages; and to begin stealing and committing other, sometimes violent crimes. Young people must learn to cope with many mental health problems, such as high rates of depression, suicidal behaviors, and eating disorders.

TABLE 8.1
THE RISKS OF ADOLESCENCE ACCORDING TO SOCIAL
PROBLEM AREAS AND AGE

Social Problem Areas	Age	Findings
Substance use	High school seniors	65% have used alcohol
		79% have smoked cigarettes
		19% used marijuana in the last 30 days
		18.6% smoked tobacco in the last 30 days
	8th graders	28% have been drunk at least once
Depression	adolescents	35% experience depressed moods
Suicide	adolescents	12% of the mortality rate is due to suicide
Homicide	10- to 14-year-olds	1.9 per 100,000; increases to 8.4 per 100,000 for African American males
Sexual intercourse	15-year-olds	27% of the girls, 33% of the boys have had sexual intercourse
	17- to 18-year-olds	50% of boys had sex by age 17.2
		50% of girls had sex by age 18.2
	13 and younger	Over 60% of sexually experienced girls had forced intercourse

	TABLE 8.1 CONTINUED	
Pregnancy	adolescents	23% of sexually active teens experience a pregnancy during the last year
HIV/AIDS	20- to 29-year-olds	Constitute 20% of the population with AIDS*
Crime/delinquency	10- to 17-year-olds	Constitute 10.9% of total arrests for crime
School dropout	16- to 24-year-olds	13–14% drop out of high school and do not complete their education
Eating disorders	12- to 18-year-olds	.5% females develop anorexia, 5-18% are afflicted with bulimia
Poverty	adolescents	20% live below the federal poverty line

From Alan Guttmacher Institute (1994); Brent (1989); Carnegie Council on Adolescent Development (1995); Dryfoos (1990); Flanagan & Jamieson, (1988); Gans and Blyth (1990); Herzog & Copeland (1985); Johnston, O'Malley, and Bachman (1994); and Petersen et al. (1993).

*The time between infection and onset of AIDS is up to 10 years.

Adolescents' Mental Health Needs: Girls' Invisible Problems

When asked to conjure a picture of the troubled adolescent, many people visualize a teenage boy. This vision may reflect our exposure to media images of boys dressed in black leather jackets or gang colors and engaged in violent behaviors. Or it may be due to a limited definition of "troubled adolescent." While it is true that more adolescent males than females are engaged in acts of delinquency (Dryfoos, 1990) it is important to note that girls in today's society face a myriad of problems—many of which have the potential to become serious life issues.

The young female adolescent in our society is particularly susceptible to what may be described as a group of "invisible" or "inwardly directed" problems including (but not limited to) depression, eating disorders, and poor body image. Although these difficulties may be less noticeable than delinquency, for example, they are quite serious, and many teenage girls are in dire need of services and help. Because these problems are easily hidden, girls who require assistance may successfully conceal them until they have reached a very serious level. In-depth analyses of these "invisible" problems are presented in other chapters. For the purposes of this chapter, however, it is important to remember three points: that problem behaviors do not usually occur in isolation; that these behaviors seem to group according to gender lines; and that gender-specific problems are not the same across cultural and ethnic lines.

In previous chapters we have presented problem behavior theory, which suggests that problems tend to occur in clusters. The National Council for Research on Women notes that girls who are depressed, for example, are more likely than nondepressed peers to develop eating disorders, become pregnant, and abuse substances (Phillips, 1998). Furthermore, within the framework of problems that tend to occur more frequently for girls than for boys, there are substantial variations across ethnic, cultural, and socioeconomic groups. Using the example of depression again, a recent study by the Commonwealth Fund (1997) found substantial variance in girls' depressive symptoms across ethnic lines, with 17% of Black girls, 22% of White girls, 27% of Hispanic girls, and 30% of Asian girls reporting such symptoms.

One study (Colten et al., 1991) examined the patterns of distress and disorder in a community sample of adolescents. The study included a random sample of 9th-, 10th-, and 11th-grade students in a northeast community. The researchers assessed 13 mental health areas and determined the presence or absence of specific problems. The results for 10th graders are summarized in figure 8.1. This table points to a number of significant considerations for adolescent girls. First, the number of girls who reported experiencing substantial difficulties in the study's 13 mental health areas was quite large. For example, psychosomatic disorders were found to occur in almost 50% of the 11th-grade girls, depression occurred in 33% of the 10th-grade girls, and anxiety occurred in 31.6% of the 12th-grade girls. Secondly, gender differences are quite pronounced in this study. Across all grades a higher percentage of girls reported problems in 8 of the 13 measures.

It is estimated that approximately 17–22% of adolescents suffer from developmental, emotional, or behavior problems (Costello et al., 1988). This figure does not include youth displaying at-risk behavior; it includes only youth with serious mental health problems, which can be defined as causing a significant impairment in the everyday functioning of the person. In numbers, 11–14 million of the 63 million youth in the United States display a significant impairment (Kazdin, 1993). There is clearly a need for mental health services for this population.

Barriers Everywhere: Finding and Accepting Help

While adolescence is a time when serious problems often begin to unfold, it unfortunately is also a time when youth face acute barriers to accessing the help

FIGURE 8.1

PERCENT OF BOYS AND GIRLS HAVING PROBLEMS

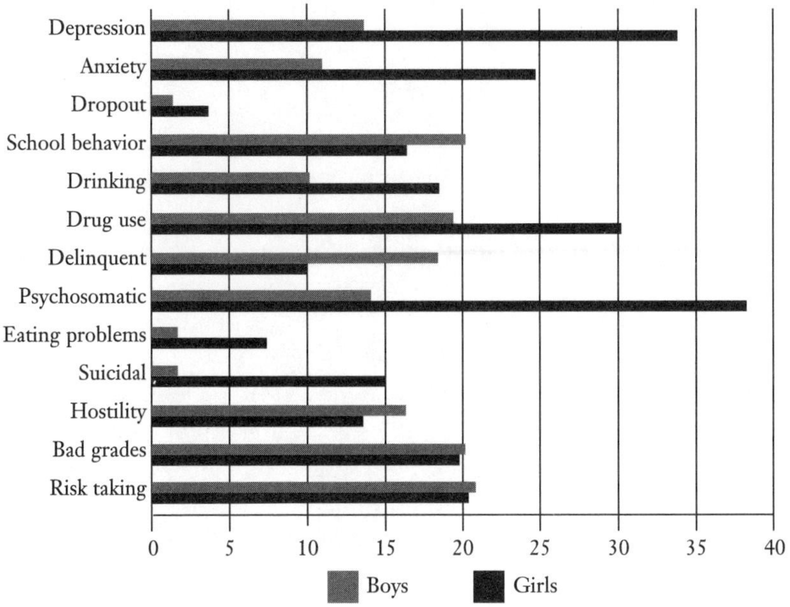

From Cohen et al. (1991)

they need. All too often, the seventh- or eighth-grade student does not know where to go or whom to trust. Locating help for adolescents is not only problematic for the youth themselves but also is a major challenge for professionals, parents, and communities. Many of the problems that girls experience demand attention outside of, or in addition to, the family. Several scenarios come to mind: the adolescent girl who is raped but too ashamed to tell her friends or parents; the girl who knows she has crossed the boundary from alcohol and drug experimentation to dependence; the girl who is trapped in a sexually intimate relationship and has not obtained birth control or STD protection; the girl who has depressed moods, feels hopeless, and experiences unhappiness much of the time; and the girl who has been adopted into a gang and is now involved in serious illegal behavior.

Given their level of need adolescents vastly underutilize systems of care (Millstein, 1988). Indeed they seek care less frequently than any other age group (Cypress, 1984). The key factors in this underutilization of services are: cost, poor organization of services, lack of availability, and concerns regarding confidentiality (Millstein & Litt, 1990). Poor utilization is more common among younger adolescents, those living in poverty, and minority group members (Millstein & Litt, 1990). Many of the serious problems confronted by adolescents (such as mental disorders, sexually transmitted diseases, and abuse) are not covered by most health insurance plans or the coverage is so restrictive that access to help is impeded (National Research Council, 1993).

Confidentiality

According to the National Council for Research on Women, "Of the adolescent girls with depressive symptoms, 46 percent cited concerns about confidentiality—or not wanting their parents to know that they were having problems—as their reason for not getting help" (Phillips, 1998, p. 25). Recent survey results reveal that under conditions where medical treatment would be confidential, adolescents would be significantly more likely to seek care for depression, birth control, sexually transmitted diseases, and drug use (Council on Scientific Affairs, AMA, 1993). Kobocow and colleagues (1983) administered personal interviews requiring substantial self-disclosure to a group of 195 seventh- and eighth-grade students. On a posttest questionnaire, "56.8% of females and 38.6% of males listed assurance of confidentiality as the most important statement made by the interviewer prior to the interview" (p. 422). These results illustrate the high value that adolescents place on confidentiality, as well as the need for increased sensitivity to adolescents' strong concerns about their privacy.

Systems of care must become more sensitive to adolescents' concerns about confidentiality. To be effective, these systems must also be tailored to an adolescent's nature. For example, many healthcare providers have no training in working with adolescents. In order to be able to ask sensitive questions and expose guarded concerns, adolescents must be comfortable with providers. And we know that providers report being unprepared to help adolescents with contraceptive counseling, evaluation of psychopathology, general counseling, and other areas (Irwin, 1986). Particularly in the current business-driven managed care environment, even practitioners who relate well to youth may not be able to take the time needed to develop rapport and provide a context for helping the adolescent disclose serious concerns.

If we want to help young people in trouble or at risk, we need to pave a road for them that is easy to follow and will lead to a successful outcome. Access to professionals who are specifically trained to work with adolescents is only one component of successful intervention for youth in trouble. Youth who need help must feel cared for and respected by a network of people. As mentioned in chapter 5, a social support group can provide an important buffer to serious problems and stress. Connections to a social support network may also make the prospect of seeking help more plausible since it is easier to acknowledge and address problems with the mutual support of others.

Providing Resources and Prevention

Providing access to resources is crucial if we are to help adolescents with the serious issues they face. It is important to remember that solutions can sometimes be simple. Not every adolescent problem requires intensive treatment. Even serious problems may be alleviated by providing access to simple resources. For example, Ackerson and colleagues (1998) found that providing adolescents with a self-help book about depression and conducting only four weekly phone calls reduced depressive symptoms.

Simple or complex, in order to access services adolescents must first know about existing resources. Schools, agencies, and communities need to engage in greater outreach, promote existing programs, and teach young people what services are available, how to access them, and how to use them effectively. Early adolescents are not mobile; they do not yet drive and public transportation to areas where services are located may be a mystery to them. It is, therefore, particularly important to consider the proximity and accessibility of services in your community. The Go Grrrls program creates a "Personal Yellow Pages" that girls can refer to for help (chapter 17). By enhancing awareness of available services and reducing barriers to ease access, we can build a community that is more responsive to the needs of adolescent girls.

Chapter 9

Planning for the Future: Barriers to Success

*There should be an all-girl place with classes on how to get jobs, like how
to go on an interview and fill out applications. If the class was all girls, you
could just be yourself.*
> —14-year-old girl, from *A Matter of Time* by Carnegie Council
> on Adolescent Development (1992, p. 11)

*I think that being a kid is the most important stage of your life. It's a time
when you start to develop a personality. It's when you start to learn about
who you are, and what you want to do with yourself. And it's a time when
you develop trust. It's a time when you learn how to be a person in society.
Unfortunately, a lot of kids don't have that. If you don't grow up learning
how to be a productive person, then you're going to have a problem once you
grow up.*
> —Sara Rosen, 16-year-old, from *Great Transitions: Preparing
> Adolescents for a New Century* by Carnegie Council on Adolescent
> Development (1995, p. 55)

During the final meeting of a recent Go Grrrls club, one participant pulled
her group leader aside to thank her privately. Emma, who wants to be a
marine biologist, explained, *"This is the first time I ever told people what I wanted
to be . . . and they didn't laugh at me!"* Because of the many advances women have
made over the last century, it may be surprising to hear that girls still face substantial barriers as they plan their futures. Emma is not alone in encountering
a less-than-supportive reception to her personal and career goals. Many girls in
today's society find that their visions and dreams for the future are discouraged
or even disparaged. Others, exposed to unrealistic media messages, may assume
that the most direct and satisfying path to success is to become a highly paid
model or actress—a goal they are unlikely to achieve. Still others, encouraged

86

by their families, fairy tales, and societal myths, believe that they will simply grow up to marry Prince Charming and live happily ever after. It is important to disabuse girls of unrealistic notions and to offer support, encouragement, and a road map to help them find their way to a successful future.

Adolescence is a critical juncture for planning the future. New pressures develop as young people examine potential roles that carry greater responsibility than the roles of childhood. A key aspect of young people's preparation for the future is their sense of achievement. As Santrock (1996) notes, "achievement becomes a more serious business in adolescence, and adolescents begin to sense that the game of life is now being played for real" (p. 453). Adolescents' experiences of success and failure are perceived as precursors to future outcomes in the adult world.

Based on this new orientation toward achievement, one might assume that adolescents become more invested in school success as they see the link between a good education and a successful life. However, as children move into adolescence their expectations for success tend to decline, their sense of competence declines, and their attitude toward school becomes more negative. Adolescents also become more focused on achieving outcomes than on gaining intrinsic satisfaction and greater competence.

What factors influence a person's achievement? Researchers point to both psychological and motivational factors, noting that intellectual ability is only one small part of the picture. In order to be successful achievers, young people need to be confident in their abilities and persistent in their efforts. Often, bright students lack these necessary confidence and planning skills and end up achieving far below their capacity.

Achievement motivation—the desire to accomplish something, to obtain a level of excellence, and to put forth the effort to excel (Santrock, 1996)—can be a critical factor in adolescents' success. Much attention has been focused on girls' declining confidence in their academic abilities as they move into adolescence. This erosion of intellectual confidence is likely to undermine girls' achievement motivation. Declining confidence is often at the root of many girls' low educational and vocational aspirations, especially in fields such as science and math (Eccles, 1994; Eccles et al., 1999; National Science Foundation, 1996). Girls who are competent in math and science may lose confidence in their abilities as they move through adolescence, which ultimately influences the types of careers they choose.

When students in a high school English class were asked to write a fantasy autobiography of their future, the differences between boys' and girls' tales were revealing (Tisdale, 1997). The boys' essays included themes of adventure, crime, and invention, including the invention of a time warp. The girls imagined very different futures. As Tisdale describes, "one after the other (wrote) of falling in love, getting married, having children, and giving up—giving up careers, travel, college, sports, private hopes, to save the marriage, take care of the children."

Moving from Middle School to Success

It is important to help girls focus on the future—on their careers and aspirations—during the middle school years. As noted earlier, the transition to middle school is often a difficult one, and it can take its toll on a girl's achievement motivation. In fact, middle school is referred to by Eccles as a "developmental mismatch" for young adolescents, as the institution offers few opportunities for youth to practice decision making and explore cognitive development. Eccles's research shows that achievement is detrimentally influenced by this transition in several ways: (1) grades often drop during the first year of middle school, (2) after the transition to middle school, adolescents become less interested in school, and (3) middle schools, as opposed to elementary schools, are more controlling, less cognitively challenging, and place more emphasis on competition.

Another reason to direct girls' attention to the future during their early-adolescent years is the real necessity for early career planning. If a young woman wishes to be a veterinarian, for instance, she will have to enroll in several upper-level math and science classes, beginning with foundation courses during middle school. She will also need to plan to spend 8 years of her life in college. Given the need for such foresight, goal setting is key to the process of future planning. It is a central component of the model used at many urban schools to help students develop talents, identify career wishes, and enhance academic skills and abilities. Many programs emphasize a self-directed career search where students learn how to map out steps for meeting their goals with appropriate timelines.

I Think I Can: Learning Attitudes and Orientations

Along with goal setting skills, another factor critical to success in middle school is how young people perceive their own abilities. Research by Henderson and Dweck (1990) found that adolescents who saw intelligence as fixed avoided tasks that challenged their abilities and chose to work only on problems they knew how to solve. But children who thought intelligence was malleable accepted challenging tasks and looked at failure as a way to learn and improve. Most critically, they saw their failures as resulting from a lack of effort rather than a lack of ability. Hendersen and Dweck (1990) refer to these two orientations as the *helpless orientation* and the *mastery orientation*. In the helpless orientation, adolescents feel trapped by the experience of difficulty. They attribute their difficulty to a lack of ability, as evidenced by self-talk such as, "I'm no good at this." Once they define themselves as failures they become trapped in a negative outlook. Mastery oriented adolescents are task-oriented. Rather than focusing on their ability, these young people focus on learning strategies. Mastery oriented children often say to themselves, "I need to think carefully and use my past experience." Rather than being threatened by new problems or difficult tasks, they report feeling challenged and excited by them.

In one study (Elliott & Dweck, 1988), fifth graders were led to believe that they had either low or high ability and then were asked to perform a novel task. They were warned that they would soon be performing similar tasks that would prove quite difficult. Fifty percent of the children worked under a *performance goal:* They were told that their performance would be compared to that of other children and evaluated by an expert. The other 50 percent were encouraged to accept a *learning goal:* They would make some mistakes, they were told, but working at the tasks would sharpen their minds and help them in school. The children who displayed signs of helplessness were those who believed they had low ability and were pursuing a performance goal. For them, continuing to work on the difficult task was a repeated demonstration of their own stupidity. By contrast, even "low-ability" students who pursued a learning goal persisted despite their failures and showed remarkably little frustration because they thought they could grow from their experience. Table 9.1 shows how achievement factors are influenced by either a mastery orientation or a learned helplessness orientation.

TABLE 9.1
ACHIEVEMENT FACTORS COMPARING A MASTERY VS.
LEARNED HELPLESSNESS ORIENTATION

Factors	Mastery Orientation	Learned Helplessness Orientation
View of Ability	Ability increases with effort	Ability is fixed
Goal	Learning goals: To try to become smarter	Performance goals: To try to show current abilities
Attribution for Success	Success due to high ability	Success due to luck or high effort
Attribution for Failure	Failure due to low effort	Failure due to low ability
Reactions to Failure	Persist, try harder	Give up, perform poorly

Girls are more likely than boys to have acquired a learned helpless orientation. Studies (Dweck & Licht, 1980; Eccles, 1987) have found that girls are less likely than boys to attribute success to ability and are more likely to attribute failure to a lack of ability. Thus, girls often fail to see their own ability as an important aspect of their success.

Not surprisingly, even gifted girls are more likely than gifted boys to underestimate their intellectual skills and their relative class standing (Strauss & Subotnik, 1991). Furthermore, this same study found that gifted girls reported more test anxiety than gifted boys. Many studies have found consistent evidence of gender differences in expectations for success and confidence in abilities. The differences depend on the domain and follow gender stereotypes—boys have higher confidence in math, science, and sports; girls have higher confidence in English and social activities (Eccles et al., 1999).

Middle school girls who have a learned helplessness orientation need coaching to help them develop a more adaptive attributional style. In one study, for example, students who became helpless in the face of repeated failures on math problems were given "attributional retraining" (see Dweck, 1975). These students first experienced some success followed by prearranged failures. After the failures they were told that they had not worked fast enough and should have tried harder. Through this retraining they learned to attribute their failures to lack of effort rather than low ability, hence developing a mastery orientation.

Girls need strong support in developing a mastery orientation. Difficult situations should be viewed as opportunities to develop better skills and competencies ("You'll be better at problem solving by working on this"). It is also critical to challenge girls to take on difficult work and seek to master it ("You're smart enough to solve those types of problems"). Last, encouragement of effort is critical ("If you persist you'll probably figure it out").

At the Intersection of Gender, Race, Social Class, and Peer Culture

In addition to gender differences, ethnic minority differences in achievement are also important to understand. In adolescence, minority youth become keenly aware of restricted occupational opportunities and this awareness can limit their life choices and plans for the future (Spencer & Dornbusch, 1990). Furthermore, many studies have found that differences in achievement are more likely to be an attribute of social class than ethnicity. For example, Graham (1990) found that middle-class African Americans had high achievement expectations and understood that failure is most often due to lack of effort rather than lack of ability, just like their middle-class White counterparts. In general, middle-class adolescents of all ethnicities measure higher than lower-class adolescents on various achievement indicators (such as expectations for success, achievement aspirations, and recognition of the importance of effort) (Gibbs, 1989).

Peer pressure can play a role in undermining achievement motivation for low-income minority students. In some African American and Hispanic peer cultures, academic achievement is discouraged as a sign of showing off, whereas many White and Asian American peer culture groups value and encourage such achievement (Steinberg, Dornbush, & Brown, 1992). Such negative peer pressure became infamous in one study when researchers (Fordham & Ogbu, 1986) found high-achieving African Americans risked rejection by their African American peers when academic accomplishments caused them to be perceived as "acting White." There is a psychological toll on such high achievers who are placed in a position of abandoning their cultural group and racial identity in order to succeed (Arroyo & Zigler, 1995). Clearly, extra consideration must be given to youth "at the crossroads," whose gender, race, social class, and peer culture may combine in unique ways to affect achievement motivation.

Career Development: Getting Girls to Think Outside the Box

How do girls decide on careers? Ginzberg's developmental career choice theory suggests they go through three stages: fantasy, tentative, and realistic (Ginzberg, 1972). Childhood career choices are numerous—"I want to be an actress, a model, a teacher, a rock star." This is considered the *fantasy stage* of career choice. From ages 11 to 17, adolescents enter the *tentative stage* of career development as they prepare for the realistic aspects of decision making in young adulthood. According to Ginzberg, adolescents in this stage move from evaluating their interests (11–12 years of age) to evaluating their capacities (13–14 years of age). The period from 17 to 18 years of age is the *realistic stage* of career choice. Early adolescence represents a key period of influence concerning career choice.

Adolescents often approach career decisions with a high degree of uncertainty and stress. Thus, many adolescents, especially girls, do not adequately explore career decisions on their own. In fact, students do not seem to know what information to seek about careers or how to seek it (Santrock, 1996). To compound the problem, few adolescents receive any direction from career counselors. In one study (Grotevant & Durett, 1980), students lacked information about the educational requirements for a particular career and the vocational interests associated with career choices.

Gender plays a very significant role in career decision making. Females continue to be constrained by traditional gender norms. Many girls are socialized to adopt nurturing or family roles rather than career roles. Although girls increasingly aspire to more professional jobs, due to cultural, peer, and family influence, many do not seriously consider traditionally male-oriented jobs (which frequently pay more than traditionally female-dominated jobs) and may even doubt their ability to attain such jobs. Furthermore, many girls do not seriously plan for careers and have not explored career alternatives (Baumrind, 1990; Eccles, 1999). Clearly, girls make different career choices because of their socialization. Figure 9.1 shows clearly how certain jobs continue to be gender-dominated.

FIGURE 9.1

PERCENTAGE OF WORKERS WHO ARE FEMALE

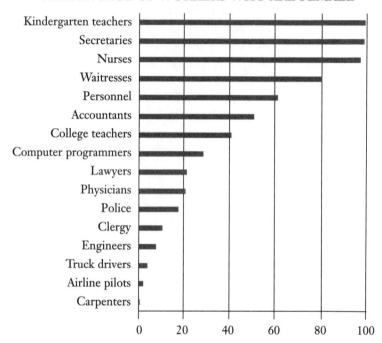

From U.S. Bureau of the Census (1995)

Research continues to demonstrate the existence of stereotypical views of gender and occupations. Consider the following scenario: A teacher walks to the front of a class and instructs the students to "get out a clean piece of paper. We are going to do a 'draw a scientist' exercise. When you are finished, hand in your picture." At the end of the day the teacher looks at all the pictures and finds that 100% of the boys drew the scientist as a man and 84% of the girls drew the scientist as a man (Wahl, 1988, cited in Mackoff, 1996). How likely is it that girls will imagine themselves as scientists given this scenario?

While media messages and cultural influences affect girls' career choices, parents are often the culprits, expecting more academic and career oriented achievement from their sons and less from their daughters (Eccles et al., 1993). They often reinforce gender-stereotypic careers by providing boys with more sports opportunities and emphasizing computers and math and science books and games. Girls are often pushed into language classes and social activities. These expectations and aspirations can have a profound effect on the future lives of adolescent girls.

In chapter 10, gender differences in assertiveness were noted. It is interesting to consider the way women's assertiveness in a job performance situation is regarded compared to men's. Negative perceptions are attached to women who demonstrate "masculine" behaviors. As the following list shows, positive "masculine" behaviors for men are often seen as negative behaviors for women.

Men	**Women**
He's assertive	She's a bitch
He's firm	She's rigid
He follows through	She's a micromanager
He's a detail person	She's picky
He's silent	She's secretive
He's directive	She's power hungry
He worked his way up	She slept her way to the top

Given these societal barriers, it is not surprising that many girls do not dream of scaling the corporate heights or becoming research scientists. One study (Simmons & Blyth, 1987) found that girls were less likely than boys to wish to work at an occupation continuously through their adult lives, while boys were less oriented toward plans of marriage and children. Early-adolescent boys were significantly less likely to say they wanted to get married and have children. And in this study, at least, a smaller percentage of girls aspired to work when they had young children than the percentage of women who actually do so in the adult population. Girls who do not expect to work while they are raising children may, then, be in for a shock when, by choice or necessity, they seek employment during those years.

Vision, Choice, and Adventure: Girls in the Future

Some programs have been developed to address the issues described in this chapter. For example, project CHOICE (creating her options in career education) was designed to detect barriers in career development. The program provides counseling and matches girls with female role models. Girls are also referred to occupational groups and career workshops. Choices (different from CHOICE) (Bingham, Edmondson, & Stryker, 1993) is a teen women's book for self-awareness and personal planning and has been used in weekly clubs or support groups for girls. Other similar programs such as Perfect Future Day and Choices have been successful in directing girls to more advanced careers (Kerr, 1992). Perfect Future Day and Choices encourage girls to share their career fantasies and discuss barriers that might block their progress. The emphasis is to help girls avoid gender stereotypes in occupations and encourage high aspirations. Results of Perfect Future Day revealed short-term success and found that girls redirected their career paths, although more long-term study is needed to examine impact over time.

Girls need support and encouragement for their career and educational goals. Emma, who we quoted at the beginning of the chapter, deserves to live in an environment where she is not laughed at for aspiring to be a marine biologist. More programs and events are needed to help girls imagine solid, rewarding careers for themselves. But even that is not enough. It is important to challenge girls to dream of adventures—mountain climbing, traveling, learning a new language—they would like to have in their lifetimes and to help them figure out how to experience those adventures. As girls begin to envision the kind of future they would like to inhabit, it is important to help them shape that future by encouraging them to participate in creative activities that can impact their community and society. By honoring the visions of girls and helping them to set goals and take credit for their successes, we will help them build strong futures.

PART II

THE GO GRRRLS CURRICULUM

Chapter 10

Working with Adolescent Girls

When I started to lead these groups I thought I had it pretty together, but every time I teach the program I learn something new myself. And every group of girls is different. You never know who you're going to get! I feel like I have about 40 little sisters all around the city, now.

—Nicki, Go Grrrls leader

Thanks for being our leaders. We think you guys are cool to come and teach us about ways to respect ourselves and feel good about who we are. You were silly and also fun, too. Bye.

—From a note written by Go Grrrls participants
Sarah and Nicole to their group leaders

As the review of girls' issues suggests, many social problems begin in early adolescence. Intervening during this period provides a ripe opportunity to both prevent the onset of problems and change new patterns of behavior that have not yet been firmly established. Early intervention allows for the introduction and enhancement of social and coping strategies that can have lifelong impact on adolescent girls. Intervention can also provide protection from negative sources of influence such as the media and some peer pressure. Involvement in the Go Grrrls program helps girls develop a lifelong perspective about living as a female in society and can provide a lasting base of information for girls transitioning from adolescent to adult life.

Our enthusiasm for working with girls has come from the sheer delight of seeing girls reach out for a greater understanding of themselves and learn better ways of surviving in today's world. Our experience in conducting groups with adolescent girls has reinforced the notion that this is an ideal developmental period for preventive intervention. The girls we see every week want to know more about who they are, their developing bodies, where they fit in society,

97

how to develop greater support among friends and parents, and how to make responsible decisions that they can feel good about. Their natural interest and desire to learn about themselves should be harnessed and developed, not wasted.

Implementing the Go Grrrls Program

The Go Grrrls program is designed to be conducted on a weekly or twice-a-week basis with small groups of early-adolescent girls. We believe that a group size of 8 to 10 participants is most effective, although groups can be conducted with anywhere from 4 to 15 girls. Each session is designed to last 90 minutes, which is enough time for participants to become involved but not enough time for them to get bored. Some situations, such as when the Go Grrrls group is incorporated as part of the school day, require that the groups be condensed to one-hour blocks. While it may be necessary to vary the program delivery in some ways, it is important that all of the content areas in the curriculum be implemented in full. This is because each session builds on the knowledge and skills learned in the previous sessions, and the total curriculum content is considered critical to the program's overall positive effects.

This program is a curriculum-based approach to prevention. As such there is a prescribed model to follow. We believe it is important to follow this model but it must be presented in a fun and exciting manner. Psychoeducational programs tend to be pedagogical and can end up being boring, and lacking in interest. We have tried to design the Go Grrrls program in a manner that is fun and exciting. However, *delivery* of the program largely affects how fun and exciting it truly is. If group leaders read from the pages or drone on like adults in a *Peanuts* cartoon, the girls will tune them out as quickly as they would an easy-listening radio station. We use discussion, role-play, and games to get the point across. As noted earlier, we sometimes suggest a game for the very end of a session. While they may seem to have little to do with course content, these games have a purpose. They are a sort of "reward" to girls for having given their attention to more serious subject matter earlier in the meeting.

Group Leaders

In our implementation of the program we have used undergraduate and graduate students from the local university. Many of these women are majoring in human service fields such as social work, education, family studies, and psychology, but dynamic leaders have also been recruited from engineering, pre-med, and business fields. We assign two female group leaders for every 6 to 10 girls. On a very practical level, two group leaders can better control the group process and sustain a higher level of energy because they can take turns "taking point" throughout a session. Coleaders also make it possible to use instructive, leader role-plays in some sessions. Group leaders can be paired so that their talents complement one another. Additionally, having two leaders provides girls with a broader range of role models. We provide close weekly supervision of the group leaders and implement an extensive training program.

In recruiting for group leaders we look for the following skills:

- *Enthusiasm and good teaching ability.* Groups need to be fast-paced and lively. Leaders need to bring a high degree of enthusiasm and excitement to the group.
- *Organization and planning ability.* Because this is a structured curriculum leaders need to be highly organized. They must come prepared for each group. They need to plan ahead and anticipate any difficulties. We help group leaders with these tasks by providing them with a Go Grrrls storage box. Inside the box are all the materials and supplies they need for each group session.
- *Good listening and interpersonal sensitivity abilities.* It is vital that Go Grrrls club participants feel like they can talk about any issues they have and be attentively listened to. The group leader and participant relationship is critical to the success of the program and good listening is the starting point for building a strong, trusting relationship. At the same time, it is important that group leaders are assertive enough to move the group on if a single participant is dominating the group time.
- *Good understanding of adolescent development and the specific issues facing early adolescent girls.* Because this program is based on developmental knowledge of early-adolescent girls it is important that leaders be familiar with the developmental basics for this age group. A significant part of the group leader training is preparing the leaders on critical developmental issues and promoting an understanding about early-adolescent girls.
- *Good social skills and comfort in role-playing and demonstrating behaviors.* The group experience is designed to be "action oriented" and therefore relies on leaders who are comfortable demonstrating a wide range of behaviors. For example, leaders are asked to "ham up" an interaction showing how not to behave and to provide a model performance of the best way to behave.
- *Sensitivity to problems and ethical issues.* Problems will invariably arise and will need to be addressed by the group leaders. Leaders need to be sensitive to these problems, anticipate them as much as possible, and feel comfortable dealing with potential ethical issues. As this is a prevention group, we do not

attempt to provide counseling services to girls, but leaders must be equipped to help link girls to needed services.

We have found that most of our group leaders are profoundly influenced by their experience in delivering the program. Most of our group leaders are young college women; many of them are still forming their own identities and confronting the stereotypes and pressures placed on them by society. Anyone supervising group leaders needs to be aware that the leaders will probably need time to process their own issues as young women in society. In this sense, the program benefits both the participants and the leaders.

Recruitment and Participation

Go Grrrls was designed as an after-school program, although we have also implemented the program during school hours. We have been successful in recruiting a large number of girls to participate. Several different strategies have been used. For example, we have signed up many participants during orientation and "parents' nights" at schools. These events are ideal because potential participants and their parents are present together. This allows us to explain program format and content to parents while getting girls excited about becoming part of the club. Other recruitment strategies have included giving presentations at special school events and actively recruiting for participants during lunchtime. Frequently, program "graduates" reach out to girls by introducing themselves and explaining the program. (Several participants have actually finished the entire program cycle twice, a few girls have completed three cycles, and one ardent fan is on her fourth round!) It is not uncommon to hear parents exclaim that they wish they had such a program when they were in middle school.

We do not describe Go Grrrls as a "prevention program" to potential participants. Instead, we ask them if they'd like to join the Go Grrrls *club*. This may seem like a small point, but girls are much more likely to sign up for a club (it sounds like fun, they get to be a member, etc.) than they are to sign up for a prevention program (which sounds like something their parents would make them do!). The biggest barrier to participation has been that the program sometimes ends up competing with other after-school activities like music lessons, clubs, or sports. Go Grrrls administrators should try to schedule the program at a time that does not overlap with other popular after-school activities. Running the program in several cycles through the school year enables different girls to participate, as sports and other clubs may be seasonal. At some schools, Go Grrrls is offered as a special elective class during the school day, which eliminates the problem of competing activities.

The Participants: Everyone's Invited

The Go Grrrls program was designed specifically for girls between the ages of 11 and 14. We have focused on intervening at an age when the program content is likely to have the most impact. Because this is a primary prevention program it is designed for *all adolescent girls*, not just at-risk youth. The goal of the program is to reach adolescent girls before they begin to experience some of the negative consequences of growing up as a girl in today's society. Most middle schools today include sixth-, seventh-, and eighth-grade students. We have found that groups run successfully when all participants are in the same grade or when there is no more than one grade level separating them.

We have successfully implemented the program with girls from a broad range of backgrounds. Many of our groups are racially mixed, with White, Hispanic, Black, Asian, Native American, and mixed-race girls. The program has also flourished in schools that are attended by an absolute majority of Hispanic students. At these schools we attempt to use group leaders who are bilingual or who come from the neighborhoods where the program is instituted. The program evaluations at these schools are as high as our overall ratings. At least half of the girls who have completed the program in Pima County, Arizona, where Go Grrrls originated, live at or below the poverty line (this is measured according to the percentage of participants who receive a free school lunch).

According to SIECUS (Sexuality Information and Education Council of the United States), 11% of self-identified gay or bisexual women surveyed on college campuses knew they were gay or bisexual in grade school; 6% knew by junior high school. This means that 17% of women who later identify as gay or bisexual had determined that fact by middle school. The Go Grrrls program defines lesbianism and bisexuality as normal and healthy. Our leader training includes a discussion on how to answer questions about sexual orientation with sensitivity and honesty.

Because the Go Grrrls curriculum encourages girls to appreciate themselves for their unique characteristics, it naturally supports respect for cultural differences. Still, because we cover so many topics, it is unrealistic to suggest that the curriculum may be applied exactly the same way regardless of participants' race, ethnicity, sexual preference, or other unique characteristics. We suggest that professionals use the curriculum as a template and make minor modifications when they are needed. There are plenty of opportunities for creative enhancement, and we encourage the girls to make the role-play dialog "their own" by ad-libbing. The students' response is tremendous.

While most of our groups are voluntary after-school clubs open to all participants, we have also conducted groups for at-risk girls (girls who have a history of delinquency, pregnancy, substance abuse, etc., and may also be at risk from poverty). These groups generally take place during the school day, and participants are referred by school counselors, teachers, and administrators. The curriculum remains basically the same for these groups; however, "sample situations" and role-play scenarios can be modified to reflect this population's experience. Importantly, we leave all incentives for participation in place even though the group is no longer considered voluntary. Consequently, at-risk participants who are mandated to join the group feel like they are participating freely and not coming to the group as a punishment.

We also have made some modifications to the program and implemented it with older teenage girls. For these students, as with the at-risk populations, it may be necessary to change the sample situations to reflect concerns of more mature girls. Some small modifications of course content may be necessary (for instance, it is not necessary to cover material about a girl's first period with a group of 19-year-olds). Most of the older participants in the program have been at-risk students or participants in a teen parent program, and these girls have expressed great enthusiasm about the program.

The Group Process: Guidelines for Success

The group process is critical to the success of effective groups for adolescents. Young people need to be actively involved in the group. When group leaders dominate the process the program becomes more like the all-too-familiar classroom presentation. The following key factors can keep the program interesting and encourage the success of the group process (Hazel et al., 1981; Rose & Edelson, 1987; Wolfe et al., 1996):

Active pacing

Leaders can make a group more engaging by maintaining a very active pace. The Go Grrrls curriculum contains a lot of material and active pacing is necessary to cover it all. Recommended time signatures for activities and discussions, as well as a time target space (example below), are given for each session.

<u>Establishing Group Standards:</u>   (10 minutes)   Time: _____-_____

We require that group leaders write out the times in the space provided. This is important because it is virtually impossible to keep track of how long "10 minutes" actually is during the session itself. If an activity is recommended to take 10 minutes and the group leader has calculated the entire group time in advance in the time target spaces, she can check to see if they are on pace, or if they need to speed up or slow down, just by checking her watch.

One of the most critical skills in active pacing is keeping the discussion on target. When one group member digresses, time is lost and other group members begin to get bored. A well meaning group leader may allow a girl to ramble on. A good group leader is able to keep the members focused on the topic at hand without offending a long-winded participant. This must be done in a positive, matter-of-fact manner. For example: "Julie, your point is important but we need to stick with today's topic or we'll get behind with the material. You and I can talk more about this when the group is over, if you like." We encourage group leaders to keep a lively pace when they are speaking and organizing the session's tasks. Being organized and clear about what needs to be accomplished in each session helps keep an active pace.

Frequent contribution

When possible, group leaders should work toward obtaining contributions from all participants. This also means that leaders should keep their comments to a minimum so group members can participate. Calling on all members to make statements keeps everyone involved. For example, when discussing the negative influence of the media selected members can be asked, "How has the media influenced you?" or, "Sandy, can you tell us in your own words how media can have a negative effect on girls?" Asking group members to contribute to the discussion facilitates involvement.

In many sessions, girls are encouraged to share responses or journal assignments out loud. We have found that if group leaders choose one person to respond and then "going around the circle" from that point, the girls at the end of the circle tend to become restless. It is better to randomly request responses by using girls' names. Once the culture of participation is established, girls will usually volunteer—and even clamor—to respond.

Use of praise

Leaders are trained to use a lot of praise in the groups. Girls feel more assertive and confident, and are more likely to apply the material to their everyday lives when they receive positive feedback about their contributions. Be as specific as you can when giving praise and praise the *behavior* not the person. A group leader should think about what it is that a member said or did that was noteworthy. An example of specific praise might be, "That was a good example of how to tell your friend how you feel without making her feel bad." Small and quick praise such as "great explanation" or "good insight" is also needed. Remember, praise is more effective when delivered in an enthusiastic and upbeat manner. Group leaders are also instructed to offer praise to each other.

Two of our group leaders perfected a special "flying high five" to praise each other and their group members. This kind of spirited praise and celebration sets an excellent example by showing girls how two women can collaborate and appreciate each other's talents and skills.

Use of names

Using group members' names makes the group experience more personal and satisfying. The name game played in session 1 not only helps members get to know one another's names, but also helps group leaders quickly learn the participants' names. Using names right away helps with early "crowd control." And because most participants are getting used to the newly large, impersonal middle school setting, they respond very positively to a small group setting with leaders who immediately take the time to learn their names.

As mentioned previously, group leaders are encouraged to call on members by name when asking questions. This is faster than waiting for group members to respond to a question thrown out to the group and keeps the group lively and more interesting. It sets the expectation that everyone should be involved and participate in the process. Furthermore, open-ended questions can sometimes lead to one person dominating the group discussion, which needs to be avoided as much as possible.

Linking the Program to Families

The Go Grrrls program uses a companion parent curriculum to involve the families of participants. This companion piece (in Appendix F) provides parents with a very brief description of each session's goals and activities, along with some recommended activities and discussion points for home use. In one instance, girls are asked to interview their parent/guardian about their opinions on dating prior to a group discussion on this topic. In this way, girls bring parental feedback into the group.

While we encourage "home participation" from parents, we discourage parents from attending the group. There are several reasons for this: Girls tend to feel constrained by their parent's presence; parental presence takes away the "club" ambience; usually only a few parents would be able to attend during group time and it is awkward to have partial parent attendance; and, practically speaking, including parents simply swells the group to an unwieldy size. When a parent is very insistent on participation, we ask for help with materials, or curriculum review, or some other task that does not involve actually attending the group.

Working with Schools: Getting Support

Most school administrators, counselors, and teachers are very supportive of Go Grrrls once they understand the content and goals of the program. When approaching new schools, it is important to find one or two "key contacts" who will help spread the word to faculty and parents, aid in recruitment, and help with logistics like room assignments and school policies. Because Go Grrrls has established an excellent reputation in our home area, we generally receive requests from schools to conduct groups; however, at the outset it may be necessary to make appointments with key school personnel. The majority of our key contacts are school vice principals (assistant principals) and school counselors. These people can sometimes help collect permission slips, notify Go Grrrls administrators of school open house nights, and help smooth over any procedural snags.

There are several small but substantial barriers to successful integration of the program in local schools. Inclusion of sexuality content can be a source of conflict. In one district, we were informed that the program would be welcome only if the sexuality content was eliminated. It is usually possible in these cases to work with administrators to come to an understanding. It can be pointed out, for example, that the program is voluntary and parental permission to participate is required; therefore, all parents give informed consent for the discussion of sexuality. It is also true that the curriculum covering sexuality is actually abstinence-based, which is a developmentally appropriate approach. Pointing this out to school personnel can ease concerns.

Another common barrier to smooth school relations involves securing rooms to use for the after-school program. It is imperative to train group leaders to establish good communication with the classroom teacher and to check on any specific requests a teacher may have (e.g., "Please put desks back in clusters at the end of the group"). It is also important to check on any school rules that are in place, even for after-school activities, at each site. At one school where we provide services, for example, there is a uniform code that requires students to keep their shirts tucked in, even after school. Most schools have some kind of dress code, and it is important to remind group leaders to dress according to these guidelines. While leaders are not expected to dress up, or to wear school uniforms, of course, they are not allowed to wear clothes that contain tobacco or alcohol ads, extremely short dresses/shorts/skirts, or spaghetti straps. We do encourage our group leaders to dress casually, though, so they can participate in all activities. Advance preparation and good communication between Go Grrrls staff and school personnel are tremendously important for long-term program success.

The Community Context: A Ripple Effect

Go Grrrls represents a primary prevention strategy that is focused directly on interaction with girls. Even though our focus is limited, the program should be seen as one component within a broader community context. The girls themselves serve as catalysts for change when they begin to spread the messages they learn in the group to the broader school population. School personnel become more aware of issues specifically affecting girls. School counselors and teachers use the group as a resource. In one instance, a small community group in a rural area heard about the Go Grrrls program and began serving youth from several different public and private schools at a central location in their area. Parents participate at home and frequently become activists on behalf of their daughters. Indeed, implementing the Go Grrrls program tends to create a ripple effect, or a new awareness of girls' needs. While the program is specific and circumscribed, the broader community context is a critical component of effective efforts to respond in a comprehensive manner to further promote the healthy development of girls and the environment in which they live.

In the curriculum that follows, each session is introduced with quotes from Go Grrrls participants and leaders. Quotes are followed by brief descriptions of that session's highlights or recommendations for the group process. The curriculum itself is presented so that practitioners can easily implement the program. Other useful tips for using the curriculum are included in the preface. We hope that your experience working with young teenage girls turns out to be as rewarding for you as it has been for us.

Chapter 11

Being a Girl in Today's Society

Session 1: Introduction to Girls' Issues

The first meeting was a little scary 'cause I didn't know anybody yet, but our leaders were nice so that helped. Then I really liked playing the name game because we got to know everybody's names and we remembered our positive adjectives for the whole time we met.

—Amber

When I signed up for this I thought it might suck, but this was actually fun. When are we supposed to meet again? Can I bring my friend Patti with me?

—Leticia, at the end of her first meeting

New experiences arouse a complicated mix of emotions. When new Go Grrrls participants walk into the meeting room for the first time, they are likely to be experiencing some combination of curiosity (*What will we do?*), nervousness (*Will I do it well enough?*), excitement (*This could be fun*), skepticism (*This might be boring*), and hope (*I hope I like this*). The first session of the program is designed to establish a supportive atmosphere and capture girls' attention and interest. This work begins even before girls walk through the door.

Depending on the facility, we arrange chairs or pillows on the floor in a circle. The important point is to establish a physical set up that will support the goal of involving every participant, and classroom-style rows of desks simply do not work. Next, we prepare to greet participants at the door.

A typical scene unfolds like this: The bell rings, signaling the end of the school day. Girls wander down the hallway, a bit unsure of where they're headed.

"Are you here for the Go Grrrls club?" we inquire as they near the door.

"Yeah."

"Welcome. We'll be meeting in this room. Come on in. My name is Jan. What's yours?"

"Marilyn."

"Thanks for coming, Marilyn. We're going to have a lot of fun."

"What are we going to do?"

"Good question! We'll tell you all about it as soon as everybody gets here."

Once the girls have arrived, coleaders take positions on opposite sides of the circle—not beside each other, and not standing at a chalkboard lecturing like classroom teachers. The initial atmosphere may range from nervous quiet to boisterous conversation. Every group is different. Sometimes girls have relationships established prior to the group. Other times, all the girls are strangers to one another. Regardless of the starting point, the goal is to mold this collection of individuals into a group where every individual is recognized, yet all feel a sense of belonging. Group leaders take turns introducing themselves.

During our group leader training, we instruct leaders to encourage participation from the very first session. For example, during the section on establishing group rules, Go Grrrls members are asked to brainstorm their own club rules. Instead of having the group leaders write these down, we train group leaders to have the girls write the rules that they suggest. This must be done carefully, however. If a group leader responds to the first girl who offers a rule by saying, "Good. Could you please write that down?" and the girl says, "No," the group gets off to an awkward start. Instead, we train group leaders to approach the first girl who offers a rule and show her a handful of colored markers. Then the group leader asks her, "What color do you want?" Once the girl has chosen a marker, the leader simply says, "Good suggestion, write it down." This is subtle, but girls will respond, and the group culture of participation is established.

Rationale

Prior to introducing the content of the group it is important to develop a comfortable and supportive group atmosphere. Establishing this supportive atmosphere will provide a sense of security and safety for group members. This is extremely important given the developmental level of early adolescents. The overall program will be briefly introduced to participants to give them a sense of the topics that will be covered during the course of the 12-session cycle.

Goals

1. Introduce the Go Grrrls program format, content, and purpose.
2. Create a comfortable and supportive atmosphere.
3. Obtain pretreatment measures for program evaluation.

Materials

Puzzle (p. 113), flip chart, markers, Go Grrrls Questionnaire (p. 211), scrap paper, pens/pencils, parent curriculum (p. 225), and workbooks.

Overview

During this session group members begin to get to know one another and leaders introduce the Go Grrrls program. The session begins with brief introductions, followed by administration of the Go Grrrls questionnaire pretest. Next, a "name game" is played to help both leaders and participants learn group members' names quickly and to break the ice. Next, group rules are set up. After the group establishes its rules, the Go Grrrls puzzle is introduced. The puzzle serves as an outline to show group members how the program will progress and how the curriculum pieces fit together to make a whole.

Procedure

Before the group begins, arrange the room so that girls can sit in a circle. Either arrange chairs in a circle or find a comfortable area where girls and group leaders can sit in a circle on the floor.

<u>*Introduction*</u>   (5 minutes) Time: _____ – _____

Begin the session by welcoming all participants to the Go Grrrls Club. Introduce yourselves and give some basic background information. This should include information about who you are, what you do, why you are doing this, and some fun fact such as what your favorite color is, what pets you have, and maybe even one thing you remember from middle school/junior high. This is an example of an introduction:

> My name is Maria and I am a college student at Arizona State University. I am one of the leaders of this group. We will be meeting in this room for the next six weeks to talk about what it's like to be a girl, what kinds of things girls go through, and all of the great qualities girls have. We will meet twice a week on Tuesday and Thursday at 3 P.M. I'll be leading this group because I love working with kids. I remember one day when I was in junior high and I dropped my lunch tray in the middle of the cafeteria. I was so embarrassed! My favorite color is purple.

<u>*Play the name game*</u>   (20 minutes) Time: _____ – _____

The purpose of playing this game is to get to know everyone's name and to create a comfortable, fun atmosphere. One group leader explains the rules:

I want everybody to take a moment to think of an adjective that describes you . . . something positive . . . that starts with the same letter of the alphabet as your first name (for example, Adventurous Andrea or Inventive Iris). The first person will say their adjective and name (Adventurous Andrea). The person to her right will go next. This person says the first person's adjective and name, then says her own adjective and name (Adventurous Andrea, Slick Sally). The person to "Slick Sally's" right will then say all of the previous adjectives and names, adding her own to the list (Merry Maria, Slick Sally, Inventive Iris). We'll keep going until each person has taken their turn. It can get pretty hard to remember everyone's name as we go along, so if you need help you can ask everyone to help you out! Who wants to start?

You should participate in this game as well. You may need to help girls with tricky first initials. The game is fun, but it can be hard for kids at the end of the group to remember everyone's name. Suggest that if a girl can't remember someone's adjective and name, she ask the person to remind her.

Taking attendance
Now you need to take attendance. It is crucial that you do this carefully for program evaluation purposes. One group leader should explain:

I am going to come around and ask you to help me fill out some information on our attendance sheet. After today, we will just record whether you are here or not, but today it may take a little while to get everybody's name and information. Thanks for being patient!

Be sure that you have written down every participants' *full name*, her correct initials, her birth date (including year of birth), and her ethnic information. Every time a new person joins the group, collect this information. You can then use it to match the pretest information with the attendance information to determine whether "dosage" of the group affected outcomes.

Go Grrrls Questionnaire   (25 minutes)   Time: _____ – _____
Do not hand out the questionnaire pretest until you finish giving the directions below. Be sure that girls have a private, comfortable place to take the test. If they are sitting close together, have them spread out around the room before you read the directions. (Answers may be skewed if girls sit too close together and check their answers with one another). This is what you can say:

Today you will be participating in a very important study. This questionnaire asks you about your attitudes, behaviors, and concerns about issues facing young girls today. The purpose of the study is to help our community understand what kinds of issues girls face. Your answers will be confidential. That means that your parents won't see your answers. Your teachers won't see your answers. Nobody will come to you later to ask you why you answered a question in a particular way.

Please read all of the questions carefully. Sometimes it seems like a question is repeated. There are questions that are similar, but not the same. This is done on purpose for the study. It is very important that you answer every question, but if a question makes you feel very uncomfortable you do not have to answer it.

Remember, this isn't a test, so there aren't any "right" or "wrong" answers. If you aren't sure about an answer, give it your best guess. Try to answer every question, and if you need help, just raise your hand and one of us will come help you.

Now pass out the pretests and pens and have the girls fill them out. Remain alert to answer any questions, but do not walk around the room "on patrol" or girls may think you're reading their responses.

Because girls will finish at different times, it's important to have something quiet to do for the girls who finish quickly. We suggest that one of the group leaders engages everybody who finishes in a silent game of Hangman, using a category like movies. Spread some markers around and have fun quietly!

Once everyone has finished say something like this:

Thank you for filling out those questionnaires. We want you to know that your opinions are really important, so thanks for helping us. We'll fill out another questionnaire like this one, but not until the very end of the club. Right now we're going to talk about what our group should be like.

Establishing group rules   (10 minutes)   Time: _____–_____
We call this section "This Is How We Do It."

1. Find a place in the room to put the flip chart (either on the floor in the middle of the group or hanging on a wall somewhere) where everyone can see it. Begin by titling the sheet with the words: This Is How We Do It.
2. Ask girls to identify what rules are, and what they feel are appropriate rules for this group. Tell them that this is their club, so they need to come up with their own rules. Have them write their ideas in different colors on the flip chart page. When the first girl volunteers a group standard, approach her with a handful of markers and say, "Great. Pick a color and write it on the

board for me." By directing (rather than asking for volunteers to write) you begin a group culture of participation. Examples of rules include:

> No interrupting while somebody else is talking
> Respect each other
> Be on time
> Don't tell other people what you hear in here
> Be nice to people
> No swearing (it's not respectful)
> Have fun!

3. When they have finished offering suggestions, be certain that you either review or add the following concepts: confidentiality, the right to "pass" on answering a question or making a contribution, listening and giving helpful feedback. Define each of these.

- *Confidentiality:* This is very important. Here is what you can say:
  Confidentiality means that what we say in the club stays in the club. Now, if you want to tell somebody about a really fun game that we played, that's fine. But if somebody in here tells us that her big sister got pregnant last year, we shouldn't talk about that with people outside of the club meetings. Does everybody see why this is important? (Take questions if they arise.)

  We (use your name and your coleader's) won't tell people what goes on in here either. There are a few exceptions to that rule, though, so we want you to know up front what they are. Our Number One, Numero Uno, Big Old, Gigantic, Main concern here is that everybody is safe. So, if one of you guys told us that you were going to hurt yourself, or somebody else, or that somebody is hurting you, we would need to tell other people so we can keep everybody safe. Does that make sense to you all? Okay, great.

- *The right to pass:* This means that if a group member does not want to talk, she has the right to say, "I pass." Here is what you can say:
  Everybody in this group is important. We want to hear from all of you. Sometimes we'll ask people what they think about something. Every now and then, though, we all have a really hard day, or we just can't seem to think of anything, or something feels too personal to talk about right at the moment. If this happens, you can just say "I pass," and we'll move on to the next person. It's important to remember that "passing" isn't something you can do all of the time . . . that's not fair to everybody else who is sharing their thoughts. But it is important to know that we can all pass sometimes.

- *Positive feedback:* It is important to respect each person by listening to what they say and not saying hurtful things back. Here is what you can say:

  Everybody in the group has their own opinions. That's good! Some people agree with us and others disagree. That's normal! When disagreements happen, it's important that we remember to be respectful. That means that we should not be mean or hurtful to another club member. For example, it's fine to say, "I disagree with that because . . .", but it's not okay to say, "You are so stupid. No way is that true!" Does everybody see the difference?

  It's also important that we try to encourage each other. For example, if you think somebody just said something really cool, it's good to say so! Or if you think that everybody in the club just did a great job at one of the games, say it out loud.

Finish up the rules and any questions, and then explain:

  Now it's time to figure out what we're going to do and talk about in our Go Grrrls club.

Go Grrrls puzzle   (10 minutes at the most)   Time: _____–_____
In this time frame, the curriculum is introduced to members using the puzzle.

  Ask girls if they remember the name of the club (Go Grrrls). Ask them to give you some ideas about what important things girls might talk about.

  Display the large "puzzle" that shows the group curriculum. Explain that you all will be talking and learning about what it means to be a girl. You will talk about choices that girls make and how to make good choices. You will talk about how important it is to feel good about yourself and how to do that. You will talk about how important it is to stay away from risky behavior and how to do that. You will play games and have fun while you do this.

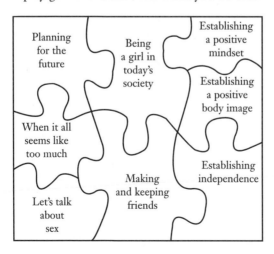

Ask group members to read each puzzle piece title aloud, and then quickly review each piece. Examples follow for eight puzzle pieces.

Being a Girl in Today's Society: In this section we will talk about what it means to be a girl. We will discuss how others see girls and women and how we see ourselves. We will talk about the messages that the media gives us about what it means to be a successful girl or woman, and we will decide if we agree with those messages or not.

Establishing a Positive Body Image: In this section we will talk about our bodies and how we might compare ourselves to others. We will consider how important it is not to rely on physical appearance as the measure of self-worth. We will talk about the ways that understanding our positive personal qualities can help us respect ourselves.

Establishing a Positive Mindset: How we talk to ourselves is important. We will learn about how we talk ourselves into a downward spiral and how we can lead ourselves to an upward spiral.

Making and Keeping Friends: In these club meetings we will learn about making friends, about good relationships, and about how to handle problems that come up in friendships and dating situations. It's important to find good friends who will support you when you make good personal choices.

Establishing Independence: We will talk about standing up for yourself so that you feel good about your decisions and other people understand you and respect you. You will learn ways to solve problems and make smart decisions.

Let's Talk about Sex: In these meetings we will learn about the facts of life and about ways to respect and protect yourself. We will also talk about how important it is to stay away from drugs and how using drugs might get you into some very risky situations.

When It All Seems Like Too Much: In this section we will talk about some problems that come up that are too much to deal with all alone. When these problems happen, it's important to know where to go to get help. We'll figure out a plan.

Planning for the Future: During these club meetings we will exchange ideas about your choices for the future. What kind of job do you want? How can you achieve your goals and dreams? What adventures would you like to have? We will talk about everything we learned and did in the club, and have a party and graduation to say goodbye to each other.

Explain that each puzzle piece contributes to the whole, and that it is very important for club members to come to every club meeting. Introduce the incentives for perfect attendance. Perfect attendance is defined as attending every group. Exceptions can be made, if a member is sick, has a family event that their parents mandate they attend, etc. Remember, this is an incentive, meaning that we want the prize to encourage attendance. It should not be made impossible for kids to achieve!

Distribute Go Grrrls journal/workbooks
and parent curriculum   (10 minutes) Time: _____ – _____

Distribute the parent curriculum. Explain that everyone needs to give a copy of the parent curriculum to their parent/guardian. This is very important because in the parent permission form we promised everyone's parents that they would get one! Then, explain that the journal workbooks are for club members to keep. Tell them they are welcome to write whatever they want in the journals, and that you will not collect them or force them to tell you what they write, but that you will ask them to voluntarily share their work. Mention that you will ask them to complete fun little assignments in their journals for each club meeting. Keep track of journal assignments completed by each member. Again, remember that we want them to complete the assignment, so if you see somebody scribbling furiously at the beginning of the group to complete it, *let them do it!*

Explain incentives for journal assignment completion. Each time they complete a journal assignment, club members can enter their name in a final-session drawing for a gift certificate or other incentive. The more assignments they complete, the better their chances of winning the prize are.

For this meeting's assignment (p. 9 in the workbook), ask the girls to make a list of the following (if you are not using the workbook, be sure to speak slowly so that they can write these down):

Your favorite color, favorite song or music group, favorite book, favorite TV show, who lives in your home with you, the types of pets you have and their names, and what your hobbies are.

Explain that you all will share these lists out loud at the next club meeting, so you can all get to know one another better.

Closing   (10 minutes) Time: _____ – _____

For the closing game, play Two Truths and a Lie. This game, like previous activities in this session, helps leaders and participants get to know one another. Give each member a piece of scrap paper and pencil. Ask each participant to write down two statements about herself that are true and one statement about herself that is a lie. Explain that you will each read these three statements out loud, and the rest of the group will try to guess which of the statements is the lie. Tell them to try to trick people. Group leaders should play, too. Here is an example:

1. I am the oldest in my family.
2. I love broccoli.
3. I have a pet skunk.

People might guess that the skunk statement is the lie, when actually the lie is in statement #1—she is not the oldest, but rather the youngest in the family.

After the game, say goodbye to all group members and remind them where and when the next club meeting is. Relax and enjoy the fact that your first session went so well!

Session 2: Media Messages

"It was good learning about stereotypes because then I got to see ways that I can just be myself instead of doing stuff like all the TV shows and magazines say. Like, I'm just not into the whole make-over thing in all the magazines. I'll make myself over any way I want, thank you. And now when I listen to music, I still dance to it if it has a good beat, but if the words say nasty things about girls I talk about it with my friends."

—Dora

"Look at this one! She look like she starving. Shit. No wonder she got that sad looking face!"

—Karel, while looking through magazines to make a collage

The girls huddle over a large piece of blank paper. We are listening to a popular rap song—not a particularly raunchy one, but one that nevertheless contains some disparaging lyrics about a woman's role in life.

"I like this song!" Melissa says while dancing around.

That's fine, of course. We are not trying to stop girls from listening to popular music. We are trying, instead, to teach them to listen for negative media messages and learn to "talk back"—think critically— about what they hear.

"Yeah, it's got a great bass line," I agree, disarming any need for the girls to defend their music. "Let's check out what they're saying . . ." We extract some of the messages in the rap tune and then we listen to a country song and go through the same process.

Meanwhile, my coleader is working with the other half of the group. They have been foraging through popular magazines, constructing a collage of media stereotypes of women. After about half an hour, we pull the two activity groups together to present our findings.

Sheena, from the magazine group, presents their collage.

"Nobody has zits and their teeth are all perfectly straight," she points out. "They're all really tall and skinny but some of them have big boobs. And they're mostly white women, except for a few." The other girls nod in understanding and agreement.

Next, Sarah, from the music group, takes the lead. "Some stuff the songs say is that you've gotta act sexy. And you're supposed to be easy, but then you're bad, like a hoochie-mama if you do it."

The girls giggle.

"I'm serious. . . . Then, other songs say you have to take care of your house and your kids, but the magazines show that you have to look really good and wear makeup while you do it."

They all nod and laugh again.

"What happens when we compare ourselves to these stereotypes?" I ask. The room grows quieter.

"Well, you feel bad," Melissa volunteers, and points to the collage. "I mean, I'm never gonna look like her."

"Yeah and it can make you kind of mad, you know, to hear all the stuff about the hos and the bitches."

Although this is only the second group meeting, the girls already feel some solidarity. We continue the discussion, moving through gender-role stereotypes of women and men. At the end of the meeting, when we ask them how many real women they know who fit the media stereotype, they admit that they don't know anybody who really does.

"My mom doesn't wear makeup when she makes us dinner," one girl says, "and neither does my Dad."

Rationale

Several studies note the powerful influence of media messages in reinforcing negative stereotypes about girls and women. Television, magazines, radio, and lyrics of popular music bombard adolescents with the message that physical attractiveness and early expressions of sexuality are the gateways to maturity, independence, and peer approval. This group is intended to promote awareness of the profusion of negative images of women and girls in popular media, and to equip girls with the ability and confidence to critically challenge these cultural myths and stereotypes.

Goals

1. To identify pressures society places on girls through media messages.
2. To examine perceptions about gender role and feelings about gender.
3. To help girls challenge the message that sexuality and physical image are the most important aspects of an individual and to teach them to "talk back" to these negative influences.

Materials

Puzzle, flip chart, magazines, scissors, glue, music cassette, cassette player, markers, pens, blank sheets of scrap paper, tape, and a group prize for 10 Stereo-types game.

Handouts: Lyrics to a popular song with some negative messages about women, "I Am Unique!" (p. 241).

Overview

During this session the club members are divided into two groups. One group leader facilitates each group. Half the members listen to popular songs in order to identify the messages about girls and women. The other half creates a collage from magazines popular with adolescent girls, identifying the message inherent in those pages. The two groups then come together and group leaders facilitate a discussion of what the girls have learned. Girls are encouraged to think critically about media messages that portray early sexual activity as glamorous, and facilitators help them arrive at the conclusion that these media messages are faulty.

Procedure

Introduction/journal/workbook activity   (15 minutes) Time: _____ – _____
After greeting club members and taking attendance, ask if anyone remembers all of the adjectives and names of the group members from last session. Then, as an ice-breaker activity, ask each girl to read her journal "favorites list" aloud (p. 9 in the workbook). This activity helps kids get to know each other and helps facilitators get to know members, too. Be sure to use the girls' names frequently.

Refer to the Go Grrrls puzzle. Ask members to identify which piece of the puzzle you are on today (Being a Girl). Give a very brief overview of what the group will focus on today. Example:

Today we are going to talk about what messages we get from music, magazines, TV, and other places—about what it's like to be a girl. We're going to see if we agree with the media images of what's important.

Identifying media messages exercise   (25 minutes)   Time: _____ – _____
Break the group into two sections (3 minutes to get kids into two groups). You may have them count off by twos. Ask each group to congregate in a separate area in the room. One group leader should accompany each section.

Music group. This group listens to some songs on tape. The first time you play the songs, allow the girls to just listen. Then distribute the song lyrics. Ask the girls to listen again while reading the lyrics. Ask them what the songs seem to say about girls. How girls are supposed to act, what they should look like, how they should feel, what their purpose is, what they should do, etc. Spread colorful markers around a big sheet of flip chart paper and explain that this group will create a "graffiti style" collage of the messages about girls/women they hear in the songs. Explain that they will present their findings to the other half of the group shortly.

Magazine group (simultaneous with music group above). This group peruses magazines to identify messages about girls/women in articles, advertisements, and photos. Spread out scissors and glue sticks around a big sheet of flip chart paper and explain that their task is to create a collage of messages these magazines are giving about what girls/women should look like, act like, etc. Explain that they will present their findings to the other group shortly.

Discussion   (15 minutes)   Time: _____ – _____
Bring the two groups together. Have one group at a time explain their findings to the other half. Highlight similarities found in both groups by making a list on the flip chart. Tell the girls that if they can come up with a list of at least 10 stereotypes of girls from the media they looked at and listened to, they get a prize (Don't tell them what it is). Some items on this list might include:

> *skinny, no zits, pretty, sexy, cheap, easy, big eyes, blonde hair, always looks happy, firm butt, only thinks about sex, good cook, etc.*

Make sure the girls list at least 10 things so you can award the prize. (For group prizes we frequently award inexpensive items like pencils, erasers, or candy). While they savor their victory, lead a discussion focusing on the possible effects of accepting this image as real or ideal. Ask the girls how many (if any!) women they know who really fit these stereotyped images. Mention the fact that not even the models look "perfect" in real life. Photos are routinely touched up to erase blemishes or to make someone appear thinner!

Media messages about guys   (10 minutes)   Time: _____ – _____
Then ask the girls what media messages they think guys deal with. What do magazines, music, TV, etc., suggest that guys look like or act like? Some possible answers include:

muscular, drives a hot car, drinks beer, plays sports like a superstar, doesn't show feelings, is always having sex, makes a ton of money, is always confident and never scared of anything, plays in a rock-and-roll band, treats girls badly, etc.

Lead a brief discussion asking girls whether they think the media stereotypes of guys are very realistic. Then talk about what is more important about both guys and girls that these messages don't say (being a good friend, having a good sense of humor, having talents and skills, being smart, funny, etc.)

Sexual harassment: What it is and why it's not okay   (5 minutes)   Time: _____–_____

When people think they should act like the stereotype of women and men, they often treat each other without respect. One real problem for many young people is a form of disrespect called sexual harassment. Ask group members if they have ever heard of the term "sexual harassment." Define the term with the group as, "when someone is teased, touched, or bothered about being female/male by another person or persons." Ask them if they can think of some examples of sexual harassment. Some examples might include:

Guys whistling at girls in the hallway.

Guys trying to touch girls' private parts.

Girls rating a boy's body when he walks by.

Guys teasing a girl about having a flat chest.

Ask the group why it's not okay to harass or to be sexually harassed. Reasons might include:

It makes you feel bad.
It makes you self conscious.
It's mean to do that.
It shows disrespect for another person.

Tell the group members that if they think they are being sexually harassed, they should tell an adult that they trust right away so they can get help. Also tell them that it's important for everyone to remember the need to be respectful of other people and not to feel like they must act like a stereotype.

Concluding remarks   (2 minutes)   Time: _____–_____

As a brief segue between today's session and sessions 3 and 4, discuss the negative effects that can result when girls/women believe the false media message that the most important thing about people is what they look like and how "sexy" they are. Point out that it's okay to try to look good. Looking good can make you feel good. But mention that feeling like you have to look *perfect* can lead to negative feelings. Similarly, it's fine to like boys. But mention how important it is to respect yourself enough to believe that you are valuable for qualities other than sex. We need to learn to accept who we are, what we look like, and our bodies as they are. We need to focus on what is important about ourselves—namely, our personalities, talents, skills, and dreams. Mention that we will talk more about this in the next "puzzle piece."

Journal/workbook assignment   (5 minutes   Time: _____ – _____

Ask the girls to make a list of five things they really like about themselves (p. 20 in the workbook). Tell them that at the next club meeting they will be asked to read three of these items out loud. Remind them to bring their journal/workbooks with them every session, and remind them about the journal incentives.

Closing   (13 minutes)   Time: _____ – _____

Hand out scrap paper and pencils. Ask each girl to write the following:

1. Her name, backwards, including first and last names. (Maria Jones becomes Airam Senoj.)
2. The name of an animal she likes, in plural form (monkeys).
3. The name of a flower she likes in plural form (daisies).
4. A human emotion, in noun, not adjective, form (happiness, not happy).
5. The name of a natural force, object, or a place she loves (the moon, granite, lightning, the Grand Canyon).
6. Her name, backwards, the same way she wrote it in number 1.

Suggest that everyone take a turn at pronouncing her "backwards name," because she will be saying it out loud. Pass out the I Am Unique! handout (p. 241) and ask the girls to fill in the blanks. You should also complete the list above and fill in the blanks of the poem. After sharing your poem with the group, ask each girl to read her poem out loud.

Say goodbye to club members, tell them when the next meeting is, and remind them about attendance and journal assignment incentives.

Chapter 12

Establishing a Positive Body Image

Session 3: Building Body Confidence

I went on a diet for the first time this year. I didn't really, really, really think I was fat, but my friend Julie still wears a size 4 and I couldn't even fit a 6 any more. I didn't like going to the mall with her because she's all, 'I'm so fat' and meanwhile I'm way bigger than she is. It was depressing.

—Jessica

The best part of this club was when I did the body tracing thing. At first I didn't want to do it at all and then (my group leader) said I could trace her, first. She made a real funny pose with her arms up. When we looked at all the pictures, everybody looked different. Mine just looked different like everybody else's.

—Miranda

This session flows smoothly, but some groups encounter barriers. One of the barriers tends to occur after we have asked the girls to trace their body outlines on cloth and we have challenged them to list five things they like about their bodies. Not only is it difficult for many girls to think of five, but even those who can are hobbled by the possibility they will be labeled conceited—"stuck up" is what they say—if they extol their own virtues. Group leaders must model the skill of self-praise to make it acceptable to the group.

In one meeting, Loretta stares forlornly at a blank handout asking her to list five positive body qualities.

"How are you doing with that?" I inquire.
"Crummy. I can't think of anything," she says.
I encourage her, "Hmm. I heard that you're a really good dancer."
"Yeah. So. . . ." she responds.

"Well, I love to dance. I love the way I can move my hips back and forth and catch the rhythm of the music." I demonstrate.

Loretta laughs, but she says, "Yeah, I like my hips, too. And my feet . . . when I dance I can move my feet really fast."

"Excellent! Write those down! Hey, I thought of another thing I like about my body: my hands. They look just like my mother's hands and when I look at them I'm reminded of her."

"My nose is just like my Aunt Agnes's." She's really cool." Loretta adds, "nose like Aunt Agnes's" to her paper. She's smiling now and needs no additional prompting to declare that she also likes her "curves" and her "strong arms."

You've got to walk the walk. That is, the group leaders' body confidence can make or break this session. It is not enough to tell girls how to begin to like their bodies. We must offer a model of self-acceptance and self-celebration.

Rationale

Adolescent girls frequently develop a negative body image, and negative body image tends to be related to low self-esteem and depression. These factors are, in turn, related to high-risk behaviors. This session challenges girls to find personal, physical characteristics that they like about themselves, and emphasizes that attractiveness is based on factors other than physical appearance. Participants are encouraged to appreciate and build on their unique qualities, talents, and skills instead of relying solely on their physical appearance for their self-concept.

Goals

1. To help girls develop a positive body image.
2. To help girls understand that being attractive isn't just based on physical looks.
3. To help girls understand that attractiveness is based on behaviors as much as appearance.
4. To help girls focus more on their personal qualities than their physical looks.

Materials

Puzzle, flip chart, cloth, crayons, pens/pencils, markers, and sticky notes.
Handout: What I Like about My Body/Women's Dissatisfaction with Their Bodies (p. 242).

Overview

First, girls participate in an exercise designed to help them accept their bodies as they are. During the course of the group, focus shifts from acceptance of physical characteristics to the importance of personal qualities, abilities, skills, and talents. Discussion relates this session to the "media messages" session by helping girls to realize the importance of inner qualities (rather than physical characteristics) in establishing lasting friendships and good dating relationships. The group ends on a positive note, with each girl describing some of the things she likes about her body and some of her favorite personal qualities.

Procedure

<u>Introduction</u>   (5 minutes) Time: _____ – _____

Begin the session by reviewing the puzzle. Ask the girls to identify which puzzle piece you are on (establishing a positive body image). Tell them that an important part of developing a positive image is developing a positive body image. It is *very* important to explain to the girls that during this stage of their physical development (early adolescence) it is normal and natural to develop more body fat than they had when they were younger. Here is an example of how to describe this:

> During puberty, a girl's body goes through what is called a "fat spurt." This is completely normal. Girls develop at different rates, and everybody's body is different. We'll talk more about physical changes in the "Let's Talk about Sex" sessions, but for today it is important to remember that the physical changes you are experiencing now are helping your body—and your self—grow into a woman.

Ask the girls why they think it might be important for girls to develop a positive body image. Go around the group and get some responses. Summarize these, and then conclude with the following:

> For a lot of girls, accepting their body is a challenge—too often their body is a source of anxiety and hurt. And while magazines and TV promote images of women with so-called perfect bodies, most girls and women cannot and will not look like these models. So we need to learn to like our bodies the way they are and not compare ourselves with the unrealistic standards set by society. Who sets these standards anyway? Can there be more than one way of looking beautiful? Remember how foolish some of the media messages we analyzed in the last session were? (There was too much emphasis on being skinny, or looking sexy, and not enough on the really important qualities of a person.) We can focus on

being healthy, exercising, nutrition, and on fun self-care. We can be the best people we can be, inside and outside.

Journal/workbook activity (10 minutes)   Time: _____ – _____

Review the "what I like about myself" journal assignment (p. 20 in the workbook). Each girl is to share three of the five items on her list with the group. Make a chart to classify the responses, but do not label the response categories until after all responses are shared. One leader should facilitate the discussion while the other leader is prepared, with four different colored markers, to write down girls' responses. As the girls offer their answers, the "writing leader" should categorize them:

How I look	How I Act & Treat Others	What I Can Do (talents, skills)	How I Think

After all responses are offered, have the girls guess the column labels. Label the categories in the girls' own words (e.g., "My Body" for "How I Look").

Point out (if true) that a number of girls identify physical aspects that they like about themselves. (Usually this is the longest list. Girls have often been taught to evaluate themselves, critically and positively, based on their physical attributes.) Point out that girls are often taught that the most important thing about them is to have good looks. Dispute this. Also, note that everyone has a different set of traits that are good. We won't all have great looks, winning personalities, special skills, and superior cognitive abilities. But all of us have strengths in some areas. Some people are good in school, while others are friendly and outgoing. This is what is truly important about people: their unique blend of qualities.

Tracing exercise (50 minutes)   Time: _____ – _____

Hand out large sheets of cloth. Divide girls into pairs. Have each member of the pair trace her buddy's outline onto the cloth with the markers. Then, ask all club members to fill out the "What I Like about My Body" handout. Writing on the handout first gives girls time to think about what qualities they will write on their cloth. If a girl is having trouble coming up with five physical qualities that she likes, be encouraging without being insulting (e.g., point out a participant's pretty hair, but do not tell a girl with obvious acne that she has beautiful skin!). Ask each girl to write the items from the handout on her cloth body outline. Then, ask each girl to add to her cloth body outline five qualities *other than physical traits* that they like about themselves.

Remember, if a girl is very uncomfortable about allowing someone else to trace her outline, it is *just fine* for her to draw her own outline freehand onto the cloth. This exercise is meant to help girls feel good, and should not make anyone feel worse about themselves! If a girl refuses to participate at all, do not force her. Often girls will join in halfway through the exercise once they perceive that they have a choice.

When everyone has finished, lead the girls on a little "tour" of each person's body masterpiece. Then get back into a circle and discuss the exercise. Ask girls if it was difficult to do or not. Point out the fact that lots of girls start off by thinking about their body in terms of the "fashion model" standard—weight, hips, breast size, etc.—but finish by focusing on other aspects of their bodies that they really like, such as their eyes, lips, hands, rounded curves, their own weight, etc. Tell the girls that they can keep these outlines and decorate them some more at home. (Some kids have embroidered them, added glitter-glue, yarn hair, etc.) If you have a long group session, you may want to provide these materials.

List of qualities exercise   (5 minutes)   Time: _____–_____

Explain to the group that women are considered "attractive" more because of how they act than how they look. This is a more positive approach than worrying about what your body looks like. Have the group brainstorm examples of attractive behaviors. Let each girl write one on the flip chart with her own choice of marker color. Examples might include:

> *smiles*
> *intelligent*
> *happy*
> *fun to talk to*
> *respect for others*
> *good sense of humor*
> *friendly*
> *self-respect*

Point out that none of these things has to do with one's physical appearance, and all of them things are something that girls can do to be attractive. By focusing on the positive, we can be more attractive and stop worrying about not having a "perfect 10," fashion-model body. Being happy and friendly will probably be a lot more attractive to another person than weighing five pounds less!

Handout exercise   (5 minutes)   Time: _____–_____

Hand out the graph of women's dissatisfaction with their bodies to the club members (p. 28 in the workbook). This study shows the changes over time in women's dissatisfaction with their overall appearance, weight, and abdomen. The study found that 89% of women wanted to lose weight, and that more than half were dissatisfied with their appearance. Unfortunately, over the last 25 years, women have become increasingly unhappy with what they weigh and how they look. Trying to live up to that fashion-model image takes them on a downward spiral. Tell the girls that we will talk about how to get themselves on an upward spiral, instead, at our next meeting. (Group leaders: You are challenged to think about satisfaction with your own bodies!)

Journal/workbook assignment   (5 minutes) Time: _____–_____
Ask the girls to make a list of five negative things they sometimes tell themselves (p. 30 in the workbook). Tell them that at the next club meeting they will be asked to read three of these items out loud. Remind them to bring their journal/workbooks with them to every session and remind them about the journal assignment incentives.

Closing   (10 minutes) Time: _____–_____
Choose one group member to step out of the room for a moment. Direct the other group members to decide on the name of a sports figure, cartoon character, or movie/TV character, and write the name of the chosen character on a sticky note. Invite the person back into the room and place the sticky note on her back (make sure it's nothing disparaging!). She then must ask only yes or no questions of the group until she figures out who "she is." There is a maximum of 20 questions.

For example: The group chooses Sporty Spice. The "it" person could ask the following questions:

Am I a cartoon character? (no)
Am I an entertainment figure? (yes)
Do I sing? (yes)
Do I sing with a group? (yes)
Do I sing with the Spice Girls? (yes)
Am I Ginger Spice? (no)
Am I Sporty Spice? (yes)

She cannot ask questions like, "What group do I sing with?"

Repeat with as many people as you have time for. Then say goodbyes, remind everyone of the attendance and assignment incentives and tell them what a great job they did.

Chapter 13

Establishing a Positive Mindset

Session 4: Rethinking Self-Statements

You want me to list five negative things I say to myself? I'm stupid, I'm too fat, I'm ugly, I'm lazy and nobody likes me. I can do a lot more than that. I bet I can do at least 10.

—Lisa

The upward spiral stuff really helped me a lot because I was always saying nasty things to myself, like, 'Lora you can't do this' and 'Lora you can't do that.' When (the group leader) got down and showed us what it looks like when you get down on yourself, I was like, 'Wow, I do that!' But now I'm learning to say stuff like, 'I can do this homework.' It's cool.

—Lora

Given the wide range of factors that contribute to girls' potential to become depressed, it is challenging to develop a curriculum that addresses self-esteem and depression. In the Go Grrrls program, we focus on teaching girls how they can change their thoughts about the many internal and external pressures they face. Participants are taught to identify negative self- talk, which includes statements that overgeneralize (e.g., *Nobody likes me; I'm never going to make any friends*) or imply unrealistic self-expectations (e.g., *I should get straight As all the time; I should look just like the skinny models on MTV*). Group leaders demonstrate how to turn negative self-talk into positive self-talk that can lead to an "upward spiral" of emotion and action. To ensure that members grasp the concept, we developed a game called Downward and Upward Spirals.

In the game, girls select a card containing either a negative or a positive self-statement. They are asked to read the statement out loud to the group and then identify whether it is positive or negative and whether it will take them on an upward or downward spiral. While most of the cards contain statements that

128

are readily identifiable as positive or negative, a few engender some doubt. This doubt is a good starting point for group discussion.

For example, as was earlier delineated, girls are frequently socialized to be "pleasers," so it is not surprising that one of the most common set of unrealistic expectations girls have is that they should like and be liked by everyone. In one group, the game plays out as follows:

The girls are standing shoulder-to-shoulder in a row across the back of the room. They look like a row of wildflowers of various heights, shapes, and sizes. Vanessa is the third to select a card from the Downward and Upward Spirals deck. She reads it aloud.

" 'I want to have a lot of friends but not everyone will like me.'
Hmm. I think that's a negative self-statement and it will lead me on a downward spiral."

"I think this is a tricky one," I suggest. "What makes you say it's negative?"

"Well, if I tell myself that not everyone will like me, that's not very nice."

"I can see how you would think that. It makes sense. But let's take a closer look at this. Does anybody here think the statement might be positive?"

Michelle, a quiet but thoughtful girl offers, "I think it might."

"Can you tell us why?" I ask.

"Well, it's just real life. I mean, not everybody is going to like you. So that's okay. So when you say that to yourself, it's like saying 'Don't get too stressed about it.' "

The other girls agree, but Vanessa says, "Yeah, but you know how you want people to like you."

Another girl joins in, "Yeah, but not everyone will. It doesn't mean you have to be totally rude to people. But if you're walking around thinking, 'Oh, everybody has to like me,' then it would be hard to just be yourself."

"That's true," Vanessa agrees. "But it was tricky. I should get an extra turn!"

I poll the group. "What do the rest of you think?"

"That was a really hard one, let her go again." Michelle votes. The other girls agree.

They are developing cohesiveness at this stage, a real esprit-de-corps. It is encouraging to watch. The group support is invaluable. And teaching girls to confront their unrealistic expectations empowers them to encourage themselves.

Rationale

An important part of our program is teaching girls about the relationship between low self-esteem, self-criticism, and depression, all of which increase girls' likelihood of engaging in risky behaviors. Girls entering middle school show a significant decline in their overall self-esteem. This session is designed to teach girls how they can give themselves positive messages to facilitate realistic goal achievement and boost self-esteem and self-efficacy. This confidence-building session serves as an important prerequisite to later skill-building exercises.

Goals

1. To help girls become aware of the "downward spiral": how negative self-perceptions can lead to self-criticism, and how self-criticism can lead to depression.
2. To help girls become aware of how they can change their self-perceptions to be more positive, and how to take the steps leading to an "upward spiral."
3. To help girls eliminate unrealistic standards that set them up for failure.
4. To help girls understand that feeling good about themselves will help them resist pressures to engage in risky behaviors.

Materials

Puzzle, markers, Spirals game cards (pp. 247, 249), Spirals game prize, blindfold for Trust game, three small Trust game prizes.

Handouts: Downward and Upward Spirals (pp. 243, 244), I Should, I Have to, I Want to: What works best?/Changing an "I Should" to an "I Want to" (p. 245).

Overview

Girls are asked to identify what they think self-criticism is and where it comes from. They can easily relate to what self-criticism is and can usually identify some of its origins. For example, girls often state that self-criticism is "when you get down on yourself" or "dissing yourself." The discussion about where self-criticism comes from typically revolves around setting unreachable or unrealistic goals, or trying to live up to others' expectations, and trying to be perfect. The group looks at ways to focus on setting attainable goals that enhance self-esteem. The way you present this material is extremely important. Group leaders must be very energetic to get this information across!

Procedure

<u>Introduction</u>   (2–3 minutes) Time: _____–_____

Point to the puzzle (p. 113) and ask the group to identify which puzzle piece you are on (Positive Mindset). Mention something like the following:

Establishing a positive mindset is a goal for the Go Grrrls program because we know that feeling good about yourself is really important, but it can be really difficult. Last time we met we talked about how to have a more positive body image. Today we are going to learn how to take a negative mental image and make it more positive. By feeling more positive about yourself, you can accomplish more and you can resist pressures to do some risky things. Today we will talk about things we say to ourselves that hurt our self-image and how to turn those statements around to help us feel good.

Journal/workbook activity   (15 minutes)   Time: _____–_____

Explain that the things we say to ourselves that bring us down usually fall into the following categories (write these on your flipchart):

- Unrealistic goals and expectations. These are *"I have to's and "I should's,"* like, *"I have to be really skinny,"* or *"I think I'm stupid because I don't get straight As in school."*
- All-or-nothing thinking and overgeneralization. These are words like *"everybody," "always," "nobody,"* or *"never,"* like *"I'm never going to make any friends."*

Ask girls to take out their journal/workbooks. Have each girl read out loud three of the negative messages she says to herself (p. 30 in the workbook). Do they fit into these two categories? For example: *"I'm fat,"* or *"I'm stupid, I'm not popular enough,"* probably fit into the unrealistic goals and expectations category. *"Nobody likes me"* fits into the all-or-nothing category.

Then describe how girls can sometimes end up feeling depressed as a result of unrealistic expectations or all-or-nothing thinking. Share the following examples with the group, and ask them to supply the self-criticism that might come from each of these unrealistic expectations:

If I Say to Myself:	Then the Self-Criticism is:
I *have to* get straight As.	I am stupid if I don't.
I *have to* get invited to *all* of the popular parties.	I'm not popular enough if I don't.
I really want to be liked by *everybody.*	*Nobody* likes me.
I can't make *anybody* get mad at me at all.	If they do, then I'm not a good person.
I *have to* get Tom to like me.	If he doesn't, then I'm not good enough.
I *have to* do *whatever* Tom asks of me so that he will like me.	I'm not worth hanging around if I don't.

Ask the group if they sometimes think this way. Help the girls recognize that unrealistic expectations and goals and all-or-nothing thinking can lead to self-criticism. Explain that these kinds of thoughts can lead to a "downward spiral." Then distribute the Downward and Upward Spirals handouts.

Example of a downward spiral   (5 minutes)   Time: _____–_____
When you introduce this section, start by standing up. As your coleader reads the passage below (with feeling!), you should begin to slump, frown, etc., until you are on the ground looking very distraught at the end. It's important that you ham it up quite a bit here to get the point across. Explain the following:

> I am going to demonstrate what happens when we put ourselves on a "downward spiral." Watch my body and my facial expressions for clues about how I'm feeling!

> First you begin to set unrealistic goals:
> *"I have to be liked by everyone."*

> Then you start to use more self-criticism:
> *"I really messed up when I talked back to Tom, and now I'm afraid of what my other friends will think."*

> Next you begin to feel depressed or unhappy:
> *"I am sad because nobody likes me."*

> Then you use even *more* self-criticism:
> *"I don't know how to be a good friend, I can't get along with others, I'm not a very likable person."*

> Finally you feel even more depressed or unhappy:
> *"I hate myself for what I have done and I'm really feeling depressed."*

Ask the girls what they noticed about the downward spiral. Then, explain that the way to confront the downward spiral is to turn it upside down and make it an upward spiral. Sometimes we have to pull ourselves out of feeling down and move upward to get out of a negative mood.

Example of an upward spiral   (5 minutes)   Time: _____–_____
When you introduce this section, start by lying down. As your coleader reads the upward spiral statements, react by rising a bit and looking happier and more confident with each phrase. By the last sentence, you should be standing up, head held high, and looking confident! You can do this!

> First you're feeling pretty low from the downward spiral you just took!
> *"I hate myself for what I have done and I'm really feeling depressed."*

Then you set a realistic goal:
"I want Tom to like me, but it's important for me to stick up for my own thoughts and feelings."

Next you shift from self-criticism to realistic and positive thoughts:
"Even though Tom is mad at me it doesn't mean I am a bad person or that I am not worth hanging around if I don't do what he says. There are lots of good things about me as a friend."

Finally you feel better as a result:
"I'm happy with almost all of my other friendships and I can feel good about that."

<u>*Downward and Upward Spirals game*</u>   (25 minutes) Time: _____ – _____
Group leaders: Again, your energy and enthusiasm are the key to the success of this game. As each girl takes a turn, shake her hand and congratulate her in a playful way—whether she answers correctly or not, whether she gets to move up or not. We play this game to demonstrate the upward and downward spiral effects. Ask the girls to stand in a line, next to each other, across the back of a room. Then read the following directions:

> The idea of this game is identify which sentences on the card are positive and lead to an upward spiral, and which sentences are negative and lead to a downward spiral. Each of you will draw one of these cards (hold up game cards) with a positive or negative self-statement on it. You must read the whole card out loud, then either say "positive, upward spiral," or "negative, downward spiral."
>
> You get to take one giant step forward *only* if you (1) get a positive statement card, and (2) you correctly identify that it is positive. If you get a negative statement card, or if you identify a positive statement incorrectly as a negative statement, then you just stay where you are. Everybody will get three turns to do this, and at the end of these three rounds, whoever is standing in front wins. If there is a tie, the contenders keep playing rounds until someone wins.

Remember, only girls who draw a positive self-statement and correctly identify it get to move forward. It is important that you do not modify the rules so that *everyone* who correctly identifies statements (positive and negative) moves forward, as this will only embarrass girls who have not grasped the concept yet, and are standing behind! The game is intentionally designed to have an element of chance!

Whenever someone identifies a statement incorrectly, be sure to clear up confusion before moving on. Often, kids will incorrectly identify statements like, *"I want everybody to like me,"* as positive. It's important not to embarrass anyone, but be sure to point out that this is an "all-or-nothing" statement that can lead to a downward spiral. Clearing up confusion is the reason we play the game!

Handout exercise:
Changing "I Should" statements   (8 minutes)   Time: _____–_____
Introduce this section to the girls by explaining the following:

> Okay, now we've talked about downward and upward spirals, and we've heard lots of examples of those. Next, we want each of you to tell us what kind of "I should" downward spiral statements you say to yourself. We'll get to see how silly these statements sound when we change the "I should" to an "I have to" statement, and then we'll "turn them upside down" to get us started on the upward spiral. We'll start with some examples we give you, and then you can add your own.

Pass out the handout titled "I Should, I Have to, I Want to: What works Best?/Changing an "I Should" to an "I Want to." Have the group members complete the handout so they can practice turning irrational thoughts and unrealistic goals into realistic statements that will take them on an upward spiral. You should go around and help kids because this can be tricky.

Ask everyone to cross out the word "should" and replace it with the words "have to." Then have a group member read one of the groups of statements. For example, *"I should get an A in math class,"* changes to *"I have to get an A in math class."* Ask the group: *"What differences do you notice when you change the 'should' to a 'have to'?"* (Answer: *"The sentence sounds silly and desperate, because nobody 'has to' get As."*) Point out that by having lots of "have to's" in our lives we are trying to live by absolutes. This is a difficult way to live.

Now, ask the group members to rework their "I should" and "I have to" statements into rational and realistic goals. Go around the room and help the girls with this, because it can be pretty hard to do. Then have one group member read a group of statements. For example,

> *"I should weigh only 100 pounds"* changes to
> *"I have to weigh only 100 pounds"* which changes to
> *"I want to be healthy and attractive, but that doesn't mean I have to weigh 100 pounds."*

Next, lead the girls through the process with the statements below:

> *"I should do whatever my boyfriend wants me to."*
> *"I have to do whatever my boyfriend tells me to."*

"I want my boyfriend to like me, but I respect myself enough to think for myself."

Go around the room and help each girl to rework the first two statements until they are like the "I want" example above. Ask them if they understand the connection between thinking positively and feeling good.

Journal/workbook assignment   (3 minutes to explain)   Time: _____–_____
Distribute the Dating Interview handout to the group (p. 41 in the workbook). Explain the following: "Use the Dating Interview to interview your dad, mom, guardian, or another adult about their opinions on dating." Tell them that they get double credit for this one for the drawing. Remind them to bring the completed interview form to the next group meeting.

Closing the Trust game   (20 minutes)   Time: _____–_____
Explain that this closing game will introduce the topic of the next club session (Making and keeping friends). Directions:

Arrange the room in a small "obstacle course." (Be sure that it is not something dangerous!) For example, it's a good idea to place desks and/or chairs in a row to create a maze; it is not okay to lead someone toward a stairwell. Divide the group into pairs. (If there is an odd number, pair someone up with a group leader or have one group of three girls, whichever feels right). Explain that one member of each pair will be blindfolded, and the other/s will guide her through the obstacle course using words alone. For example, the guider could say, "Take three small steps forward then stop. Turn to your left. Put your right hand out in front of you and feel the wall. Walk by the wall for five steps." One group leader should time each pair of girls, and a group member will help record the time for each pair. Each time a blindfolded person bumps into something, 5 seconds get added to the team's time. The pair (or trio) with the fastest time wins a little prize.

Say goodbyes, and remind them about attendance and journal/workbook assignment incentives. Congratulate them for working hard today and remind them to give themselves positive messages tonight and tomorrow.

Chapter 14

Making and Keeping Friends

Session 5: Meeting People and the Qualities of a Friend

Anne is my best, oldest friend. She and I have known each other since we were 7 years old. We aren't the most popular at our school, but we don't care too much. I mean, we have slumber parties with each other and we talk about EVERYTHING together. I could tell her anything at all.

—Sierra

At our school, the popular girls are like this little army. They command people to do things. I mean, they say, 'I don't like her anymore so you can't either', and people do it! It's not fair. I used to try to get them to like me, but then I realized that I don't like them.

—Nicki

For a middle school girl, life can sometimes seem like one big popularity contest. While real friendships are a source of support, the pressure to be popular can influence some girls to act against their better judgment. This session is designed to help girls refocus on the important qualities of a friend. The discussion is then extended to include desirable qualities in a boyfriend, to emphasize that the bases for friendship and romantic friendship are the same. In a recent group, the girls talked over the qualities they want in a friend.

"Somebody who laughs a lot," Jessica suggests, and writes the words in purple marker on a large piece of paper. "But they don't laugh at you."

"Yeah, you have to be able to talk to them," Karen adds, "You have to be able to tell them your secrets and not worry that they'll tell the whole school."

"Oooh, I had this friend, once," Maria says, "and I told her that I liked this guy, you know? And she told some girl who was a friend of

136

his. Everybody found out. I thought I was going to die. He quit talking to me and I felt really stupid. I couldn't believe she did that to me. Then later, I was talking to . . ."

"Pardon me, Maria," I interrupt, "good job, all of you." Maria's comments are appropriate, but I know from past meetings that if I don't bring the topic back to friendship qualities, we could be listening to this tale for more than an hour. "So everyone agrees that it's important that a friend can keep a secret?"

The girls all agree on this point.

"Okay, try to fill in the blank. . . . What is it called," I ask them, "when we (blank) somebody enough to tell them secrets and not to laugh at us?"

"Trust!" Jessica shouts.

Finding someone to trust turns out to be the centerpiece of the discussion for this group. For these girls, social interactions are a gamble where they may find either support or ridicule. This session helps them identify the kind of people who are likely to give them the support they want and highlights the qualities rather than the social status of that group.

Rationale

Adolescents are social beings. Adolescent girls in particular value close friendships. Not surprisingly, association with risk-taking peers places adolescents at greater risk. Healthy friendship, on the other hand, provides a social support system that helps bolster self-esteem, lessen depression, and ameliorate hard times. The goal of this session is to teach girls to focus less on achieving "popularity" and more on developing intimate, satisfying friendships with friends and boyfriends who will support their healthy life choices. Brief consideration is also given to helping girls identify signs of an unhealthy relationship with a boyfriend and what to do if they find themselves in such a relationship.

Goals

1. To move girls away from their focus on popularity and toward developing intimate friendships.
2. To give girls practice in identifying healthy qualities in a friend and boyfriend and recognizing positive friendships.
3. To emphasize the importance of friendship as support and how it contributes to girls' well-being.
4. To teach girls to form healthy, supportive friendships in which they can encourage each other to make positive life choices.
5. To help girls identify and learn how to end unhealthy dating relationships.

Materials

Puzzle, magazines, scissors, glue, pens, markers, Dating Values game cards, Dating Values game prize.

Handouts: My Friendship Want Ad (p. 251), My Response to the Friendship Want Ad (p. 252), I Am a Friend (p. 253).

Overview

This session helps girls pick out what we believe are important qualities in a friend and boyfriend. Each girl writes and responds to a friendship want ad. Then the group talks about how the qualities they look for in a boyfriend are similar to the qualities they want in a friend. In the final exercise, girls read, decorate, and discuss a short passage about friendship. The session provides an opportunity for girls to think about friendship and its purpose.

Procedure for part I: Qualities of a friend

Introduction   (5 minutes) Time: _____–_____

Point to the puzzle and ask the girls to identify the puzzle piece that you are on today (Making and Keeping Friends).

Ask the girls to share a story about one good friend they have and explain what makes this person a good friend. As the girls describe their friend's qualities, one group leader (or a volunteer from the group) writes a list of the group's suggestions on the flip chart.

Then ask the girls, "What are some things you can think of that friendship does for you?" On the same flip chart page, write down their answers, which might include: Developing new interests, learning something new from a friend, meeting other new friends through one friend, helping each other do the right things and make the right choices, and understanding different points of view and different cultures from your friends.

Handout exercise   (20 minutes) Time: _____–_____

Pass out My Friendship Want Ad handout. Have each group member write a friendship want ad. Tell them not to write their names on the ad. Wait a few minutes, collect the ads, shuffle them, and pass them back out (make sure that no one gets her own ad back). Have each girl read the ad she received out loud, and tell the other girls not to say when their own ad is being read. Based on these ads, make a list in your flip chart of qualities the group is asking for in a friend. As you go around the circle, listen to the want ads and summarize the main points. Help the girls develop their concept of a good friend. For example, you can say: "Ann, you said a good friend is someone who is really nice. Can you tell us more specifically what a really nice person would be like?" Here are some possible examples: sharing, helpful, giving, someone to do fun things with, someone to talk to about important and silly stuff.

Response   (20 minutes) Time: _____–_____
Then pass out My Response to the Friendship Want Ad handout. Have each girl write a response to the ad she received when you shuffled and passed out the ads. To accomplish this, each girl needs to think about what she has in common with the person who wrote the want ad. Have everybody read the want ad they received and their response out loud. Now people can identify themselves!

Discussion   (10 minutes) Time: _____–_____
Now introduce the topic of what qualities the girls would like to find in a boyfriend or partner. Have them write these down with markers on a big sheet of paper. Lead a discussion that helps girls arrive at the conclusion that being sexually active is not the main focus of a relationship. Help them to conclude that healthy relationships are about sharing, learning, having someone fun to talk to, etc.

Ask them to identify what might be signs of an unhealthy relationship. Examples include: someone who bosses you around, doesn't listen to you, teases you, tells stories about you, abuses you verbally or physically, etc. Ask them why they think some girls might stay in a relationship with someone who treated them badly. Ask them if they think there are any risks involved in staying in an unhealthy relationship. Talk about how staying in an unhealthy relationship can increase the risk for unwanted sex. Ask girls to brainstorm ways to get out of an unhealthy relationship (e.g., tell an adult they trust about what is happening, talk with other friends they respect, end the relationship, get involved with a special hobby or activity instead of dating the person, contact an agency that specializes in helping girls and women leave unhealthy relationships, etc.).

Procedure for part II: Dating

Dating Values game   (20 minutes) Time: _____–_____
The following questions should be printed on cards. Have each person in the group choose a card and answer the question. Other kids can join in on the discussion after the person whose turn it is gives an answer. One question card has a special mark on it, and whoever chooses that question wins a small prize. Be sure to incorporate information that the girls received from the interview with their parents into the discussion.

When is a person old enough to date or go out?

Do you think it's okay to date more than one person, or should you date only one person at a time?

Do you think that parents and kids agree on what a good age to begin dating is?

What do people do on a date?

Who should plan a date? Who should pay?

Is there a difference between a guy who is a friend and a boyfriend?

Who do you feel more comfortable with, a friend or a date?

How does a person decide whom to go out with?

If a guy pays for a date, should he "expect something" in return?

How would you react if a guy you have seen, but don't really know, asked you to go out on Friday night?

What are some problems that can happen when kids start dating?

Should a guy try to get a girl to "go farther" (sexually) than she says she wants to?*

Do you think this ever happens?

Should a girl try to get a guy to "go farther" (sexually) than he says he wants to?*

Do you think this ever happens?

Can you "go out" with someone if you just hang out together but don't really "date" yet?

Be very clear in leading this discussion. Emphasize the fact that "no" means "no."

Journal/workbook assignment   (5 minutes) Time: _____–_____

Ask the girls to write about one time they had a fight with a friend who is not in this group (p. 53 in the workbook). What was the fight about? How did you know you were fighting? How did you work things out?

Closing   (10 minutes) Time: _____–_____

Pass out the I Am a Friend handout. Have the members take turns reading lines of the poem out loud. Then ask each girl to decorate the handout by cutting out words and images from magazines that show what friendship means to them. (The handout is set up so there is enough room to add decorations around and under the poem). Briefly review each "work of art." Relax and let the girls take their time with this. This can be a good time to get to know more about individual group members and their interests. You can play some music in the background if you have a boom box with you. Talk about all of the fun things you can do with friends while you work on your poem decorations. (Group leaders should participate!) Congratulate the girls for their laughter, work, and creativity. Say goodbyes and remind them of attendance and journal assignment incentives.

Session 6: Building Friendship Skills and Dealing with Peer Pressure

The best part [of Go Grrrls] was learning about how to fix friendships that break. It helped me make up with my friend who I had a big fight with. I wanted to make up with her before, but I didn't know what to do.

—Moira

We had fun with those [friendship role plays] because we did them like [our leaders] did. We were really acting silly. But then I was in the cafeteria after that and I was all quiet next to some new girl when I remembered that I knew how to start a conversation. It worked.

—Kelly

For a less-than-confident teenager, approaching a new person can be a very stressful situation. Conversation skills are seldom formally taught. Some people seem to have a natural knack for conversation, but many people could use a refresher course in how to start, continue, and end a conversation. Role-play is an excellent tool to allow girls to rehearse these skills. This tool is particularly effective at this midway point in the program, since the girls are comfortable enough to really let loose.

It is important to start this session with a role-play where the leaders demonstrate "less than perfect" conversational skills. Participants feel reassured by this as it removes the pressure for them to perform perfectly. It also provides a contrast to the follow-up, "good skills" role-play, so group members can clearly see the difference.

My coleader Patti and I have rehearsed our role-plays in advance, and when we present our first skit, the girls are laughing at us—just the response we hoped for.

"So what did we do in that role-play that didn't work very well?" I ask.

"*Everything.* You were mean to each other!" Tania offers, still giggling.

"When you say we were mean to each other, what were the tips that gave you that idea?" I ask.

"Your voice was mean . . . like your tone. And when Patti asked you a question you just said like one word and nothing else."

"Good. How about you, Julianna? What did you notice that didn't go so well?" I ask.

"You didn't even look at each other the whole time. You were looking down at your feet and Patti was looking up at the ceiling," Julianna observes.

"Excellent. You're really observant. We didn't make any eye contact at all," I echo, naming the skill.

"You've thought of the really important things about the way we spoke to each other," Patti interjects, "How about what we said to each other?"

"Well, you were just saying stuff about yourself," Jacqueline notices. "Like, 'I'm so good at this' and 'I'm so great at that.' It just sounded braggy and hard to say anything back to."

"Absolutely," Patti nods. "It's fine to tell someone about yourself, but it's also important to ask some questions about them."

We run the role-play a second time, but this time we use good verbal and nonverbal skills. The girls are able to list what we did right much more successfully than if we had merely played the "good" skit first. And when we ask them to pair up and play roles of their own, they are eager to begin. After all, they have seen their coleaders risk appearing foolish, and it looks like fun.

Rationale

Making and keeping friends requires social skills that some girls lack. This session is designed to teach friendship skills and provide group members with an opportunity to practice these skills. Much of this session focuses on basic conversational techniques. These skills are essential for girls to learn so that they can build a solid peer support system and so that they can be more at ease in expressing themselves. A supportive, active peer group of same-sex friends can help girls to resist pressure to begin early dating, which is another risk factor for teen substance use and early sexual activity. Another important goal is to develop a positive prosocial peer norm.

Goals

1. To teach girls the skills of starting conversations, communicating positive feelings, being kind, and dealing with friendship friction.
2. To give girls practice in utilizing friendship skills.
3. To teach girls how to stand up to peer pressure and to support each other in upholding their personal values.

Materials

Puzzle, flip chart, plastic 3x5 card boxes for "friendship toolboxes," stickers, markers, 3x5 cards.

Overview

This session covers a lot of material, so it is important to keep the group moving swiftly. Role plays will allow the girls to rehearse social skills involved in friendship. Activities will build confidence in using these skills, and will also teach girls that they have the power to make new friends, resolve fights with old friends, and resist peer pressure from both friends and acquaintances.

<u>Procedure</u>   (2 minutes)   Time: _____ – _____
Ask the girls to identify which piece of the puzzle you are on today (Making and Keeping Friends). Introduce the topic by saying something like the following:

> Today we'll learn and practice some friendship skills. Knowing how to be a friend involves a number of important skills. Some people find it easy to make new friends, but most people find it difficult. We are going to talk about ways to start conversations, ways to say positive things to your friends, and ways to solve friendship problems. We will also talk about how important it is to stick to your values even if your friends or acquaintances try to get you to do things you do not want to do.

Procedure for part I: Starting a conversation

<u>Introduction</u>   (2 minutes)   Time: _____ – _____

> In our last session, you all had an opportunity to think about what kinds of friends you would like to have. That's important because you want to be able to seek out new friends whom you have something in common with and would like to get to know. So, let's say that in your friendship ad you were looking for someone who is fun to be with, maybe more outgoing than you are, and someone you can really trust. You've thought about some new friends and you decide there is a girl in your art class that you don't know very well and you would like to get to know better. You need to start a conversation! Conversations have three parts: (1) starting the conversation, (2) keeping the conversation going, (3) ending the conversation.

Role-play example   (3 minutes)   Time: _____ – _____
Group leaders: if you do this role-play well, this can be really funny.

> We're going to demonstrate how starting a conversation, keeping it
> going, and ending it are more complicated skills than they might seem.
> We're going to role-play an example for you where these skills are not
> used appropriately. *(It is important to ham it up during these role-plays to set
> the tone for the day! Be sure you do this one really badly. Don't make eye contact
> with each other, leave some long pauses before you say some lines, etc.)*

> 1: Uh, I um, my name is Laurie. What's yours?
> 2: I'm Sally.
> 1: *(Long pause. You're quiet and don't know what to say. Finally you say)* I like
>   track.
> 2: So?
> 1: Well, um, I also really like playing the violin. Do you play an instru-
>   ment?
> 2: No.
> 1: Oh, that's too bad. Well. See you later.

Discussion   (2 minutes)   Time: _____ – _____
Ask the group what went wrong in this example. Help them recognize some of
these important errors:

- Not knowing what to say
- Stumbling over words
- Talking only about yourself (I like track)
- Not asking the other person questions
- Not ending the conversation appropriately

Model the skill   (3 minutes)   Time: _____ – _____
Group leaders role-play again. Remember, ham it up!

> Now we're going to role-play an example where conversation skills are
> used. Watch carefully to see what we do well. You might want to watch
> our eye contact and tone of voice, too.

> 1: Hi, I'm Laurie. What's your name?
> 2: Hi, I'm Sally.
> 1: You play on the basketball team, don't you?
> 2: Yeah. That's the thing I like best about school.
> 1: I'm not very good at basketball but I like playing soccer.

2: I like to play soccer, too.

1: I've gotta go to class, but I'm glad I got to meet you. Let's practice soccer sometime.

2: Okay. That would be great.

Discussion/skill review   (2 minutes)   Time: _____ – _____

Ask the group, "What did we do well in this role play?" and encourage them to recognize the following elements:

• Good nonverbal skills. Looked the person in the eye and was attentive.
• Good introduction. Said her name and asked other person her name.
• Asked a question about the person.
• Ended the conversation and made a plan to get together with the person.

Generating ideas   (3 minutes)   Time: _____ – _____

Generate ideas with group by saying: "As you can see, starting a conversation can be difficult. What are some ideas you can think of for how to start a conversation with another person? What are some ways that would make it easier?" Help the group recognize some of these ways:

• Say something positive about the other person.
• Ask the person if you can help her.
• Invite the person to do something, like sit next to you at lunch.
• Ask the person if she watches one of your favorite TV shows.

Practice opportunity   (8 minutes)   Time: _____ – _____

Have the girls pair off and begin role-playing while you go around and give positive feedback about their attempts at starting conversations. Make sure each girl gets a chance to be the conversation starter. Give each pair one of these two scenes.

Situation #1: Start a conversation with a girl that sits next to you in social studies, but whom you haven't gotten to know yet.

Situation #2: Walk up to the new guy in the cafeteria at lunchtime and start a conversation.

Discussion   (2 minutes)   Time: _____ – _____

Acknowledge that these skills take some time to learn and practice. You might say, for example:

When starting conversations, a lot of girls feel afraid of how they will look to others. That's normal. As you can see, starting conversations and new friendships is often a little awkward at first. Try to remember that in general, people love to get to know each other. Just be yourself!

Procedure for part II: Communicating positive feelings and being kind

Introduction   (1 minute)   Time: _____–_____
Another important skill in friendship is being able to communicate positive feelings and be kind to others. Friendship is an opportunity to provide support to another person. You are a good friend when you can support the other person and share *positive* feelings with them. Friendship is mutual support—if you share positive feelings with others they are more likely to share positive feelings with you.

Discussion   (2 minutes) Time: _____–_____
Ask the group: "Why do you think it is important to share positive feelings with others?" Encourage them to recognize the following points:

- Sharing positive feelings will help your friend feel better and provide her or him with support.
- When you share positive feelings your friends will like you because it feels good to hear positive things.
- People get put down a lot by others—friends, parents, teachers—so it is important to be a positive source of support.

Present an example   (2 minutes) Time: _____–_____
Each group leader should describe a situation from her own life when she used the skill of sharing positive feelings. Here is an example:

> I was at school last week, and a friend of mine gave a presentation for the class. Afterwards I went over to her and told her that she did a great job. She was really thankful, and told me that she'd been pretty nervous, and that it made her feel really good to hear me say that I liked what she did. Then *I* felt good about making her feel happy.

Use your own example, but include these parts:

- Where did it happen?
- Who was there?
- What positive statement did you say?
- How did the other person react?
- How did you feel afterward?

Model the skill   (2 minutes) Time: _____ – _____
Group leaders will role play.

> Now we're going to role-play another situation. We want you to observe
> and tell us what you see us doing well. Do we make good eye contact?
> What is our tone of voice? Can you tell us what positive statement we
> use? Did we say it once or more than once?
>
> 1: Hi, Nikki, how are you today?
> 2: Hi, I'm fine.
> 1: I really liked the way you answered the teacher's question in class
>   today.
> 2: Thanks. It always makes me nervous when I have to speak up in
>   class.
> 1: Well, you did a really good job.
> 2: Thanks.

Ask the group, discussion/skill review   (2 minutes) Time: _____ – _____
"What skills did we demonstrate?" Help them to recognize:

- Good nonverbal skills—eye contact, tone of voice, etc.
- Clearly communicated the positive statement to the other person.
- Continued to show positive support for the other person ("Well, you did a
  really good job").

Practice opportunity   (8 minutes) Time: _____ – _____
Pair girls up and have everyone practice at the same time while you go around
and give them positive feedback. Use these situations:

> Situation #1: Support a friend of yours who is feeling down because her
> boyfriend just left her.
> Situation #2: Tell someone who just helped you with your homework why
> you appreciate them as a friend.

Procedure for part III: Friendship friction

Dealing with friendship friction: (5 minutes) Time: _____ – _____
Introduce the topic of friendship friction.

> Having friends means that sometimes you will run into problems with
> your friends. That's part of friendship—dealing with both the good and
> the bad times. Just like husbands and wives fight, friends also get into
> fights. Today we want to talk a little bit about dealing with friendship
> friction.

Journal/workbook exercise

Ask for volunteers to tell about one fight they had with a friend (p. 53 in the workbook). Then ask the whole group: "What types of problems do you think you are likely to have with your friends?" Help the group generate a list that includes the following:

- Arguments over who is a "best" friend
- Having a friend that is too demanding or controlling
- Having a friend that shares some secret information about you with others
- Having a friend who talks mostly about herself and doesn't give you time to share
- Having a friend who says something that hurts your feelings
- Having a friend who does something that you are not comfortable doing
- Having a friend who tries to get you to do things that you are uncomfortable with and that go against your values (like smoking, drinking, or having sex)

    As you can see there are lots of reasons why we might have problems with our friends. The important thing is knowing how to deal with those problems. There are some tools that you can use to deal with problems with friends.

Building a friendship toolbox   (30 minutes)   Time: _____–_____

Pass out "toolboxes" and decorations (stickers, markers, etc.). While the girls decorate their boxes, have them brainstorm some "friendship friction tools."

    We're going to spend some time talking about ways to solve friendship problems. After we list some of these tools, we're going to write them down on cards and put them in our toolboxes. Each card will be one tool that we might want to use to help ourselves with a friendship problem. What do you think some of these tools might be?

Group leaders can write suggestions down on the flip chart. Help the group come up with these and other important tools:

- Don't yell at your friend.
- Don't call your friend names.
- Be calm, even if you're mad.
- Try to listen to what the other person is saying.
- Talk about the problem with your friend.
- Don't wait for the other person to make the first move.
- Remember that all friends have problems that need to be worked out.

- Do something nice for the other person (They can list a bunch of things for this one; like writing your friend a note or card, buying a small gift, or giving her something personal).
- If your friend is asking you to do things that go against your values, then the best way to solve the problem may be to stop seeing that friend.
- Don't be afraid to say you are sorry. ("This is one of the very best ways to solve friendship problems. Of course, you should only say you're sorry if you truly mean it. If you did or said something wrong, let the other person know. We all sometimes say and do things we wish we hadn't—so if you realize that you did this, don't be too proud to stand up and say, 'I'm really sorry.' ")

Procedure for part IV: Ways to deal with peer pressure

(5 minutes, simultaneous with decorating)　　　　　Time: _____–_____
Start while the group is still working on boxes—about 20 minutes into the toolbox activity, when kids are mostly decorating. Ask them if they have ever had a friend who has tried to get them to do things they were not comfortable doing, like maybe smoking cigarettes, or sneaking out. Ask them if they have ever heard of the phrase "peer pressure" and if so, what do they think it means.

Help them define peer pressure: "Peer pressure is what happens when friends and acquaintances of your own age try to get you to act a certain way using some kind of influence, like teasing or challenging." If applicable, remind them of the Friendship Trust game they played at the end of the self-image session. Explain that some friends who try to get them to do things that are against their values or that they know to be wrong are acting like "bad guides" in the Friendship Trust game. These are friends who will lead them into walls, bump them into barriers, and can generally put them in dangerous situations.

Peer pressure exercise　　　　　(10 minutes)　Time: _____–_____
In this exercise, the girls are given hypothetical situations by group leaders. Ask the girls to act out smart ways to react. Tell them they will be learning some assertiveness and problem solving skills in the next sessions, but these exercises will help them figure out some ways to react when they feel "peer pressure." Ask other group members for feedback. Here are some situations:

Situation #1. A friend of yours offers you one of her mom's cigarettes, and when you say no, she tells you that everyone is trying smoking just to see what it's like. What do you do or say?
Situation #2. You are out with a bunch of kids and everybody starts pairing up into couples and making out. You are uncomfortable, but you are kind

of paired up with a guy who is looking at you like you should go make out, too. What do you do or say?

Tell the girls that at a future meeting, you will talk about how to refuse if someone pressures you to do something you're not comfortable with.

Journal/workbook assignment   (5 minutes)   Time: _____–_____

For the next club meeting, ask girls to write down two problems that they have run into so far this school year (p. 54 in the workbook). Be sure to indicate that they should be serious problems that are real, but not really, really, serious personal problems like feeling sad about a parent's divorce. Give examples such as the following:

> The kind of problem we want you to write down:
> *"I am having a really hard time with social studies, and there is a test next week and I don't know what to do."*
> *"My friends all say that I should go to this party next week, but I know the guy's parents aren't home, and I don't know what to do."*

> The kind of problem that is very important, but that won't work for our club activities at the next meeting:
> *"My mom is drinking really hard."*
> *"My grandmother just died and I'm really sad."*

Explain that you will talk about how to deal with bigger problems, too, but not in the very next meeting. During the next meeting they will figure out ways to solve serious "small-, middle- and large-size" problems, but not deep personal problems. There is no time for a formal closing activity in this session. Tell the gals how wonderful they are, and remind them of the attendance and journal assignment incentives. Tell them you are really looking forward to learning from them at the next session!

Chapter 15

Establishing Independence

Session 7: Problem Solving Strategies

My mom wants to control my entire life. If it was up to her I'd live my whole life locked in my room. When I asked her how old a person should be when they start to date she said, '95'! I'm really going to ask her for help with problems . . . as if!

—Melissa

After teaching the five step problem solving process through two sessions of Go Grrrls, I noticed that I was starting to use it a lot myself. I'm getting really good at the brainstorming part– I can think of all kinds of possibilities now that I've trained myself to do that–and that helps me teach the girls better.

—Angela, a Go Grrrls leader

In this program, our goal is not to tell girls to behave in one particular way, but to teach them how to make good choices for themselves. In early adolescence, girls develop the ability to use metacognition—that is, to think about their thought process. In this session, we are particularly interested in using this new capability as we teach a problem solving *process* they can then apply to a variety of life situations. It is important to supply girls with a problem that has relevance in their lives. The process steps and one sample situation are shown below:

The five-step problem solving process:	Sample problem:
1. Define the problem	Your best, oldest friend asks you to come
2. Brainstorm choices	over to her house when her parents aren't
3. Evaluate the choices	home. She tells you that she is going to
4. Make your decision	invite two boys from school and they might
5. Reevaluate your decision	bring some beer. What do you do?

151

Each of the five steps requires a nuance of emphasis. In step 1, for example, it is important to teach girls to define the problem in the simplest way possible. In the sample situation above, one way to define the problem is: *"My friend asked me over but it might be a risky situation."* In step 2, the challenge is to free girls to list as many choices as they possibly can *without criticizing them.* If, for example, a girl suggests that one possible choice in the sample situation is to *"try to talk her out of asking the boys over, but still try to get some beer,"* and the other group members begin to protest, it is important to remind everyone that in the brainstorming stage, all possibilities should be considered without any criticism.

In step 3 girls are encouraged to evaluate all of the possible choices. In our groups, we ask girls to tell us both the positive and negative aspects of each possible solution. Some girls resist offering positive aspects of the "bad" solutions on the brainstormed list. Others like to test the group leaders by emphasizing the benefits of these "bad" solutions. Since it is the process itself that we are trying to teach, it is important to take participants through the criticism stage carefully. The process may unfold like this:

"The next possible solution on our list is to *'go to my friend's house and get totally loaded.'* What's positive about this choice?" I ask.

"Nothing," Madeline says. "You'll be in deep shit is what will happen."

"I don't know about that," Rachel objects. "You could have a really good time if you do that. That's what I'd do. I mean, her parents aren't home, so it's cool."

"So the positive thing about this choice is that you might have a good time?" I ask. The girls nod, and I write down "possible good time" on our paper. Then I ask, "What's negative about this choice?"

"Like I said, you could get in deep shit," Madeline reminds us all. She is enjoying using the word "shit," but I am intentionally ignoring that. "What if her parents come home early and catch you?"

"You could also get in worse trouble," Chantelle adds. "You could get all drunk and get carried away with the guys. Uh-uh. Not me."

"So the negative things about this choice are that you could get in trouble and it might not be safe?" I paraphrase. The girls agree and I write it down as the negative aspect of this choice.

When we have finished evaluating each possible solution on the list, I ask the girls to move to step 4 by writing their initials next to the solution they choose. Most of the girls choose "good" solutions. I am not surprised, though, when Rachel signs her initials next to the *"go to my friend's house and get totally loaded"* choice. She looks up at me to see how I react.

I do not directly challenge her. "Did everybody make a choice?" I ask. When they have all finished, I move on to step 5 in the process. "All right, it's time for the last step. If your decision isn't working out, start back at step 1. Madeline, you chose, *'Tell my friend I'm busy and I can't come over.'* What if you tell her that and she still pushes you to come?" I ask. "What is the problem you have then?"

"Then I have to decide if I want to really tell her what I think. I could just still say I'm busy, or I could tell her I don't want to get in trouble, or I could ask her to come over to my house instead." She's definitely getting the process.

"Rachel, you chose, *'go to my friend's house and get loaded.'* What if you go over there and your friend and the two guys are already loaded. One of the guys is throwing up in the bathroom, and the other one just seems out of control. What are some of the things you could brainstorm to do?" I ask calmly.

"I don't *have* to stay there if I don't want to," Rachel says defiantly. "I could call my sister for a lift, or I could just walk home. I could try to kick the guys out and take care of my friend," she brainstorms.

By focusing on the options in the process of problem solving, group leaders can teach even resistant girls how to think through their decision making process.

Rationale

Often, adolescents make decisions impulsively without considering the impact of their choices. Their decisions are "experimental" attempts to acquire skills for dealing with new situations or attempts to maximize immediate pleasure. Unfortunately, these attempts may have serious consequences. This session teaches girls how to use a basic problem solving process and allows them to practice avoiding situations in which they will be tempted to engage in substance use, sexual activity, and other risky behaviors.

Goals

1. To teach girls when and how to use problem solving skills.
2. To give girls practice in applying a problem solving process to sample situations of increasing severity.
3. To teach girls how to use problem solving skills in everyday life and to resist involvement in risky behaviors.
4. To teach girls the importance of good problem solving skills to help them avoid risky situations.

Materials

Puzzle, flip chart, markers, pens/pencils, Choice and Consequence game board (p. 256), cards (pp. 257, 259, 261), and dice, Choice and Consequence game prize. Handouts: Did You Know? The Five Steps to Problem Solving (p. 254), Making Decisions and Solving Problems (p. 255).

Overview

Learning how to solve problems is an important skill for early adolescents. They are at a point in their lives where they will be facing a lot of difficult decisions—decisions that can have life long consequences. Today's meeting teaches girls a problem-solving method. They can practice using this method, and future uses for problem solving in their daily lives are suggested. The board game used in this session is designed to help kids understand the connection between choices and consequences.

Procedure for part I: The five-step problem solving process

<u>*Introduction/journal/workbook activity*</u>   (12 minutes) Time: _____–_____
Point to the puzzle and ask the girls which session you are on (Independence). Tell them that during the next two sessions you will be talking about problem solving and assertiveness.

Explain that there are different kinds of problems. Some problems we can figure out on our own, and some other problems we might need to find help to solve. Ask the girls to share some of the problems they wrote about in their journals (p. 54 in the workbook). Have them try to identify which problems are the kind they can probably work on alone, and which kind they might need to find help for. (Remember, it's always okay to ask for help!) Then point out that all people have problems. Ask them, "What are some not-so-hot strategies people use when they have a problem?" You can let the girls write some of these on the flip chart. Ideas might include:

* Ignore the problem and hope that it will go away.
* Blame someone else.
* Keep the problem bottled up inside.
* Do what somebody else says to do.

Mention that we have all tried these methods before, and they don't help us solve the problem.

<u>*Defining the problem solving process*</u>   (8 minutes) Time _____–_____
Group leaders explain the problem solving process, then help the girls work through a sample problem together.

Today we are going to talk about one really helpful way to solve problems. Sometimes decisions are hard to make. For example, what if a really cute guy asks you to meet him after school, but you have basketball practice? How would you decide what to do?

Pass out the Did You Know? The Five Steps to Problem Solving handout. You will work out the problem solving process on a flip chart page in front of the group. Use a different color marker for each of the five steps. Ask for volunteers to read each part of the problem solving process and write them on the flip chart.

1. *Define the problem:* What is the problem? It's a good idea to write it down. Keep it as short as you can. For example, in the example about basketball practice, how would you define the problem? (Example: I want to play basketball and meet the "phine" guy, but I can't do both.)
2. *Brainstorm choices:* The next step is to think of all the possible choices you could make to solve the problem. It's a good idea to write down as many as you can think of, and make sure you let yourself come up with some silly or outrageous choices, too! *One rule during this step is that you don't eliminate any choice or criticize any idea.* Let's try that now. What are all the possible choices you can think of to solve the basketball/cute guy problem? (Group leaders should list these. Remember to encourage some silly responses, and to keep kids from criticizing any ideas at this point.)
3. *Evaluate the choices:* This is the part where you figure out the pros and cons of each choice. It might help to put a + or - next to your brainstormed ideas. Let's do that now. What are some of the pros and cons of our brainstormed ideas? (Help kids evaluate the brainstormed solutions.)
4. *Make your decision:* Now that we've evaluated the ideas, it's time to select the best idea from the list. Which one do you think would be best for you?
5. *If your decision isn't working out, start back at number 1!* The last step is to keep an eye on how your decision is working for you. You might need to go back to the beginning or your decision might work out really well! Either way, give yourself a pat on the back for doing a great job at problem solving!

Handout exercise   (15 minutes) Time: _____ – _____

Pass out the Making Decisions and Solving Problems handout. Divide the group into two teams. Tell the girls that they are now going to work on some more serious problem situations. Provide each group with a "problem" to solve.

Problem #1:
Your best, oldest friend asks you to come over to her house when her parents aren't home. She tells you that she is going to invite two boys

from school, and they might bring some beer. What do you do?
Problem #2:
Your mom says you are not allowed to go out on dates with older boys.
She will allow you to go to events where kids are in groups, but not to go
out alone with a guy, especially when he is older. A really fine guy who is 4
years older than you asks you to meet him at the mall so you can go drive
around and get to know each other. What do you do?

Check on the groups to see how they progress. Pay attention to the "no-criti-
cism" rule in the brainstorming process. Make sure the "evaluation" step is
being used. When they are finished, have each team read its "problem card" out
loud, then read through the five steps.

Content discussion   (5 minutes) Time: _____-_____
Discuss the content of each group's problem and decision. Encourage them to
consider the consequences (the positive and negative possibilities) of each of
their brainstormed ideas. It is important to help girls make the link between
action and consequence. It is also important to help them think of many positive solutions to these dilemmas as possible, and to reinforce the fact that they
will reap the benefits for their smart decisions.

Process discussion   (2 minutes) Time _____-_____
Ask girls the following questions:

- Was the problem solving process easy to use?
- Do members think they can use it themselves?
- Was "brainstorming" fun? Did they think of some funny possibilities?

Clarifying the usefulness of the
problem solving process   (5 minutes) Time: _____-_____

The five-step problem solving process that we just learned is really great
to use for a lot of problems that happen in our lives. Sometimes, though,
people run into some problems that are too complicated or serious to be
able to solve alone with this method. When this happens (and sooner or
later, everybody has to deal with some kind of serious problem), it's
important to know who you can talk to, where to go, and what to do.
Mention that we will talk about how to deal with more serious problems
in a different session of the program.

Ask the girls what kinds of problems might be too hard to solve using only a
five-step problem solving process? (depression/sadness about parents' divorce,
using alcohol, having unwanted sex, not talking to old friends).

Procedure for part II: Choices and consequences

<u>*Game Introduction*</u>　　　　　　　(2 minutes)　Time: _____ - _____

Point out the fact that the examples of problems that you just worked through had elements of peer pressure to them. For example, in the sample situation where the friend was having a party, one of the things that would make it hard to say no is the fact that other kids would try to get them to come to the party anyway.

Explain that the choices girls make when they run into problem situations will have *consequences*. Explain that you are now going to play a game that will help demonstrate some of the positive and negative consequences of our problem solving choices.

<u>*Choices and Consequences game*</u>　　　　(30 minutes)　Time: _____ - _____

The purpose of this game is to help kids imagine possible consequences if they let friends pressure them into risky behaviors. Early adolescents are just beginning to possess the cognitive capabilities to understand this concept well, so it is important that you demonstrate the choice/consequence connection in several different contexts and sessions. Tell group members that you're going to play a game about the consequences of giving in, or not giving in, to peer pressure. Examples will include peer pressure to engage in sexual activity, alcohol and drug use, and other risky behaviors.

Directions: Get out your Choices and Consequences game board and dice. Have each group member choose a magic marker, pen, or crayon as their game piece. Choose who goes first by writing down a number between 1 and 20 on a paper and having group members guess the number. Whoever is closest goes first. The directions on the game board are easy to follow. When someone is sent to the "You're Grounded" or "Detention" areas, she must roll either a 1 or a 6 to go back to the space she was on before, and resume their turn. Whoever finishes first wins a small prize.

Finish today's session by asking the girls what the three main things you did today had in common: Problems: How to solve them, get help for them, or prevent them from happening!

<u>*Journal/workbook assignment*</u>　　　　　　　Time: _____ - _____

(2 minutes to explain. They need to do this at home)

Ask each group member to write about one time when they wished they would have spoken up for themselves or someone else, but didn't (p. 63 in the workbook). For example, *"Once everyone was making fun of my friend on the bus and I wanted to defend her but I didn't say anything because I felt too scared."*

Say goodbye to everyone, tell them what a great job they did, and remind them of the attendance and assignment incentives before they leave.

Session 8: Assertiveness Skills

It's hard for me to say what I want to sometimes. I feel like I'll just make people mad and then I'll get even more nervous. Mostly I just keep quiet and let them think they know what I think.

—Mina

Learning about being assertive was good because then I was brave enough to say things to my friends that I wouldn't say before. Like, now, I can tell somebody if I disagree with them. It's all about respect. You have to respect yourself and the other person, too.

—Samantha

Many girls have never heard the words "assertive, aggressive, and passive" before this session, but once they are given examples of each of these behaviors they grasp the concepts very quickly. While many girls in today's society are socialized to be passive, it is important not to overgeneralize. Out of frustration, or modeling what they have seen in adults and peers, plenty of girls choose aggressiveness as a style of communication as well.

To introduce the concept, group leaders act out a sample scene. One group leader plays a boy who is mixing all the chemicals in a science experiment and the other plays a girl who is responding to his "hogging" the experiment. The scene is played three times, with the girl responding passively, aggressively, and finally assertively. We capture the girls interest by demonstrating the behaviors rather than starting with bland "dictionary" definitions of the terms.

"I'm gonna mix this stuff together and you can be the secretary," my coleader says in a feigned male voice.

"Well, okay." I respond, sighing, with an expression of vague dissatisfaction on my face.

"What did you notice about my response in this role-play?" I ask.

"You were wimpy." Jordan says. "You looked like you really wanted to do it but you just let him do it anyway."

"That's right. Now watch the next role-play." This time we play out the aggressive scenario.

"I'm gonna mix this stuff together and you can be the secretary," my coleader says again.

I push her out of the way and shout, "Move over butthead. This experiment is mine!"

The girls are all laughing at this point. I take a bow, then a curtsy, and say, "Thank you, thank you. So what did you notice about that scene?"

"You pushed him—I mean her—you know," Sarah offers, still laughing.

"I did, didn't I? What else did I do?" I ask.

"You were really loud and you called him butthead!" Mary giggles.

"Okay. Now watch this scene and see what I do differently." I request. We work the scene once more, this time modeling assertiveness.

"I'm gonna mix this stuff together and you can be the secretary," my coleader demands once more.

"No, I don't want to be the secretary. I want to mix the chemicals, too." I say firmly but calmly.

"What did you notice about this scene?" I ask.

"Well, you just told him," Amber says. "You didn't shout or anything, but you just said what you wanted to do."

"Good job. Which of these three scenes do you think worked the best for the girl?" I ask them.

"That last one was the best one because you weren't wimpy and you weren't mean." Jordan explains. "It's like Goldilocks . . . finding the thing that is just right."

I use Jordan's analogy to introduce the words "assertive," "aggressive," and "passive." Because they have seen the demonstration (and thanks to Jordan's metaphor) these complicated-sounding terms are no threat at all. The girls jump into their own role-play scenes with enthusiasm.

Rationale

Girls are often socialized to be accommodating to others. One potentially negative result of this socialization is that girls may not assert themselves in a difficult situation. Assertiveness is an important component in girls' education, since one risk factor for early sexual activity includes adherence to traditional patterns of female submissiveness and male dominant behavior (Jorgenson & Alexander, 1983). Role-play situations allow girls to practice assertiveness skills in a safe, same-sex environment.

Goals

1. To teach girls the difference between assertive, aggressive, and passive actions and words.

2. To teach girls appropriate situations in which they may use assertiveness skills.

3. To give girls actual practice in being assertive.

Materials

Puzzle, plain 8½ x11 paper for Communication game.
Handouts: Assertive, Aggressive, or Passive? (pp. 263–264).

Overview

This session is a real skill-building session. The girls learn the definitions of the terms "assertive," "aggressive," and "passive," and practice identifying the associated behaviors and using assertiveness skills through role-plays of increasingly stressful situations. They are introduced to the idea of how to refuse sexual advances, which will be reinforced in session nine. It takes a lot of practice for most kids to really use these skills, so it is important to introduce them now and practice them throughout the remaining sessions.

Procedure

Introduction/journal activity   (5 minutes)   Time: _____–_____
Ask girls to share their journal activity from the previous session (p. 63 in the workbook). Ask them what kind of factors prevented them from speaking their minds in these situations. (Fear? Not knowing how to say what they wanted to? Worry about getting involved in a fight?) Tell them that today they will learn about a way to respect their own opinions and the opinions of other people at the same time.

Ask girls to identify which topic we are on from the puzzle (Independence). Introduce the session by telling girls that communicating what we want from people in a clear way is sometimes harder than it seems. To demonstrate this you are going to play a little game.

Building What You Hear game   (20 minutes)   Time: _____–_____
Provide each club member with an 8½ x 11-inch piece of paper. Divide the group into pairs. If there is an odd number of participants, someone may join a group as a third. Explain that in each group there will be one Sender and the others will be Receivers. Then have the partners turn their backs to each other. Inform them that they are not allowed to see each others' faces, reactions, or how they are manipulating the paper. The Sender is responsible for providing the Receiver with instructions about how to manipulate the paper. The Sender should give the Receivers at least 5 and no more than 10 instructions about how to manipulate the paper. The Sender should be as creative as possible.

During this time, the Receivers are not allowed to ask any questions or ask the Sender to repeat the instructions. After the Sender is finished, have them compare their final products. Chances are very good that no one's final products match.

Process the game by asking some of the questions below:

1. What was hard in this game?
2. What was hard for the Sender?
3. What was hard for the Receiver?
4. Which position is hardest?
5. Which position is most important?
6. Which position is easiest?
7. How is this about communication?

Close the discussion by explaining that effective communication can be difficult. It is important to be clear and straightforward.

Assertiveness role-play   (8 minutes)   Time: _____–_____

Explain to the girls that one important way to communicate clearly with people is by being assertive. Then tell the girls that today they are all going to be actors! You may want to explain something like this:

> When we take a part in a play, we learn a lot about how our character thinks and acts. In the last session we talked about ways to make decisions and solve problems. You learned some really valuable skills to help you do this. Today we're going to do some acting to learn about another kind of skill.
>
> The skill of being assertive is a really important one to learn. When you act assertively, it means that you stick up for your rights in a way that shows respect for yourself and others. For example, what if you're doing a science experiment and a boy in your group keeps doing all the fun parts and asks you to be the secretary? Would you be able to stick up for yourself in a clear (and not rude) way? We are going to act out three ways that kids might respond in this situation:

One group leader plays a boy who is mixing all the chemicals in a science experiment; the other plays the girl who is responding to this. (Remember, ham it up!)

> Boy: I'm gonna mix this stuff together and you can be the secretary.
> Girl: Well, okay. *(Even though you really want to mix the chemicals.)*
> Ask the girls what they noticed about this response.

> Boy: I'm gonna mix this stuff together and you can be the secretary.
> Girl: Move over, Butt-head, this experiment is mine.
> Ask the girls what they noticed about this response.

Boy: I'm gonna mix this stuff together and you can be the secretary.
Girl: No, I don't want to be the secretary. I want to mix the chemicals, too.
Ask the girls what they noticed about this response.

Defining the terms   (15 minutes)   Time _____–_____

You did a great job analyzing the three responses we just acted out. Now we're going to talk about what those different ways of reacting reflect. There are three ways we can choose to act in any situation:

Passive:
When you act passively, you don't respect your own right to express your ideas, needs, wants, feelings, and opinions. Sometimes people act passively because they are afraid to risk the consequences if they say how they really feel. Sometimes people act passively because they don't know how to speak up for themselves. Being passive might help you avoid a conflict in the short term, but in the long run it can cause you bigger problems. You might feel like other people are taking advantage of you. You might get really angry with people later because you don't think they respect you. In the example we role-played about the science experiment, the passive response was the one where the girl said "Well, okay," even though she really wanted to do the experiment.

Aggressive:
When you act aggressively, you disregard another person's right to be respected. An aggressive response is one that is mean, hurtful, or a put-down. You might get what you want in the short term, but in the long run you might make other people really angry and cause bigger problems for yourself later. In the science example, which response do you think was the aggressive one? (Butthead response.) Right.

Assertive:
Being assertive means that you say what you think, feel, want, or believe in a way that isn't mean or disrespectful to another person. You stand up for your own rights, and treat other people with respect. In the science example, which response do you think was the assertive response? (I want to mix the chemicals, too.) Right. What makes that response assertive? (It is assertive because the person who said it is standing up for her own rights without being rude or disrespectful.)

Assertiveness exercises   (25 minutes)   Time: _____–_____

Have the girls break into two groups. Give an Assertive, Aggressive, or Passive handout to each group. Instruct them to practice acting out the little plays on their scripts, as a pair from each team will put on a play for the whole group to identify assertive/aggressive/passive responses. Make sure pairs read the "introduction to the situation" sections out loud when they present their scene. Ask the group to guess whether each response is assertive, aggressive, or passive.

After each group's presentation, conduct a content discussion appropriate to the scenario. Content discussion will touch on the importance of rejecting risky situations and of continuing to engage in activities that are important to you no matter what other kids may say.

Process these assertiveness scenes by emphasizing that sometimes it will take more than one assertive statement to avoid or get out of a risky situation. Tell the girls that today you practiced some basics and they will learn more about assertive behaviors and both verbal and nonverbal refusal skills in the next session.

Journal/workbook assignment   (10 minutes)   Time: _____–_____
The journal assignment for the next meeting is to write down at least three questions that you have about sex or sexuality, or some myths and rumors that you've heard and don't know whether to believe or not (p. 71 in the workbook). At the next club meeting everyone will be asked to put some of these questions in an anonymous question can.

Closing   (10 minutes)   Time: _____–_____
We've probably all played the Telephone game before, but it is a classic. Have the girls line up across the room. One of the group leaders should whisper the following statement into the first girl's ear: *"I heard that Sarah McLachlan started the Lilith Fair three years ago."* The girls must then whisper the sentence to each other, one at a time. No one is allowed to repeat the sentence. At the end, have the last girl say the sentence out loud and see if it is the same! If you have a bit of time you can talk about some of the conclusions this game leads to, such as don't believe everything you hear, gossip is not reliable, if you can't ask questions to clear things up it's easy to misunderstand other people, etc. But keep it fun and light. If you have time, you can do another one. Say goodbyes and remind girls of the journal and attendance incentives!

Chapter 16

Let's Talk about Sex

Session 9: Sex 101 and Refusal Skills

When we talked about sex it was good because I didn't know about how everything worked . . . I mean I knew, but I didn't know everything. It was easy to talk to [my group leaders] because they were more like your sisters than your parents. They didn't get nervous or mad when we asked them the questions. They made me feel like it's a good thing to take my time and to remember that I am somebody special.

—Chelsea

I started going out with this guy who was 5 years older than me. He wasn't a creep or anything, and he didn't force me to do it. I could just tell that he thought I would, so I let him. It was weird. After a while he stopped calling me. I was really sad, but I didn't want to tell my friends because I thought they'd just say, 'you're so stupid.' So then I let the next guy, too, because I already lost it, right?

—Amy (spoken privately to a group leader)

Girls are usually really eager to talk about sex by the time this session rolls around. The Go Grrrls curriculum places an emphasis on pregnancy prevention within a broader program context that is both educational and skill-based. The program includes two group meetings (sessions 9 and 10) devoted specifically to the topic of sexuality, but it is the cumulative effect of the entire curriculum that is most likely to make a difference in a young person's behavior. The skill-building sessions included in the curriculum (assertiveness training, problem solving, making and keeping friends, positive self-talk, and setting reachable goals for the future) all serve as important components in reducing teens' likelihood of engaging in early, unhealthy sexual activity. Psychoeducational components of the curriculum (confronting media messages and establishing a positive body image) boost girls' understanding of the effects of broader cultural trends on their individual lives.

This is an abstinence-based curriculum, which is developmentally appropriate for middle-schoolers for many reasons. While some 11- to 14-year-olds have already had sexual intercourse, the vast majority have not. Many girls need to be reassured that their decision to wait is not unusual, but is actually the norm. Another reason to focus on abstinence is that younger adolescents are notoriously poor users of contraception. (One mother commented to me that she couldn't rely on her 13-year-old daughter to feed the hamster, let alone take a pill at the same time every day.) Finally, the potential physical and psychological side effects of engaging in intercourse at a young age can be catastrophic. Because of these factors, the emphasis in this session is on helping girls truly believe that they have the right to control their own bodies. Girls who do need to know more about birth control methods are given information and referrals.

We begin this session by clearing up any confusion girls may have about reproductive physiology. Group leaders provide candid answers to girls' questions about sex and sex-related matters. We are no longer surprised by the questions we receive. Here are some samples:

Is it true that if you stand up right after you do it you won't get pregnant?
What's sperm?
Can you get AIDS the first time you have sex?
If you have sex before you have your period could you get pregnant?
If you only have sex for 5–10 minutes, can you get pregnant?
How do you get AIDS?
How does a boy's dick go into a girl?

After we answer girls' questions and describe anatomy and reproductive physiology, we introduce the term "abstinence." Group leaders then teach girls refusal skills, building on the assertiveness role-plays from the last session. The tone of the session must be one of empowerment and choice, not of shame.

In one section of the curriculum, we ask girls to brainstorm reasons why they think some teenagers choose to have sex and why some teens wait. This discussion affords group leaders the opportunity to affirm that there are positive things about sexuality. In one group, the discussion focused on the range of behaviors that comprise sexuality.

"What is another reason that some teens might have sex?" I ask the group. (They have already listed several, including: *They don't know how to say no, they don't want to let their partner down, they want to have a baby*(!), *and they are curious*.)

"I have one but I'm not sure if I can say it," Leesa says, giggling.

The other girls encourage her to speak up.

"Okay, okay. Well, I think people do it 'cause it *feels* good. I mean, I haven't done it yet, but I've done *some* stuff and it can be nice." She smiles and blushes a bit.

"You're right, Leesa," I acknowledge. "It's really important to know that sexuality is good and healthy. This is all about trying to figure out what *you* want, what is going to be good and healthy for you."

Melissa says. "Leesa, you said you've done some stuff. How do you decide when to stop? I mean, I want to know how you're supposed to decide how far to go,"

"I haven't really figured that out yet," Leesa admits.

"What do you all think?" I throw it out to the group.

"I think you kind of know when to stop if you're getting nervous," Arletta offers. "You know, if you're all into it but then part of you is watching yourself thinking, uh-uh, don't do it!"

"Does it help to talk about setting limits before 'you're all into it'?" I ask.

"Maybe," Leesa says. "I guess I kind of do that already. Like I know I'm not going to go all the way. And then I also know that it just is not okay for anybody to touch me . . . well, you know."

"Below the waist?" I offer as a way for her to describe her limits.

"Yeah, that's it." She looks relieved to have found language she can use. "No touching below the waist."

"Me, too. I mean I wouldn't do that, either," Arletta adds, "but it is so nice to mack [make out]."

"So I have a question for you all." I want to see if they are getting the idea that sex is more than merely intercourse. "What does 'sex' include? I mean, if you hold hands with a guy is that sex?"

"Not really," Joyce says, "I mean, if you hold hands with a guy it's not like you *had* sex with him, but it's still sexy."

"How about if you kiss somebody?" I ask.

"Same thing. It's not having sex but it's . . . it's having some kind of sex." Leesa says.

"Okay. So sexuality can include a range of behaviors." I move the discussion on. "Let's talk for a little while about sexual intercourse."

Once sexuality is defined as healthy and normal, it is much easier to lead a discussion about the responsibilities and possible consequences of engaging in sexual intercourse.

Rationale

At this point in the group cycle, girls have acquired and practiced skills related to problem solving and assertiveness. Furthermore, group cohesiveness has been established, which creates a "safe" environment for discussion of sexuality. Basic mechanics of sexual reproduction are discussed to be certain that girls have a base of understanding for the remaining skill-building exercises. Girls will have practiced using assertiveness skills earlier in the program, and these skills are reviewed in role-play situations specifically designed to give girls practice in refusing suggestions to have sex.

Goals

1. To equip girls with a basic knowledge of both female and male sexual development and the mechanics of reproduction.
2. To help girls explore their own values and broader societal attitudes about sexuality.
3. To give girls practice and build confidence in their right to decline unwanted sexual activity.
4. To offer a forum to clear up sexual myths and rumors that girls have heard.
5. To create a relaxed forum for the discussion of the onset of menarche.
6. To teach girls about resources for obtaining birth control information and supplies.

Materials

Puzzle, flipchart, markers, male and female reproductive posters (supply your own), question can.
Handouts: Having Sex: Why or Why Not (p. 268), Verbal and Nonverbal Refusal Skills (p. 269), Tricky Situation (p. 267), and Starting My Period (pp. 265–266).

Overview

This session reviews myths and facts about sexual activity. Girls discuss reasons why some teens have sex and why some do not. Role-play activities give girls practice in using refusal skills, and community resources for obtaining birth control information and supplies are pointed out. This session builds on several previous sessions, including assertiveness training, problem solving, and dealing with peer pressure. While it may be useful as a solitary exercise, it will be of the greatest power in combination with the previously mentioned topics.

Procedure

Introduction/journal/workbook activity   (5 minutes)   Time: _____–_____

Point to the puzzle and ask girls to identify which piece you are on today (Let's Talk about Sex). Ask girls where they first learned about sex. Ask them to take out their journal/workbook and have everyone take a moment to write some of the myths, rumors, or questions they've heard about sex onto a slip of paper. *Make sure that they have some space to work confidentially!* Tell them that if they don't have any questions or myths, they still have to put three folded, blank pieces of paper into the can. After collecting the papers, group leaders may want to set the tone, by offering a rumor that they heard when they were younger and then explaining the truth. For example: *"I heard that you can't get pregnant the first time you have intercourse,"* or *"I heard that you can only get diseases like AIDS and stuff if you have sex with more than one person."*

Explain that these rumors are not true. Set the can aside for a moment, and explain that you're going to do a quick review of the facts. This review will help the girls better understand the answers to the questions in the can.

Sex 101: A review of the basics   (10 minutes)   Time: _____–_____

Explain that even though the club members probably know many things about the basic facts, you are going to explain some of the essentials quickly for a review, just to be sure that everybody has the same information. Pass around diagrams of female and male reproductive physiology. Pronounce the words out loud as you point out key bodily features.

Answering group questions   (20 minutes)   Time: _____–_____

After you complete the review, bring the can into the center of the circle. Have each member of the group draw a question out of the question can. As the group leaders take turns reading these myths and questions, it is important to respond in a relaxed manner. Use anatomically correct language in an unembarrassed tone.

Important: If there is a question in the can that you do not feel comfortable answering you can say, "I'm not comfortable answering that question right now. Let me think it over until the next meeting and then I will respond." If you just don't know the answer to a question, please say so. "I don't know how to answer this question. I'll do some research and get back to you next time." It is far better to admit ignorance than to misinform the girls.

Starting My Period: One Girl's Story   (10 minutes)   Time: _____–_____

Pass out this handout. Introduce the topic by stating something like this:

One of the subjects that girls usually have a lot of questions about is menstruation. Even though you learn about getting your period in health class, and you may have talked with your mom about it, there are still some common questions that a lot of girls have. Here is one girl's story about getting her period for the first time.

Take turns reading the story out loud. If necessary, a group leader can read it. When you are through, go over the "Tips" section at the bottom and help girls figure out where they might go if they need supplies or help.

Mention the fact that even though it might sound corny to them, it is really true that when you get your first period it is a special event. Ask if they have any ideas about how they might want to celebrate! For example, they might want to write a special journal entry on the day it happens, or they might want to go out for lunch with their mom, or they might want to drink a sparkling apple cider toast with their big sister, etc. (We don't want girls to leave this group feeling afraid of menarche. We want them to feel that this is a first step into the community of women!)

It's okay if you want to share a "period story" of your own, just make sure that it's not one that will make kids scared.

Facts about abstinence: The right to say no   (5 minutes)   Time: _____ – _____
Define the term abstinence, and ask girls if they have ever heard of it before. Here is one definition of abstinence:

> When you abstain from something, you choose not to do it. If you chose not to eat pizza, for example, you would be "abstaining" from eating pizza. When you choose not to drink and take drugs you are choosing to abstain from substance use. When you choose not to have sexual intercourse you are choosing to abstain from having sex. Abstaining from something is called "abstinence."

Briefly review and lead a discussion reminding girls of the media messages they learned to think critically about. Ask them if they think media messages make people believe that it is glamorous or "mature" to engage in sexual activity at a young age. Then move onto the following:

> Some people believe that "everyone" is having sex, but there are strong personal, medical and relationship-building reasons for teenagers not to have sex—that is, to abstain from sexual intercourse. Many teens know that. Let's look at the statistics and see the percentage of teens who are saying no to having sex.

Refer to the Facts about Abstinence chart on your flipchart (write these down in advance). Ask the group members for their estimates of the percentages of teens not having sex. Then fill in the blanks with the correct figures.

*Facts about abstinence:

At age 15, about <u>82%</u> of all young people have not had sex.

About <u>48%</u> of males and <u>64%</u> of females under 17 report never having had sex.

Most teens will guess that more people have had sex than is really the case. Take a moment to ask for reasons why this might be (e.g., TV shows showing kids having sex, people lying about having sex so they will seem cool, etc.).

<u>*Brainstorming about having sex:*</u>
<u>*Why or why not?*</u>   (15 minutes)   Time: _____ – _____

Ask the girls to brainstorm reasons why they think teens have sex. Have them write these ideas on the flip chart. Their reasons may include some "positive" outcomes such as, "it's fun," or "it makes them feel good." *These responses should be acknowledged, not put down!* Mention that these "positive" reasons can make it difficult for teens who choose not to have sex to stick with their choice. Also, discuss whether the positive responses are always true. Ask what circumstances might make them true or not true.

Some examples of reasons teens have sex are:

Because they don't know how to say no.	Because they think it will make them grown up.
Because they think that everyone is doing it.	Because they want to keep their boyfriend/girlfriend and they're afraid he/she will leave if they don't have sex.
Because they think it's fun or feels good.	Because they want to have a baby.
Because they're curious about sex.	Because they love their boyfriend/girlfriend and want to share themselves.

Discuss these reasons, reminding girls of the problem solving skills they have learned. Ask them to evaluate the positive and negative consequences of the decision to have sex.

Positives might include:
- *It feels good.*
- *It satisfied my curiosity.*
- *Other people might think I'm cool.*
- *I might feel closer to my boyfriend/girlfriend.*

Negatives might include:
- *I'm scared of pregnancy and STDs (especially HIV).*

- *I'm not really ready.*
- *Now he expects me to do it all the time.*
- *He wants more out of the relationship than I do.*
- *I'm afraid to break up with him even though I don't like him anymore because he will tell people that we "did it."*

Next, ask the girls to brainstorm reasons why teens abstain from sex. Some reasons that they might come up with are listed below. When they have finished brainstorming, add these reasons if they missed any:

Because they have religious or moral reasons not to.	Because abstinence can be a real sign of emotional maturity and integrity. It takes maturity to not have sex before you are ready.
Because abstinence is the only absolutely certain way to avoid out-of-wedlock pregnancy, STDs, and HIV.	Because abstinence reduces the risk of cervical cancer. (You may need to go back to the female anatomy chart to remind girls where the cervix is.)
Because abstinence shows you are stronger than peer pressure.	Because it might hurt your parents and other people in your life if they found out you were having sex.
Because abstaining may lead you to have a deeper relationship with your boyfriend, because you have time to really develop a friendship.	Because if you get pregnant you could mess up your goals and dreams and even hurt your baby's and your own chances at health and economic security.

Ask the girls to evaluate the positive and negative consequences of the decision to be abstinent. Be clear, calm, and firm in reinforcing the benefits of abstinence. Introduce the idea that if anybody in the group has already had sexual intercourse, that doesn't mean that they can't choose to be abstinent now. It is possible to decide to stop having sex until you are more ready for the responsibilities.

Handout   (5 minutes) Time: _____ – _____
Pass out the Having Sex: Why or Why Not handout. Help girls fill out the advantages to themselves if they do not have sex. Help them figure out what might make it difficult to not have sex. Use this section as a segue to discuss the refusal skills topic that follows.

Refusal skills exercise   (15 minutes) Time: _____–_____

In this section, you lead a discussion about verbal and nonverbal aspects of refusal skills. Begin the section by reminding girls of the assertiveness role-plays they did in session 8. Also remind them of the resisting peer pressure theme in previous sessions. Explain that in today's session, they will use these skills in role-plays about how to refuse unwanted (and maybe even wanted!) sex. Explain the following:

> Everybody has the right to control her own body. Every single one of you has the right to control your own body. Part of this control means that you all have the right to refuse sex. Another part of this control means that if you decide to have sex, you have the right to protect yourself from pregnancy and diseases that can be passed through intercourse. Today we will focus on ways you can say no to having sex. Next time we meet we will talk about places you can go to get birth control information and supplies.

Important: Tell the girls that one serious problem that some kids have had to get help for is that somebody—it could be someone they know or a stranger—forced them to have sex against their will. Explain that this is called rape, and that people who have been raped did not choose to have sex. Also say that sometimes when people are raped, they feel scared or embarrassed to tell anybody, but that *it is never their fault*. Tell them that if this should ever happen, or if it has already happened, the important thing to remember is to get help right away. Remind the girls of specific resources in your community where help is available.

Acknowledge that it is sometimes hard to say no to having intercourse, especially to someone we care about. Ask girls to brainstorm a list of "refusals" that would be effective. Have them write these on the flip chart. Answers should include the following:

1. Say "no!"
2. Repeat the refusal.
3. Suggest an alternative.
4. Use body language that says "no!"
5. Explain that you care about the relationship and are afraid that having intercourse would ruin it.

Turn to the verbal and nonverbal "Refusal Skills" (p. 269). Challenge the girls to see how loud they can shout a "no!" all together. Group leaders should demonstrate the nonverbal refusals and then have the girls stand up and act these out together. Again, ham it up. When you put on your best "I mean it" face, really exaggerate.

Role-play (10 minutes) Time: _____ – _____

Introduce the role-play situations. Break the girls into smaller groups and have them turn to the Situation handout. By now, the girls should be comfortable doing role-plays. Have the other group members give feedback on how well the role-players use the verbal and nonverbal refusals.

Finally, summarize the content of today's session. Remind the girls of the important reasons to abstain from sexual activity. Congratulate them on learning the skills so well. Encourage them to share the day's discussion with their parents/guardians.

Journal/workbook assignment (5 minutes) Time: _____ – _____

Ask the girls to make a list of the names of alcohol products they see advertised in magazines or on TV (p. 85). Have them list and critically evaluate some of the media messages they see in these ads. Remind them of session 2 when you talked about how to think critically about media messages.

Closing (whatever time is left)

For this session's closing, open up the floor for questions and answers. Afterward, say goodbyes and congratulate everyone on how great they did! You may play a game if there is time. Remind everybody about attendance and journal assignment incentives.

Session 10: Risky Business: Alcohol, Drugs, and Unwanted Sex

My friend went to a party and drank a lot of tequila. She didn't really get raped, but some guys at the party took off some of her clothes and people were going in and looking at her. Everybody in the whole school heard about it. It's like nobody can talk to her anymore because she's the slut. I feel bad for her, but I don't talk to her much either.

—Maria

The ads for beer are always showing dumpy guys with beautiful girls all over them just because they drink [a certain brand]. I think the girls in the ads must be drunk to be hanging around with such losers!

—Jocelyn

Young people are risk takers. The process of growing up consists of a series of risks as teenagers try new things. Unfortunately, some of the risks they take can have lifelong negative consequences. This session is devoted to helping girls understand some of the risks involved in using alcohol and other substances. We discuss the fact that substance use can lead to impaired judgment. One way we emphasize the link between substance use, the potential for unwanted sexual activity, and negative consequences is to play a game about sexually transmitted diseases (STDs). The game teaches girls about the "chain" of transmission possible with STDs.

In the game, group members (including leaders) are given an index card. One of the cards has a discreet *X* marked on the back. Each participant shakes hands with three group members and writes their names on her index card. The atmosphere is usually jovial and boisterous as girls wander around the room shaking hands during this part of the game.

> "All right, has everybody got three signatures?" I ask. The girls say yes and begin to settle back into the circle. "Good. Now everybody turn your index card over and look on the back. Who has an X on her card?" I ask. I intentionally chose who would get this card in advance. Some girls can joke about being the X person and others would be deeply embarrassed by the designation.
>
> "I do!" Cheri shouts. "Do I win something?"
>
> Even though I know Cheri is a "good sport," it is important to proceed carefully from this point. "Actually, no, Cheri. In this case, you don't win. Everybody remember this is just a game, right?" I remind them.
>
> "Uh-oh," Cheri says. "This isn't gonna be good."
>
> I walk over to stand beside her and say, "I'll explain things in a minute. For now, I want you to stand up," I give her a hand, "and read the three names on your card. Whoever's name Cheri calls should stand up."
>
> "Okay. Gina, Caitlin, and Sonya," she recites.
>
> The three girls stand up. Each of them reads three names from her own card out loud, and those girls stand up. In a short time, all of the group members are standing, including my co-leader and me.
>
> "So are you gonna tell us now?" Cheri jokingly moans.
>
> "I sure am." I reply. "We're pretending that the person with the X had a sexually transmitted disease . . ." I begin.
>
> "Oh, man. That's gross," Cheri protests, but she is laughing.
>
> "Yep, and guess what happened here?" I ask them all.
>
> "We all got it!" Gina says. "Thanks a lot, Cheri!"
>
> "All right, it is just a game, right?" I remind them.
>
> "It's okay. I don't mind," Cheri says. "Wow, did you see how quick everybody stood up?"

The game is a dramatic illustration of how STDs can be transmitted. Because they have been participants in the chain, the memory of this experience makes more of an impact on the girls than simply sharing STD statistics. Still, we share the statistics after the game, with the hope that the personal experience will make the numbers more real.

Rationale

Covell and colleagues (1994) noted that in early adolescence girls, not boys, are attracted to tobacco and alcohol advertisements that promote the product with an attractive social image. Girls are beginning to smoke and drink at younger ages. In this session, participants practice refusal skills for these substances. The "myth of glamour" surrounding substance abuse is deposed, and the increased risk for unwanted sexual activity among users of drugs and alcohol is clearly outlined. STDs are defined and the importance of personal protection through refusal or safe sex practices is stressed.

Goals

1. To teach girls to avoid using alcohol, tobacco, and other drugs and to give them practice in refusal skills.
2. To teach girls the link between use of these substances and risk for unwanted sexual activity.
3. To define STDs, make girls aware of their prevalence, and teach them how to protect themselves through refusal or safe sex practices.

Materials

Puzzle, flip chart, markers, drawing paper, and crayons.
Handouts: Respect Yourself. (You must create this handout. It is a list of local resources for birth control information and supplies.)

Overview

In this session girls are encouraged to be drug-free. They make a list of why some girls use drugs, why some girls don't use drugs, and of activities kids can get involved in instead of using drugs. Each girl designs an advertising campaign that shows alcohol or other drugs as glamorous, and then she draws an "anti-advertisement" that responds to the first ad, debunking the glamour myth and highlighting the link between alcohol/drug use and risky sexual behaviors. A game demonstrates the link between alcohol/drug use and risky sexual behaviors and emphasizes the real risk of exposure to STDs. After the game leaders explain ways to reduce the risk of exposure to STDs.

Procedure

Introduction   (1 minute)   Time: _____–_____

Ask the girls to identify which piece of the puzzle you are on today (Let's Talk about Sex). Tell them that today's session is called "Risky Business: Alcohol, Drugs, and Unwanted Sex."

Group leader disclosure   (4 minutes)   Time _____–_____

At the beginning of this session, it is very effective for group leaders to disclose one incident when alcohol affected their lives in a detrimental way. Be reasonable about this disclosure. You do not want to portray the incident in a way that might sound glamorous or exciting. *If you have any questions about what is or is not appropriate, talk with your supervisor.*

This is an example of an appropriate disclosure:

> When I was in high school, two cars full of kids from my grade were trying to get to a New Year's Eve party before midnight. They crashed into one another, and three kids were killed. One other kid was paralyzed. The kids who didn't get badly hurt were really depressed, and the whole school was grieving. The commercials for alcohol don't talk about these stories. It was so sad.

Journal/workbook discussion   (5 minutes)   Time: _____–_____

Ask the girls to take out their journal/workbooks. Go around the circle and have them read some of the ads they saw for alcohol (p. 85 in the workbook). Ask them to suggest some of the media messages they thought the ads were trying to give them. Examples:

- It's cool to drink.
- If you drink, guys will want to be with you.
- Alcohol makes you "cool."
- Drinking is the only way to have fun.

Then ask the girls if anything in the advertisements addressed the fact that use of alcohol and other drugs increases the risk for engaging in unwanted sexual activity, illness, drunken driving accidents, embarrassment, etc. Ask them why they think you would talk about alcohol and drugs in a session about sex. Explain that many answers will unfold over the next hour and a half.

Exercise   (10 minutes)   Time: _____–_____

On your flip chart, make three columns with the headings, "why," "why not," and "what to do instead." Have the group brainstorm reasons why girls use drugs. Try to draw out some of the following examples:

- to feel good
- to have fun
- to feel more relaxed
- to be part of the crowd

Have the group generate a list of reasons why girls would choose not to use drugs. Try to draw out some of the following examples:

- don't want to
- want to have fun and feel good naturally
- afraid of getting hooked
- afraid of getting caught
- bad for my body
- expensive
- can kill you
- might end up doing something you don't want to do (unwanted sex)

Lead a discussion that emphasizes the dangerous link between alcohol, drugs, and unwanted sexual activity. Ask girls to think about situations where this might happen (parties, alone with a guy, etc.). Describe the potential health risks (STDs, AIDS, pregnancy) and the mental health risks (no control over your own body, embarrassment, depression, ruined reputation, not knowing what happened).

Have the group list what to do instead of using drugs and alcohol. Try to draw out some of the following examples:

- join a club
- do my homework
- join a religious/spiritual group
- volunteer
- help coach a team
- sports
- hobbies (reading, hiking, sewing, collecting rocks, etc.)

Ask the girls what they notice about the list on the flip chart. If it is not said, point out that some girls use drugs to belong and to have fun. Emphasize the fact that by joining clubs or getting involved in their communities and after-school activities, girls will feel less tempted to use drugs because they will already "belong" and they will already be having fun!

Ad campaign exercise   (25 minutes)   Time: _____ – _____
Explain the exercise as follows:

Imagine that you have been hired by a company that makes an alcohol product (beer, wine, whiskey, etc.). Your job is to design an advertising campaign designed to get young people to drink! Be creative, and design one ad that you think will do this. Then, on a second piece of paper, draw an ad that exposes the important information that most alcohol ads, including the one you just designed, *don't* include—like the risk of sexual activity, health risks, mental health risks, death, drinking and driving, etc.

Go around and encourage girls to really "shout back" at the first ad in their second ad. When they are finished drawing, have each group member show her first ad, and act "smooth and glamorous" while she reads it. Then have her read her "reality" second ad in a real, or angry, voice. Encourage them to talk to their parents about ads they see in the coming week, about what the myths and messages are, and about what the ads don't tell you.

Handshake Game   (20 minutes)   Time: _____–_____
From J. S. and L. A. Wodarski (1993).

Pass out one index card to each group member (including yourselves). There is a very small *X* on one of the cards. Plan in advance who will receive the marked card. It should be someone who isn't too easily embarrassed. Be discrete as you hand out the cards. Read the following directions out loud:

> We're going to play the handshake game. Shake hands with someone in the club (including group leaders) and then write down that person's name on your card. You should do this with three different people. After you have shaken hands and have three signatures on your card, sit down in the circle.

After the girls have collected their signatures, read these instructions:

> I want everybody to look on the back of her card to see who has an *X* marked on it. If you have the *X*, please stand up and read all the names on your card out loud. Everyone whose name is called must stand up.

Continue with this until everybody is standing. Then explain that the *X* symbolizes a sexually transmitted disease. Every person who shook hands with the person who had the *X* has been infected. They, in turn, infected people on their cards, and so on. The point to get across is that a sexually transmitted disease travels far and quickly.

At this point, process the game. Have the person who had the *X* talk about what it felt like to read off the names on the list. Have group members talk about how it felt to stand up when their names were called. Ask them if they can imagine telling someone that they had given him a disease, or telling someone that they are pregnant.

Now explain that being drunk can increase your risk of engaging in risky behavior. Ask girls how alcohol and drugs might increase the risk of engaging in sexual activity.

Reemphasize the links between drug and alcohol use and irresponsible sexual activity. Explain that you care about every person in the group, and it is important to you that they grow up to be healthy and happy.

*Facts about STDs**   (5 minutes)   Time _____–_____
Tell the girls you're going to ask them to guess some numbers.

How many teenagers get infected with a sexually transmitted disease (AIDS, syphilis, gonorrhea, etc.) each year? Answer: 3 million per year (National Commission on AIDS, 1994). That is one out of every eight teenagers!

In 1989, how many new cases of gonorrhea were there among adolescents aged 10 to 14 years old? Answer: 11,820.

The lag time between infection and the onset of AIDS is up to 10 years. In 1993, how many people between the ages of 20 and 29 had AIDS? Answer: 55,120.

How old do you think they were when they were infected? Answer: Could have been as young as 10 years old.

Process this information by asking girls if they think this is a lot of kids.

Protecting yourself from STDs   (10 minutes)   Time: _____–_____
Ask the girls what they think the best strategy for avoiding getting an STD is (abstinence!). Point out that not having sex is the only 100% sure way to avoid getting an STD or getting pregnant. Pass out the Respect Yourself handout listing local resources for birth control information and supplies. Then explain the following:

> Even though we think it is a good choice for you to not have sex yet, it is really important to remind everybody again that we all need to take control of our bodies. So, if any of you decide that you are going to have sex, it is really important to protect yourself from diseases and from getting pregnant. One way to do this is to be sure to use a condom. Condoms provide a barrier, usually made of thin rubber, between a man's penis and his partner's body. When they are used in the right way, they protect both partners from germs that can be spread when people

---

*These statistics are taken from J. M. Wallace and D. R. Williams (1997).

have sex. Using condoms, along with other kinds of birth control, can help you avoid getting pregnant or getting diseases. There are two things we really want you to remember right now, though:

1. The only 100% absolutely positively sure-fire way not to get pregnant or get an STD is to not have sex at all.
2. If you are going to have sex, you need to take control of your body and protect yourself. Here is a handout that lists people and places in town where you can get birth control information and supplies. Respect yourself!

Alcohol/drug refusal skills exercise   (5 minutes) Time _____ – _____
Remind the club members of the (verbal and nonverbal) refusal skills taught during the last session. Then ask the girls to gather around a piece of poster paper and create a "graffiti style" poster with every verbal and nonverbal refusal for alcohol, tobacco, drugs, and sexual activity that they can think of. Some examples follow:

> *No thanks. I'm in training.*
> *Not now.*
> *I'm not ready.*
> *No, I'm allergic.*
> *I don't do that stuff.*
> *I want to wait.*
> *I don't have time.*
> *I don't need that to feel good.*
> *That crap is too dangerous.*
> *No thanks, I'd rather live.*
> *Walk away.*
> *Go "cool off."*

Journal/workbook assignment   (5 minutes) Time: _____ – _____
Ask the girls to write down the names of three adults who they really trust (p. 84 in the workbook). What is it about these people that makes them trustworthy? Could they contact these people if they needed to talk about an important issue in their lives?

Closing   (5 minutes) Time: _____ – _____
This is a fun and relaxing closing activity after a few sessions of very serious work. Tell girls to gather in a semicircle in front of you. They are going to play Rainstorm. Here is how it goes:

The person (group leader at first) in the front of the semicircle directs the action by turning slowly and making eye contact with each person in the circle.

Each group member imitates the director as soon as the director makes eye contact with them. The director turns towards the entire circle eight times, in this order, to create the rainstorm:

1. Face each person while rubbing your palms rapidly together.
2. When facing the first person again snap fingers.
3. When facing first person again, slap thighs.
4. When facing first person again, slap thighs, and stomp feet.
5. When facing first person again, slap thighs.
6. When facing first person again, snap fingers.
7. When facing first person again, rub palms together.
8. When facing first person again, turn in silence.

The rainstorm is now over.

Ask club members to start thinking about how they would like to celebrate during the party for the last club session, which is two sessions away. Remind them of attendance and journal assignment incentives.

Chapter 17

When It All Seems Like Too Much

Session 11: Seeking Help, Locating Resources

A couple years ago, when I was in fifth grade my uncle raped me when my mom wasn't home. When I told her about it she cried really hard and then she called the police. It was really bad. They put him in jail, and for a little while I went to counseling. Then my mom told me that counseling was really expensive and we couldn't afford it and she asked me if I was okay now. I told her that I was, but I'm not. I think about it all the time. I can't talk to my other friends about it because I'm afraid of what they'll think or tell other people. And I can't talk to my mom because she wants me to just be done with it.

—Naomi

My friend, Gina, is always trying to get me to try stuff. We used to be really good friends but now she's starting to scare me. Last month she got suspended for smoking pot on the field after school and she just said she didn't care. Some of my other friends are saying they won't go near her, but I know she's a nice person. I think that her dad drinks a lot. How can I help her?

—Heather

During the course of conducting these groups, several instances have arisen in which girls disclosed weighty concerns and shared sensitive stories with group leaders. We have heard girls tell of physical abuse at the hands of parents, stories of sexual coercion by older males, confessions of eating disorders, and acknowledgment of substance abuse problems. Frequently these stories emerge during this session. For this reason, it is important to review the limits of confidentiality (from session 1) at the outset of this meeting.

182

"Does everybody remember the rule about confidentiality from our first meeting?" I ask the group.

"What's said in the room stays in the room." Alicia responds.

"That's right, Alicia. How about any exceptions to that rule?" I prompt.

"You can tell people about stuff like games that we play," Hannah says, "but not really personal stuff that we talk about."

"Good, that's absolutely correct. I'm thinking of something else, right now . . . " I fish for responses.

"Oh, I know. That stuff about how you have to tell if we said we were gonna hurt somebody or hurt ourselves," Alicia remembers.

"That's right. There were three exceptions to the confidentiality rule. If anybody here told us they were going to hurt themselves, hurt somebody else, or that somebody is hurting them, we couldn't keep it a secret because we want to be sure that you're safe. Does everybody remember that now?" I ask.

They nod.

"It's also really important for everybody to know that if any of those things—or other serious problems—are on your mind, we can try to hook you up to the help that you need. Sometimes keeping these secrets takes so much energy that it seems impossible to solve the problem. Today we're going to talk about where to go to get help."

My coleader joins in. "Sometimes people think that they should be able to solve all their problems alone. But getting help is such a smart and brave thing to do." We finish the confidentiality reminder by inviting girls who need to talk more to come see us when the group is over.

Adolescents frequently assume that they have the right to confidentiality even in circumstances when they don't. If we do not warn girls of the need to disclose certain information, they may (rightly) feel betrayed when we later announce that their confidence will not be kept. Still, we want to inform girls without scaring them away from sharing serious problems. Informed, respectful consent is called for.

Rationale

While it is important to encourage girls to take responsibility for solving manageable problems, it is just as important to teach them that some problems can be too big or too serious to handle all alone. An adolescent who is struggling with serious issues can truly profit from learning about personal and community resources. Teaching girls where to go for help and encouraging them to seek that help when necessary can help them to establish a "helping protocol" before the need for such services arises.

Goals

1. To teach girls that some situations may require outside help.
2. To teach girls how to tell when a problem is too serious to handle all alone.
3. To teach girls where and how to get help for serious problems when they need it.

Materials

Puzzle, markers, flip chart, game, team prize for Solve It or Seek Help game. Handouts: My Personal Yellow Pages (pp. 270–271), Who Can Help? (p. 272).

Overview

This topic can evoke some major issues for girls; leaders can begin by reviewing confidentiality and limits to confidentiality with the group. Next, girls participate in an exercise designed to help them discern the difference between problems that they can solve on their own and problems for which they need to seek help. The group establishes a set of general guidelines to indicate when a problem requires outside resources to solve. Next, girls are encouraged to think about the adults they trust, and to consider these adults a part of their personal resource list. Leaders then pass out the "Personal Yellow Pages" of community resources (health and social services, recreational activities, etc.) available to girls in their own area (these must be constructed locally for obvious reasons). Girls can practice using the resource guides by reading through sample problems and suggesting appropriate agencies or individuals to contact in each situation. Finally, girls are encouraged to view "resource seeking" as a sign of intelligence and strength rather than a sign of weakness. Leaders should be alert during and after the group for girls who are ready to disclose serious problems.

Procedure

Introduction   (2–3 minutes) Time: _____–_____

Point to the puzzle and ask the group to identify which puzzle piece you are on (When It All Seems Like Too Much). Mention something like the following:

> We already learned how to use a five-step problem solving process to help figure out what to do when we are facing a challenging process. But some problems are too big or too complicated to handle by ourselves.

Sometimes we have problems that are very serious and we need to get help before we can really solve them. Today we're going to talk about how to do that.

Review the limits of confidentiality with the group before going any further in this session. See the introduction to this chapter for an illustration.

Procedure for part I: How to tell "when it all seems like too much"

<u>Solve It or Seek Help game</u>   (20 minutes)   Time: _____-_____

Explain that today they will learn how to tell if a problem is one that they can try to solve on their own or if it is one that they should try to seek help with right away. You will play a game to help girls learn the difference. Here are the instructions for the game:

> We are going to divide into two teams. I have a list of some problem situations. I will read each problem situation out loud. Each team will have 30 seconds to discuss whether they think it is a "solve it" or "seek help" kind of problem and why. When 30 seconds are up, we'll ask each team for its answer, and what made them decide which kind of problem it is. Whichever team has the most correct answers at the end of the game wins a prize. If it is a tie, both teams win a prize!

Group leaders should help the girls gather into two team circles so they can talk about their answers. One leader should stand near each group to monitor the discussions. When the teams answer, the group leaders should help the girls bring out some of the reasons they chose their response. Leaders should take turns reading the following problem situations out loud:

1. Anne can't decide whether to go to her friend Shelley's house after school or to the mall with her mother. If she goes to Shelley's she'll get to see Shelley's new kitten. If she goes to the mall, she might get a new pair of shoes. Should she "solve it" or "seek help?" (solve it)
2. Marilyn thinks her mom might be drinking too much. When Marilyn came home from school yesterday, her mom was asleep on the couch with a bottle lying next to her. Marilyn's 3-year-old brother was sitting on the floor playing with some toys all by himself when Marilyn got home. She is starting to feel worried about her mom but doesn't know what to do. Should Marilyn "solve it" or "seek help?" (seek help)
3. Loretta is confused. First she told Madeline that she would help her with her homework after school, but then Erik asked her if he could walk her home.

She really likes Erik but she feels like she might be letting Madeline down if she doesn't stay to help her. Should Loretta "solve it" or "seek help?" (solve it)

4. Faye has been spending a lot of time lately thinking about her friend Sara. Sara just doesn't seem to be acting like her old self. Faye notices that Sara seems tired all of the time. Whenever Faye asks her to go out, Sara says she's not in the mood to go anywhere. Sara is even starting to look kind of different. She seems to be getting skinnier and she hardly ever smiles anymore. Should Faye "solve it" or "seek help?" (seek help)

5. Sophia doesn't know what to do. She hasn't been feeling very good lately. Her stomach aches and she thinks she feels kind of dizzy sometimes. Her mom has been pretty busy lately, so she doesn't want to bother her about this stuff, but it's getting hard for Sophia to concentrate on school and her friends. Should she "solve it" or "seek help?" (seek help)

Guidelines for seeking help   (5 minutes)   Time: _____–_____

Place the flip chart where everyone can reach it easily and title the page "Seek Help." Lead a discussion focusing on signals we can look for to find out if a problem is a "seek help" kind of problem. These signals should include:

- You spend a lot of time worrying about the problem.
- So far the things you tried to solve it haven't worked.
- It seems like no matter what you do you can't solve it.
- You are worried that someone else might find out about the problem.
- You feel scared when you think about it.
- You feel kind of "lost" when you think about the problem.

Congratulate the girls for coming up with "seeking signals." You might want to point out that many of the signals are emotions, like worry, fear, hopelessness, anger, and frustration. Remind them to use these emotions as guides to decide if they need to seek help.

Procedure for part II: Where to go "when it all seems like too much"

Journal/workbook activity   (15 minutes)   Time: _____–_____

Introduce this piece by explaining the following:

We just talked about how to tell the difference between problems we can try to solve on our own and problems that are too complicated or serious and we need to seek help with. When we run into a "seek help" kind of problem (and sooner or later, everybody has to deal with some "seek help" problems), it's important to know whom you can talk to, where to go, and what to do.

Ask the girls to take out their journals/workbooks. Their assignment was to write the names of three adults they really trust (p. 84 in the workbook).

On a flip chart page, write the title "People we trust." Then ask the girls to write the name of at least one person from their journal list. Under that person's name they can write down one quality about the person that makes him or her trustworthy. (Example: *Tia Jessica: She always really listens to me when I talk to her,* or *Mrs. Walsh: She always acts really calm and makes fair decisions.*) Encourage the girls to color and decorate the page (join them!) while you all discuss some of these special people in the world.

Personal Yellow Pages exercise   (15 minutes) Time: _____ - _____

Pass out the My Personal Yellow Pages handout. Explain that everyone is to fill in the blanks on this handout. If they don't know some of the phone numbers it's okay; they should fill in the missing numbers by asking their parents or guardians.

Group leaders should explain that the people on this list will also be concerned about the girls' safety, so if they confide that they are thinking of hurting themselves or someone else, or that someone is hurting them, these adults may also need to tell someone else. Go around the room helping girls think of some people who they can list in their yellow pages. (Do not give the girls your phone number. Explain that you will be in their school for a short time, but it is important to you that they list people who will be there for them for the long haul.)

Who can help?   (15 minutes) Time: _____ - _____

Next, distribute the Who Can Help? handout. Ask volunteers to read each of the two situations out loud. After each one is read, ask the girls to suggest as many helping resources from the yellow pages list as they can for that particular problem.

Conclusions   (5 minutes) Time _____ - _____

Wrap up the day's session by explaining:

Many problems can be solved by using the five-step problem process we learned earlier, but some problems are too serious or too difficult to solve by yourself. It's important to think about where you might go for help if one of those problems happens to you. Friends are helpful, but sometimes they don't have the answers you need. Adults you trust are important resources in your life. There are also lots of agencies in town where you can get specialized help for specific problems. Remember that it's not a sign of weakness to ask for help, but a true sign of strength and intelligence to reach out when you need to.

Journal/workbook assignment   (5 minutes) Time: _____–_____

Ask the girls to write about three goals they would like to achieve as an adult (p. 95 in the workbook). Explain that one goal should be about an adventure, another should be about a career, and a third about schooling. Some examples might be: to become a teacher or an engineer, to hike Mount Everest, or to graduate from college.

Chapter 18

Planning for the Future

Session 12: Visions for a Strong Future

Nobody ever asked me what I want to be before.

—Judi

I used to say that I wanted to be a model, but I'm not sure now. I still might try that, but I started thinking about how I'm good at other stuff, too. Like maybe I could be a lawyer, because everybody always says I'm really dramatic and I can talk people into doing things.

—Jennifer

Many participants in the Go Grrrls club start the group with a "fantasy" desire to be a model but end the group with a real plan to explore the educational requirements for becoming a physician, teacher, engineer, social worker, or physicist. In this session, we teach girls how to set short-term objectives to achieve long-term educational, career, and adventure goals. We also try to help girls find a connection to the future by having them evaluate a list of "value" statements about world issues (e.g., environment, education, racism, etc.) and consider ways that they might truly make a difference in the future world that will be theirs.

This is a fairly simple session to conduct, but some girls have trouble figuring out what objectives they might be able to set to help move them toward a long-term goal.

> "Does anybody need help filling out the What I Will Be Doing handout?" I ask.
>
> Mayra raises her hand. "I'm not sure I get it," she says.
>
> "Let's take a look. Your goal is to explore being a veterinarian. Wow! I love animals." I take the pressure of the task off for a moment.

"Yeah, I do too. I have three dogs, two cats, a gerbil, and an iguana," the aspiring Doctor Mayra relates. "And my uncle is a veterinarian."

"Do you ever visit him?" I ask.

"Not very often. He lives about an hour away from here so we don't get to see him very often," she tells me.

"Hmm. Do you ever talk with him about his job? Could you call him?" I ask.

"Yeah, I guess I could." She looks at me and raises her eyebrows. "That could be one goal. I could call him in the next 5 days and talk to him about what it's like to be a vet!"

"Excellent. Write it down. I bet you can come up with the other goals, too." I tell her.

"For the next-5-months goal I could try to go visit him at his office. He let me hang around once before when I was little." Mayra is excited now.

"That would be really fun for you, I bet. You'd probably learn a lot, too," I encourage her. "How about the next-5-years goal?"

"That's kind of hard," she thinks for a moment. "Maybe I could check out what classes to take if I want to be a vet. I could talk to my guidance counselor."

Mayra may never become a veterinarian. That's not important. Not every middle school girl has a specific vocational desire, nor do they need to. It is important for girls to begin to think about their life goals, and to see that they have support to explore their interests. The emphasis in this session is on helping girls figure out how to set goals and explore their connection to the future. It is just as important, though, to give them encouragement by truly believing that they can accomplish their goals and follow their passion.

Rationale

During this session, group facilitators encourage each girl to develop a positive vision of what her future might look like. Girls practice realistic goal setting and facilitators help outline the importance of education. Research shows that girls who have future educational and career goals are less likely to engage in risky behaviors. We discuss the importance of having personal goals and the potential for girls to experience success.

Goals

1. To encourage girls to establish educational, vocational, and other healthy goals.

2. To identify ways that girls can establish goals and then make plans to achieve those goals.
3. To instill a sense of confidence and enthusiasm in the process of teaching these skills.
4. To encourage the development of a mastery orientation to learning.

Materials

Puzzle, flip chart, markers, pens.
Handouts: What I Will Be Doing (p. 273), What's Important to Me (p. 274), Community Hookups (p. 275).

Overview

This session is designed to be very positive and encouraging. We hope that the exercises and activities will help girls truly believe that they can set and attain goals. The tone of this session should be very uplifting, and group leaders should make certain they give strong encouragement to every member of the club.

Procedure

Introduction/journal/workbook activity   (15 minutes) Time: _____–_____
Ask the girls to point out which piece of the puzzle you are on today (Planning for the Future). Congratulate them on getting to the last piece! Start the discussion by emphasizing the fact that it is very important for girls to set goals for themselves. Mention that often setting goals for ourselves, gives us a clearer sense about what we want from life. In thinking about what goals are right for you, review what your needs and interests are. Think about what things might help improve your life.

Ask the girls to take out their journal/workbooks. Have them read some of their goals (p. 95 in the workbook). Be very encouraging, and cheer each girl on in her interests.

Handout exercise   (8 minutes) Time: _____–_____
Have the group complete the What I Will Be Doing handout. In the circle, have each member read their responses out loud. Point out that getting more out of life means making plans to do things, and doing them! After the girls fill it out, one group leader should create the following categories on the flip chart:

For my personal self
For others and society
For my career

For my family
For my creative self

Then ask each girl to look at her What I Will Be Doing handout, and to use a marker to write ideas under the appropriate categories on the flip chart. They may come up with new ideas to write under categories they hadn't considered before.

Hooking up with positive activities   (20 minutes)   Time: _____–_____

Pass out the What's Important to Me handout. Give the girls about 5 minutes to fill out the form. Then, when they are all finished, write the numbers 1–10 on the flipchart. Read each statement out loud and ask anyone who circled that statement as one of their top three concerns to raise her hand. Count the hands and have someone record that number next to the question number on the poster. Do this for every statement on the list.

Break the kids into two "interest groups" according to two of the items on the list that many people circled. One group leader works with each group. Have kids brainstorm some ways that they could "hook up with positive activities" to make a difference in their own communities about these two issues. Pass out the Community Hookups handout. Help them to come up with an action plan. (What can they do tomorrow to make this happen? Next week? Next month?)

Briefly stress the importance of remembering safety rules when doing volunteer work. For example, kids should not just go door to door offering services. They need to tell an adult and take someone with them.

Bring the two groups together. Ask the girls to describe why working to build their communities could help them create a positive self-image. Ask them to describe why using drugs or joining gangs would not help them create a positive self-image. Encourage them all to take the next step in getting involved. Also, ask them to speak with their parents, social studies teachers, counselors, etc., to link up with school-based activities that promote leadership.

Planning for the Future game   (30 minutes)   Time: _____–_____

Place the flip chart so it is propped up on a chair in front of the group. Explain the directions for the game as follows:

We are going to play the "planning for the future" version of Pictionary. Using your What I Will Be Doing handout, decide on one goal you can draw on the flip chart. Using your other handout, Planning for the Future, choose another goal to draw. Last, pick whatever you want to draw just for fun. You will be given one minute to draw your goal. During that time, the group will try to guess what your goal is. Someone needs to keep time. Whomever's drawing is guessed in the shortest amount of time is the winner. Remember, no talking and no writing words. Have fun!

Journal/workbook assignment (5 minutes) Time: _____–_____
Ask the girls to write (on p. 110 of the workbook) about what they liked best about the Go Grrrls club, what they liked least about it, and finally, what they would do differently if they were a group leader.

Closing (8 minutes) Time: _____–_____
For the closing section, summarize the messages about the importance of planning for the future. Reinforce the value of all participants' educational, career, adventure, and community goals and dreams.

Have the girls plan some special details for their final session party. What food do they want? Do they want music? Games? Be sure everyone knows how important it is to come to the last session! Tell them all what great work and fun they've accomplished and say good-byes.

After the session

The two group leaders should organize their attendance record and journal assignment records in preparation for next session's drawing.

Session 13: Review and Closure

It was fun to just talk and hang out and play the games and have fun. I learned more about not hating my looks and how I act. Thanks.

—Kristen

We talked about things I wanted to know. It was cool working together. I'm telling my little sister that she has to do this next year. I'm really going to miss my group leaders.

—Trina

The final club meeting is always bittersweet. By the end of the group, leaders and participants have shared their knowledge, emotions, and talents with one another. We want girls to leave the group feeling proud of their accomplishments and ready to encounter new challenges.

For some girls, though, the last meeting can be very emotional. Girls who have developed strong connections to group leaders may be tearful. The way group leaders handle closure is very important.

Cori and Whitney stand arm-in-arm, swaying to an R&B song playing loudly in the room. "When will we see you again?" Whitney asks. "You can't just go away!"

"We'll be around next semester to recruit some more girls to join the club." I tell her. "You two can help us—tell them how great it is and bring them over to the sign-up table for us." I suggest.

"Yeah, but it's not the same," Cori complains. "What are we going to do on Tuesdays and Thursdays now?"

"Didn't you say that you wanted to join the drama club? You should do it. You did such a great job with all of the role-plays!" I compliment her.

"Thanks." She is beaming. "But we're going to miss you."

Some leaders are tempted to tell girls that they will keep in touch. Usually, this is not advisable and/or possible. It is better to speak honestly about the end of the experience.

"I'm going to miss you, too." I tell the girls . . . and I mean it. "You taught me a lot. Thank you for being so honest and smart, and so much fun. Remember the things we learned here!"

"We will," Cori assures me as she and Whitney dance off together.

Rationale

End the group with a final session and provide a sense of closure and accomplishment. Group facilitators distribute certificates of achievement and personalized goodbye notes to all participants.

Goals

(1) Review and summary of topics covered during the course of the group
(2) Collect final data for program evaluation
(3) Provide participants with a sense of closure and accomplishment at the end of the program.

Materials

Puzzle, posttest (pp. 211–216), program evaluation (pp. 217–221), markers, pencils, graduation certificates (p. 277), food, decorations, drawing prizes.

Overview

This session is very important. Group leaders do a *brief* review of all of the subjects covered during the 12-session program. Girls then complete the posttest. Finally, the girls gain a real sense of accomplishment when they receive the graduation certificates and congratulatory notes from leaders. They will then eat, play, relax, and finally say goodbyes.

Procedure

First, place the Go Grrrls puzzle in front of the group. Very briefly remind the girls of all the topics you've covered during the club meetings. This should take no more than about 5 minutes. It is important to do this so that they all remember how much material we've covered before they take the posttest and fill out the program evaluation.

Posttest and evaluation administration   (25 minutes)

Even though the girls will be excited, remind them that we need their honest, thoughtful answers on this test so we can make the program even better for all the kids who come after them. Tell them that we truly value their opinions. Remind them to work privately and to ask you if they are unsure of what any questions or words mean. Finally, remind them that their responses are confidential.

Graduation ceremony

Call out each girl's name and present her with a graduation certificate. Congratulate every girl for something very specific and personal that you know about her from the course of the group. Make it special! Congratulate every girl on how hard she worked to learn about making good personal decisions about her life.

Party

Based on what your group decided to do at the end of last session, you can now relax and have fun dancing, playing games, etc. While the general merriment goes on, be sure that you make a special effort to mingle with each participant. You may want to ask each girl if she thinks differently about anything now that the group is over. Have fun and reinforce the messages from the entire program, at the same time!

Closing/Goodbyes

Thank the girls for participating in the Go Grrrls program. Conduct the drawing for the attendance and journal assignment. Tell them that they are all winners. Emphasize the importance of making good life choices. Send them on their way as stronger young women!

Relax and pat yourself on the back for your own hard and fun work!
Well, it's almost the end . . . now you have to clean up the room!

APPENDICES

Appendix A

Building a Girls' Movement: A List of Books and Other Resources

Several people have worked hard to help restore girls' strong voices by listening to what girls have to say and writing about topics that matter to them. We would like to acknowledge some of those people with the hope that readers will connect with other important works on girls' issues. Two early efforts came from England: *I Like to Say . . . What I Think* (Simmons & Wade, 1984) and *Bitter-sweet Dreams: Girls' and Young Women's Own Stories* (Goodings, 1987). Gilligan's work, *Making Connections: The Relational Worlds of Adolescent Girls at the Emma Willard School* (1990) and *Meeting at the Crossroads* (1993), are classics in building an understanding of the complex issues girls face. Many of the quotes in our book came from *Girl Power: Young Women Speak Out* (Carlip, 1995), a wonderfully diverse collection of girls' voices. Shortly after she teamed up with Gloria Steinem to create Girls Speak Out, a program that brings girls together to talk, Andrea Johnston wrote *Girls Speak Out: Finding Your True Self* (1997), which documents the lessons they learned from listening to girls speak about their true selves. A similar book is *Ophelia Speaks: Adolescent Girls Write About Their Search for Self* (Shandler, 1999).

Girls themselves also are beginning to take back the podium. Their yearning to find a voice is well represented by over 300 "zines," self-made publications created by and for girls. This underground culture is well represented by *A Girl's Guide to Taking Over the World: Writings From the Girl Zine Revolution* (Green & Taormino, 1997). Increased access to the Internet has led to the creation of online girl zines such as CyberGrrl, Gurl, Geek Girl, and Fat Girl. Many of the zines capture the strong voice of girls, as is depicted in such titles as *Alien, My Life and Sex Thrive in the J. Crew Catalogue*, and *Angry Young Women* (Green & Taormino, 1997). Commercial magazines created as alternatives to the successful glitzy teen magazines include *New Moon: The Magazine for Girls and Their Dreams* (published six times a year) and *Teen Voices: Because You Are More Than a Pretty Face*.

While girls work hard to reestablish their voices in the world, women have been laboring to shape a broader understanding of girls in contemporary society. Writing about how women rediscover their true selves, Hancock (1989) gleans important insights in her study of the life stories of 20 women. Peggy Orenstein (1994) made famous the American Association of University Women study's finding that, as young girls reach adolescence, their self-esteem plummets. Orenstein spent a year in two California middle schools and her prose in *School Girls: Young Women, Self-Esteem, and the Confidence Gap* brings to life the many ways American society shortchanges women and girls.

American society is obsessed with women's bodies. Brumberg (1997) explains why in her book *The Body Project: An Intimate History of American Girls.* This historical account chronicles the way growing up in a female body has dramatically changed over time and why it is more difficult to inhabit the emerging female form today than in the past. Girls increasingly define themselves through their appearance—hence their body has become their primary "project." Nancy Friday has contributed a personal and comprehensive examination of the power and mystique of beauty in *Our Looks, Our Lives: Sex, Beauty, Power, and the Need to Be Seen* (1997). And to round out the social implications of being female, Tanenbaum's (1999) *Slut! Growing Up Female With a Bad Reputation* describes how good girls are turned into "sluts" and the imputations this epithet carries.

Some authors sought to offer clear advice about healthy ways to parent a girl. Examples include Mackoff's (1996) book, *Growing a Girl: Seven Strategies for Raising a Strong Spirited Daughter,* Bingham and Stryker's (1995) *Things Will Be Different for My Daughter: A Practical Guide to Building Her Self-Esteem and Self-Reliance* and Rutter's book, *Celebrating Girls: Nurturing and Empowering our Daughters.* Mann's early book (1994) *The Difference: Growing Up Female* in America is a popular book in this vein. A columnist for the *Washington Post,* Mann was inspired by her own experiences with her daughter. The book is written primarily for parents and is based on extensive interviews with experts and teenage girls.

Amid all these important books, one clearly tipped the first domino of the girls' movement: Mary Pipher's *Reviving Ophelia: Saving the Selves of Adolescent Girls* (Pipher, 1994). This *New York Times* bestseller struck a cord with American women by describing the "girl-poisoning culture" that young girls grow up in today.

Finally, several professional women have responded to the girls' movement by creating self-help books for girls trying to survive in this toxic culture. One popular book for teenagers is Abner and Villarosa's (1996) *Finding Our Way: The Teen Girls' Survival Guide.* This book is a down-to-earth manual about life as a teenage girl, covering topics that range from eating healthily to dealing with abuse. Or consider Catherine Dee's (1997) *The Girls' Guide to Life*, an action-oriented self-help book with exercises and ideas about how girls can face the issues that affect them. Lynda and Area Madaras, the mother and daughter team who wrote *What's Happening to My Body? Book for Girls* also teamed up to create *My Feelings, My Self* (1993), a self-help book that attempts to answer basic questions adolescent girls ponder about parents and relationships. A more thoughtful than self-help–oriented work is an edited paperback by Tonya Bolden (1998) called *33 Things Every Girl Should Know*. This volume contains stories, advice, and poems by 33 different women. A more specialized book written specifically for preteens is Mavis Jukes' (1996) *It's a Girl Thing: How to Stay Healthy, Safe, and in Charge*.

As you can see, the long path to the girls' movement includes a wealth of information about girls from a variety of perspectives. In addition to books there are conferences, including teen zine conventions, the National Girls Conference, the Riot Grrrl convention, and so forth. Organizations have blossomed as well. Particularly significant is Girls Incorporated, which was formed in 1945 as Girls' Clubs of America. Girls Incorporated is dedicated to helping girls and young women overcome discrimination and develop their capacity to be self-sufficient, responsible citizens. This organization also serves as an advocate for girls and has promoted programs to expand girls' career opportunities, encourage math and science abilities, discourage the use of alcohol and drugs, and prevent teenage pregnancy. In 1992, Girls Incorporated outlined a "Girls' Bill of Rights" (see page 5 in workbook), an important beginning in the effort to improve the culture in which girls live.

The explosion of effort to help girls function more effectively was accompanied by new research studies that shed light on the unique problems girls face, as well as resources and prospects available to help them succeed. Scholars such as Carol Gilligan, Jacquelynne Eccles, Roberta Simmons, Jeannie Brooks-Gunn, Anne C. Petersen, Carol Beal, and Ruth Striegel-Moore, to name only a few, have helped shape the understanding about girls that forms the foundation of the Go Grrrls program.

Empowering Adolescent Girls incorporates the knowledge and practical wisdom accumulated from these important sources and offers a succinct, scholarly review of current literature on the major issues girls face. However, our goal is not merely to inform, but also to provide a practical guide for practitioners interested in preventing some of the most common problems girls face in today's society. We know of no other programs that have been systematically developed based on an empirical understanding of girls and have shown successful outcomes using a randomized control group design. We hope that this work will serve as another important stepping-stone on the path to understanding and empowering girls.

Appendix B

Outcomes: A Brief Review of Our Research

In 1997–98 we conducted an evaluation of a 12-session version of the Go Grrrls program. Volunteers were recruited to participate in the Go Grrrls club as an after-school activity. Participants came from three schools, two junior high schools, and one alternative school for high-risk youth. Participants were randomly assigned to a treatment or wait list control condition. A total of 108 girls completed pre- and posttests (see the Go Grrrls Questionnaire, pp. 211–216). The treatment and control groups were similar: There were no statistically significant differences between them on any of the demographic measures. Also, there were no significant differences between the groups on the pretest measures. The demographic breakdown of the girls follows.

TABLE B1
DEMOGRAPHICS OF GO GRRRLS TREATMENT
AND CONTROL GROUPS

Treatment Group (n=68)	Control Group (n=40)
Mean age: 14.18	Mean age: 13.33
Mothers attended college: 32.3%	Mothers attended college: 34.6%
Fathers attended college: 27.1%	Fathers attended college: 27.1%
Single parent family home: 49%	Single parent family home: 53%
Hispanic: 15.8%	Hispanic: 11.2%
Caucasian: 55.8%	Caucasian: 68.8%
African American: 2.1%	African American: 1.6%
Native American: 4.2%	Native American: 2.4%
Mixed race: 22.1%	Mixed race: 15.1%
Receiving free school lunch: 43.2%	Receiving free school lunch: 42.5%
Started their period: 73.4%	Started their period: 68.3%

Devising a Measurement Model

Because the Go Grrrls program is conceptualized as a broad-based prevention program, it was challenging to develop adequate measures to assess its effectiveness. We decided to use multiple measures to tap into the various aspects of the program, hypothesizing that different program content areas would reflect differently across various measures. A list of these eight measures follows.

- The body-image scale: based on previous measures (Simmons and Blyth, 1987). Five items that measure satisfaction with body image, including "How happy are you with your overall figure?"
- The assertiveness scale: seven items that measure anticipated assertiveness, including items such as, "If a friend wanted to give me alcohol I could say no."
- The peer self-esteem scale: (Hare, 1985) ten-item scale that measures self esteem by asking subjects to assess their friendships, e.g., "Other people think I am a lot of fun to be with."
- The attractiveness scale: eight items that measure girls' perceptions about attractiveness. A sample item is "I think girls need to be skinny to be attractive."
- The self-efficacy scale: a nine-item scale that measures girls' perceived gender-role efficacy. For example, "I feel good about being a girl" is one item.
- The self-liking and self-competence scale: (Tafarodi & Swann, 1995) measures perceived personal efficacies and self-esteem. A sample item is "I perform well at a number of things."
- The hopelessness scale: (Kazdin, 1993) measures hopelessness/helplessness. A sample item is "Someday I will be good at doing the things that I really care about."
- The help endorsement scale: fifteen items. Essentially, a list of people and agencies that might offer help to teenagers. Girls circle all possible sources of help they might use if they need it. Examples include school counselor, self-help book, information hotline.

While some of these scales tap into the effectiveness of very specific sessions, others measure more global program effects. Table B2 portrays the relationship between program content and the eight measurement scales just noted.

As the table reveals, some measures were common to several program content areas (for example, body image, self-esteem, and self-efficacy). While we were satisfied that most of the measures selected reflected specific program content, it was more difficult to determine what measure would best tap the overall program. In the end we concluded that girls' sense of self-efficacy was

TABLE B2
PROGRAM CONTENT AREAS AND RELATED MEASURES*

Program Content Area	Related Measure
Being a girl in today's society	Body image Attitudes about attractiveness Self-esteem Self-efficacy
Establishing a positive body image	Body image Attitudes about attractiveness Self-esteem Self-efficacy
Establishing a positive mindset	Body image Attitudes about attractiveness Self-esteem Self-efficacy Hopelessness
Establishing independence	Self-esteem Self-efficacy Assertiveness
Making and keeping friends	Self-esteem Self-efficacy Assertiveness Peer self-esteem (friendship)
When it all seems like too much	Self-esteem Self-efficacy Assertiveness Helping resources
Planning for the future	Self-esteem Self-efficacy

the measure that best reflected total program content. Since no such measure existed, we had to develop this scale. Each measure was tested for reliability and the results are presented in Table B3.

* Sexuality is not covered here, as these measures were instituted prior to the inclusion of sexuality as a topic area.

TABLE B3
RELIABILITIES FOR GO GRRRLS MEASURES

Measure	Pretest
Satisfaction with body image	.72
Assertiveness	.72
Friendship esteem	.80
Attitude toward attractiveness	.76
Self-efficacy	.92
Self-esteem	.89
Hopelessness	.80

Positive results were documented for the Go Grrrls program. First, all pretest to posttest changes were in a positive direction: participants' self-esteem increased and how much girls valued attractiveness decreased. The pretest to posttest changes were all significant for the treatment group. As the following figures show, there were few changes from pretest to posttest for the control group.

The overall effectiveness of the program was tested by examining the differences in change scores between the treatment and control groups. In other words, given two equivalent groups of girls, did the treatment group show more positive change than the control group? The randomized experiment found significant between-group change for seven of the eight measures in Table B4.

TABLE B4
SIGNIFICANT BETWEEN-GROUP CHANGE

Body image $F(1, 116) = 6.03$, $p < .008$

Assertiveness $F(1,116) = 4.75$, $p < .01$

Attractiveness $F(1,116) = 8.75$, $p < .002$

Self-efficacy $F(1,116) = 3.42$, $p < .03$

Self-esteem $F(1, 113) = 6.30$, $p < .006$

Hopelessness $F(1,113) = 1.70$, $p < .09$

Help $F(1,116) = 1.84$, $p < .08$

Overall, the program had positive outcomes across a number of measures (figure B1). The strongest impact was on the measures of value of attractiveness, self-esteem, and body image. The measures of hopelessness and help were significant, but only at the .10 level. Only one measure did not obtain significance and that was friendship esteem. What is encouraging from these results is that the significant effects reflect more of the "core content" of the program: The program emphasizes body image, self-esteem, and self-efficacy throughout, whereas only two sessions deal directly with friendship esteem.

We have included evaluation tools in Appendix C. It is our hope that ongoing evaluation will be conducted as Go Grrrls programs take place across the country.

FIGURE B1
OUTCOMES OF GO GRRRLS PROGRAM

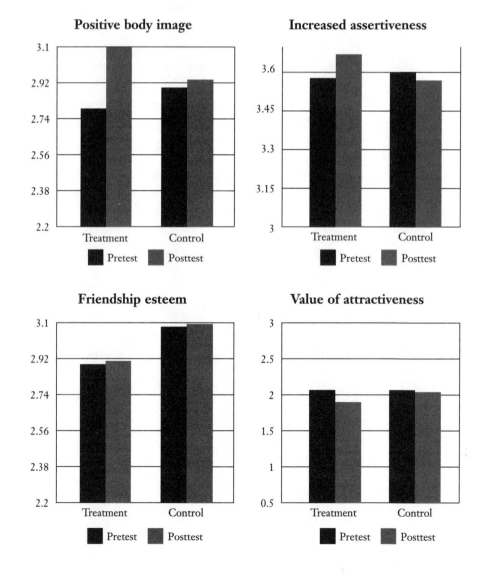

FIGURE B1 (CONTINUED)
OUTCOMES OF GO GRRRLS PROGRAM

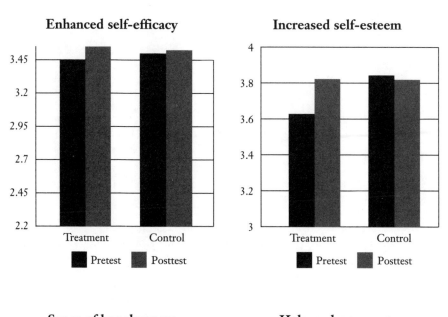

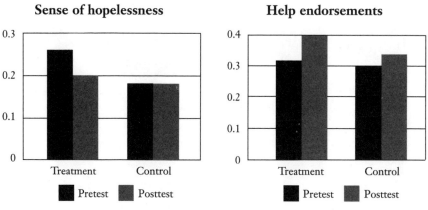

Appendix C

Using the Evaluation Tool:
The Go Grrrls Questionnaire

The Go Grrrls Questionnaire evaluation instrument includes eight sub-scales that measure different aspects of the Go Grrrls program:

Body image scale: "Your Body," questions 1–5 on page 211
Assertiveness scale: "What Would You Do," questions 1–7 on page 212
Peer self-esteem scale: "Friends," questions 1–10 on page 212
Value of attractiveness scale: "Attractiveness," questions 1–8 on page 213
Self-efficacy scale: "Being a Girl," questions 1–9 on page 213
Self-liking and self-competence scale: "About Me," questions 1–20 on page 214
Hopelessness scale: "Feelings," questions 1–17 on page 215
Help scale: "Getting Help," questions, a–o on page 216

The questionnaire also includes a confidential tracking system by having the girl supply information such as her initials, date of birth, school, and grade. This information is used to match pretest and posttest questionnaires. At the end of the questionnaire are additional questions about the participant's background.

How to Score the Questionnaire

Body-image scale: Add scores from questions 1–5 together. Higher scores indicate higher positive body image.

Assertiveness scale: Add scores from questions 1–7 together. Higher scores indicate greater assertiveness.

Peer self-esteem scale: Reverse the score for negatively worded questions 2, 4, 6, 8, 10 (e.g., 1=4, 2=3, 3=2, 4=1). Higher scores indicate greater peer self-esteem.

Value of attractiveness scale: Reverse the score for questions 3, 4, 8 (4=1, 3=2, 2=3, 1=4). Add items together. Lower scores indicate a decrease in the value of attractiveness.

Self-efficacy scale: Add scores from items 1–9 together. Higher scores indicate a positive sense of efficacy about being a girl.

Self-liking and self-competence scale: Reverse the score for negatively worded questions 3, 6, 7, 9, 11, 14, 17, 18, 19, 20 (1=5, 2=4, 3=3, 4=2, 5=1). Add items together. A higher score indicates positive self-liking and competence.

Hopelessness scale: Items are true or false. True questions are 2, 8, 9, 10, 12, 13, 14, 15, 17. Remaining items are keyed "false." Scoring is based on the number of items answered in agreement with the key. Higher scores equal greater hopelessness.

Help scale: Add number of items circled for a total score.

Appendix D
Participant Satisfaction

In addition to collecting data on program effects, it is important to gauge participants' satisfaction. During the final Go Grrrls meeting, girls fill out an evaluation form in which they must rate each of the sessions on a scale of 1–5 (with 5 being the highest approval rating). Our program goal is to have participants rate all sessions, on average, as a 4 or higher. Thus far, we have achieved this goal. It is also important to solicit qualitative feedback about the groups. To accomplish this, we ask the girls open-ended questions. Here is a sample of responses we've received:

> *"We got to express our opinions to someone who would listen."*
> *"I had someone to talk to and trust."*
> *"We talked about how we are going to plan for the future."*
> *"It taught me how to be more independent."*
> *"It taught me how to make new friends easily."*
> *"I learned more about me!"*
> *"I learned more about not hating my looks."*
> *"I got to talk about what I wanted to do in my life."*
> *"It was cool working together."*
> *"Is there going to be another one?"*
> *"I hope you come back."*

The participant satisfaction evaluation form follows.

The Go Grrrls Questionnaire

Print the first letter
of your first name.

Print the first letter
of your middle name.

Print the first letter
of your last name.

Please answer some questions about
yourself below and on the following
pages. For each statement or question,
circle the number that seems most appropriate for *you*.

Your Body

What is your
date of birth? _____
                    MONTH   DAY   YEAR

What school do you attend?

_____

What grade are you in?
(Circle one.)   6   7   8

How old are you? _____

	No	Yes	Don't know
Did your mother attend college?	0	1	2
Did you father attend college?	0	1	2

	Not at all	A little	Somewhat	Very much
1. How happy are you with how good-looking you are?	1	2	3	4
2. How happy are you with how much you weigh?	1	2	3	4
3. How happy are you with how tall you are?	1	2	3	4
4. How happy are you with your overall muscle development?	1	2	3	4
5. How happy are you with your overall figure?	1	2	3	4

What You Would Do   ## *Friends**

	Definitely could not	Probably could not	Probably could	Definitely could
1. I could go up to someone my age and start talking to that person.	1	2	3	4
2. If a friend wants me to do something that I don't want to do, I could tell my friend that I don't want to do it.	1	2	3	4
3. If a friend wanted to give me alcohol, I could say no.	1	2	3	4
4. If a friend wanted to give me marijuana, I could tell my friend that I didn't want any.	1	2	3	4
5. If friends did something that I didn't like, I could ask them to change what they were doing.	1	2	3	4
6. If some of my friends are playing a game, I could ask them if I could join.	1	2	3	4
7. If a friend wanted to give me some cocaine or crack, I could say no.	1	2	3	4

	Stongly disagree	Disagree	Agree	Strongly agree
1. I have at least as many friends as other people my age.	1	2	3	4
2. I am not as popular as other people my age.	1	2	3	4
3. In the kinds of things that people my age like to do, I am at least as good as most other people.	1	2	3	4
4. People my age often pick on me.	1	2	3	4
5. Other people think I am a lot of fun to be with.	1	2	3	4
6. I usually keep to myself because I am not like other people my age.	1	2	3	4
7. Other people wish that they were like me.	1	2	3	4
8. I wish I were a different kind of person because I'd have more friends.	1	2	3	4
9. If my group of friends decided to vote for leaders of their group I'd be elected to a high position.	1	2	3	4
10. When things get tough, I am not a person that other people my age would turn to for help.	1	2	3	4

*Reprinted with permission from Hare, B. R. (1985). The HARE general and area specific (school, peer, and home) self-esteem scale.

Value of Attractiveness

	Strongly disagree	Disagree	Agree	Strongly agree
1. I think girls need to be skinny to be attractive.	1	2	3	4
2. The way I look is more important than the way I act.	1	2	3	4
3. I am attractive just the way I am today.	1	2	3	4
4. There is more pressure for a girl to be pretty than for a boy to be handsome.	1	2	3	4
5. The most important thing for a girl to be considered attractive is how her body looks.	1	2	3	4
6. How I look is more important than who I am.	1	2	3	4
7. Looking like a model is the most important way to be attractive.	1	2	3	4
8. I can attract boys in ways other than how I look.	1	2	3	4

Self-Efficacy

	Strongly disagree	Disagree	Agree	Strongly agree
1. I am comfortable being a girl.	1	2	3	4
2. I am an effective girl.	1	2	3	4
3. I feel confident about myself as a girl.	1	2	3	4
4. I feel good about being a girl.	1	2	3	4
5. I am a successful girl.	1	2	3	4
6. I am a caring and confident girl.	1	2	3	4
7. I feel I will be an effective girl and woman throughout my life.	1	2	3	4
8. I am proud to be a girl.	1	2	3	4
9. I think now is an exciting time to be a girl.	1	2	3	4

*About Me**

	Strongly disagree	Disagree	Neither agree nor disagree	Agree	Strongly agree
1. I have much potential.	1	2	3	4	5
2. I feel comfortable about myself.	1	2	3	4	5
3. I *don't* succeed at much.	1	2	3	4	5
4. I have done well in life so far.	1	2	3	4	5
5. I perform very well at a number of things.	1	2	3	4	5
6. It is often *unpleasant* for me to think about myself.	1	2	3	4	5
7. I tend to *devalue* myself.	1	2	3	4	5
8. I focus on my strengths.	1	2	3	4	5
9. I feel *worthless* at times.	1	2	3	4	5
10. I am a capable person.	1	2	3	4	5

	Strongly disagree	Disagree	Neither agree nor disagree	Agree	Strongly agree
11. I do *not* have much to be proud of.	1	2	3	4	5
12. I'm secure in my sense of self-worth.	1	2	3	4	5
13. I like myself.	1	2	3	4	5
14. I do *not* have enough respect for myself.	1	2	3	4	5
15. I am talented.	1	2	3	4	5
16. I feel good about who I am.	1	2	3	4	5
17. I am *not* very competent.	1	2	3	4	5
18. I have a *negative* attitude toward myself.	1	2	3	4	5
19. I deal *poorly* with challenges.	1	2	3	4	5
20. I perform *inadequately* in many important situations.	1	2	3	4	5

*Reprinted with permission from Tafarodi, R. W., & Swann, W. B., Jr. (1995). Self-liking and self-competence as dimensions of global self-esteem: Initial validation of a measure. *Journal of Personality Assessment, 65*, 322–342.

Feelings

In this section there are sentences about how some kids feel about their lives. Write down if the sentence is true for you or false for you. If the sentence is how you feel, you would say it is true. If the sentence is *not* how you feel, you would say it is false.

	True	False
1. I want to grow up because I think things will be better.	T	F
2. I might as well give up because I can't make things better for myself.	T	F
3. When things are going badly, I know they won't be as bad all of the time.	T	F
4. I can imagine what my life will be like when I'm grown up.	T	F
5. I have enough time to finish the things I really want to do.	T	F
6. Someday I will be good at doing the things that I really care about.	T	F
7. I will get more of the good things in life than most other kids.	T	F
8. I don't have good luck and there's no reason to think I will when I grow up.	T	F

	True	False
9. All I can see ahead of me are bad things, not good things.	T	F
10. I don't think I will get what I really want.	T	F
11. When I grow up, I think I will be happier than I am now.	T	F
12. Things just won't work out the way I want them to.	T	F
13. I never get what I want, so it's dumb to want anything.	T	F
14. I don't think I will have any real fun when I grow up.	T	F
15. Tomorrow seems unclear and confusing to me.	T	F
16. I will have more good times than bad times.	T	F
17. There's no use in really trying to get something I want because I probably won't get it.	T	F

*Reprinted with permission from the American Psychological Association. From: Kazdin, A. E., Rogers, A., & Colbus, D. (1986). The hopelessness scale for children: Psychometric characteristics and concurrent validity. *Journal of Consulting and Clinical Psychology, 54,* 241–245.

Getting help

Where would you go if you needed help or had a question about a problem? (Circle all that apply.)

    a. mother

    b. father

    c. brothers or sisters

    d. uncle or aunt

    e. friend your age

    f. older friend

    g. teachers

    h. kids who are leaders

    i. books

    j. hotlines or crisis centers

    k. medical doctor

    l. police

    m. minister or rabbi

    n. school counselor

    o. social service agency

	No	Yes
Do you get a free school lunch?	0	1
Have you started your period yet?	0	1

Who lives with you? Circle all the adults that live with you.

    a. mother

    b. father

    c. stepfather

    d. stepmother

    e. grandfather

    f. grandmother

    g. aunt

    h. uncle

    i. foster father

    j. foster mother

What is your ethnicity?

    1. White

    2. Hispanic (Mexican American, Latino, Puerto Rican, etc.)

    3. African American

    4. Asian

    5. Native American

    6. Mixed race (for example, Hispanic and White)

How much does your mother work?

    1. Employed full-time

    2. Employed part-time

    3. Doesn't work

    4. Unemployed

    5. Don't know

What Did You Think about Go Grrrls?

Y ou're almost done filling out questionnaires! Just read the reminders of what we did in each session of the Go Grrrls group. Think about how much you liked or didn't like each session, and circle a number from 1 to 5. Here is a list of what the numbers mean.

1= I didn't like this session at all.
2= I didn't like this session very much.
3= I thought this session was okay.
4= I liked this session a lot.
5= I thought this session was great.

Session 1: *Introduction.* In the first session we introduced the Go Grrrls program and explained the "puzzle." We played the name game to remember each other's names and set up our group rules. We passed out the journal/work-books.

1	2	3	4	5
(didn't like at all)	(didn't like much)	(it was okay)	(liked it a lot)	(it was great!)

Session 2: *Being a girl in today's society.* In this session we talked about what society expects from girls. We split into two groups. One made a collage and the other listened to songs. Then we all talked about the media messages girls get and how to think critically about those messages.

1	2	3	4	5
(didn't like at all)	(didn't like much)	(it was okay)	(liked it a lot)	(it was great!)

Session 3: *Establishing a positive body image.* In this session we talked about developing a positive body image. We shared lists of qualities that we like about ourselves. We made outlines of our bodies on cloth and wrote about things we like about our bodies and our personalities and talents.

1	2	3	4	5
(didn't like at all)	(didn't like much)	(it was okay)	(liked it a lot)	(it was great!)

Session 4: *Establishing a positive mindset.* In this session we talked about self-criticism. We played the Downward and Upward Spirals game, and we talked about changing "I should" statements into realistic "I want" goals.

1	2	3	4	5
(didn't like at all)	(didn't like much)	(it was okay)	(liked it a lot)	(it was great!)

Session 5: *Making and keeping friends.* In this session we talked about qualities we like in friends. We filled out a friendship want ad and answered that ad. We decorated the friendship poem by cutting up magazines. We played the Dating Values game.

1	2	3	4	5
(didn't like at all)	(didn't like much)	(it was okay)	(liked it a lot)	(it was great!)

Session 6: *Making and keeping friends.* In this session group leaders acted out examples of not using skills like eye contact, tone of voice, and saying positive things. Then they acted out examples of using the skills. Then we all acted out scenes and made a friendship tool-box to help us solve friendship problems. Last, we talked about ways to deal with peer pressure.

1	2	3	4	5
(didn't like at all)	(didn't like much)	(it was okay)	(liked it a lot)	(it was great!)

Session 7: *Establishing independence.* In this session we learned about the five steps to use when solving problems. We worked through examples of problems (like what to do if your friend asks you to come over for a party when her parents aren't home).We played the Choices and Consequences game.

1	2	3	4	5
(didn't like at all)	(didn't like much)	(it was okay)	(liked it a lot)	(it was great!)

Session 8: *Establishing independence:* In this session we played the Communication Game. We learned about the difference between assertive, aggressive, and passive ways of acting. We acted out some scenes to help practice being assertive.

1	2	3	4	5
(didn't like at all)	(didn't like much)	(it was okay)	(liked it a lot)	(it was great!)

Session 9: *Let's talk about sex.* In this session we reviewed the basics about human sexuality. We put questions in the question box and then answered them. We talked about why some kids have sex and others choose to be abstinent. We acted out some situations and practiced using verbal and nonverbal refusal skills. We talked about where to go for more information about sex.

1	2	3	4	5
(didn't like at all)	(didn't like much)	(it was okay)	(liked it a lot)	(it was great!)

Session 10: *Let's talk about sex.* In this session we talked about ways that alcohol and other substance use can lead to unwanted sex. We drew advertisements designed to make kids think that drinking is cool, and then we drew ads to talk

back to the fake "glamorous" myths about alcohol. We played a game to show how quickly sexually transmitted diseases can travel.

1	2	3	4	5
(didn't like at all)	(didn't like much)	(it was okay)	(liked it a lot)	(it was great!)

Session 11: *When it all seems like too much.* In this session we talked about where to go for help when you have a really serious problem. We filled out the personal yellow pages and brainstormed ways that people can find help.

1	2	3	4	5
(didn't like at all)	(didn't like much)	(it was okay)	(liked it a lot)	(it was great!)

Session 12: *Planning for the future.* In this session we talked about goals and dreams for the future. We tried to picture where we want to be in 5 weeks, days, and years. We talked about steps we could take to help reach our goals. Finally, we played Pictionary with our goals.

1	2	3	4	5
(didn't like at all)	(didn't like much)	(it was okay)	(liked it a lot)	(it was great!)

Session 13: *Planning for the future.* Today! Party! Congratulations!

1	2	3	4	5
(didn't like at all)	(didn't like much)	(it was okay)	(liked it a lot)	(it was great!)

Which session did you like the very best (not including today's party)?
(Fill in the blanks. You can look back at the questions you just answered to help you remember the session numbers.)

I liked session number _____ because _____

_____

_____

_____

Which session did you dislike the most?

I didn't like session number _____ because

_____

_____

_____

_____

Circle all of the *things that you liked* about the club from the list below.

Circle all of the *things that you didn't like* about the club from the list below.

a. The subjects we talked about

b. The games we played

c. The group leaders

d. The way we got to know other club members

e. The way we got to talk to each other

f. The discussions that we had

g. The journals and assignments

h. Talking with my parents about the club

a. The subjects we talked about

b. The games we played

c. The group leaders

d. The way we got to know other club members

e. The way we got to talk to each other

f. The discussions that we had

g. The journals and assignments

h. Talking with my parents about the club

What was the best part of being in the Go Grrrls club?

What was the worst part of being in the Go Grrrls club?

Was there anything that you really wanted to talk about that we didn't bring up during our meetings? If so, what was it?

Did your parents ask you to do any activities from the parent curriculum?

YES   NO

What Go Grrrls activities did you do with your parents?

If you were a group leader, what would you do differently?

If I were a group leader I would talk about_____

_____.

If I were a group leader I would act like _____

_____.

If I were a group leader I would do_____

_____.

Is there anything else you want to tell us? If so, just write down your thoughts here. Thanks again!!!

Thank you for answering these questions!

Appendix E

Parent Notification and Permission Form and Information Sheet

The information and activities of the Go Grrrls program were chosen to teach girls how to: critically evaluate media messages, develop assertiveness skills, develop problem solving methods, build healthy friendships, understand basic sexuality facts, locate resources, and plan for the future.

The program will begin on _____ and will last until _____. All Go Grrrls groups are conducted by female leaders, with all female participants.

Please read and complete the section below and return this form to

_____

Child's name _____

Child's age _____ Child's date of birth _____ Child's grade _____

I have read and understand this form.
☐ My child has my permission to participate.
☐ My child does not have my permission to participate.

I understand that I have the right to review the curriculum and all material used in the education program and that I have the right to revoke this permission without notice at any time.
Comment:

_____

Parent/guardian name (printed)

_____

Parent/guardian signature

_____

Student's signature

_____

Telephone number _____ Date_____

If you don't have a phone, a contact number_____

Parent address (street) _____

(city) _____(zip)_____

Program contact _____ Phone number _____

Parent Information Sheet

Dear parent/guardian:

The Go Grrrls program teaches girls how to build their personal strengths, feel good about themselves, and resist pressures to engage in risky behaviors. Go Grrrls is a prevention program designed specifically for *all* preteens and teens, (not just "at-risk" girls). There are 13 meetings that address the following topics:

Being a girl in today's society: Confronting media messages

Establishing a positive body image: Learning to appreciate our unique appearance and talents

Developing a positive mind-set: How to give ourselves encouragement to succeed

Establishing independence: Learning problem solving and assertiveness skills

Let's talk about sex: Learning the facts, respecting ourselves, and staying safe

When it all seems like too much: Where to go to get help with serious problems

Planning for the future: How to set long-term goals for education, careers, and adventures

You will receive a brief parent curriculum at the beginning of the program. This curriculum provides a short summary of the topics covered in each session and suggests topics and techniques for discussion at home. Your involvement is important!

Thank you for allowing your child to participate in this excellent program.

Sincerely,

Go Grrrls Staff

Appendix F

The Go Grrrls Parent Curriculum

Dear parent/guardian of a Go Grrrls participant:

Thank you for taking the time to use this companion curriculum.

We look forward to working with the Go Grrrls participants. It is always rewarding for us to watch young people learn and gain self-confidence during the course of the program. If you have any questions or comments during your child's participation in Go Grrrls, please call us.

We think we already know two things about you . . .

1. You are truly interested in your daughter's healthy future, and
2. You are very busy.

Because of this, we tried to make this guide brief and informative. We describe the activities of each session in about one paragraph. After that description, we offer suggestions for home activities or discussions relating to the Go Grrrls program topics. These activities or discussions usually can be incorporated into your day quite easily.

Again, thank you for your participation in Go Grrrls. We will mail you an evaluation form at the end of the program, and we welcome your comments at all times. Have fun!

Sincerely,

Go Grrrls Staff

Topic: Being a Girl in Today's Society

Session 1: Introduction to girls' issues

In this session, we try to create a fun and comfortable group atmosphere for all club members. We play some games and have the kids set up some basic rules for the group. Participants fill out a preprogram questionnaire. We briefly introduce the topics we will cover in the coming sessions. Finally, we pass out journals or workbooks for the girls to keep. At every club meeting, we will be giving one journal assignment, which the girls are to complete before the next meeting.

Suggested topics for discussion or activity:

1. Simply ask your daughter whether she enjoyed the first club meeting. Why or why not?
2. Ask about the club incentives. Let your child explain the system to you.

Journal assignment:

Girls are asked to make a list of some of their favorite things, which they then share with the other members and the group leaders at the next session. This helps everyone get to know one another.

Topic: Being a Girl in Today's Society

Session 2: Media messages

In this session we help girls understand and criticize the stereotypes about women and men that abound in the media. They listen to music and browse magazines to come up with these stereotypes, and then we discuss why these messages are unrealistic and perhaps harmful.

Suggested topics for discussion or activity:

1. Watch one TV show with your child tonight. Together, make a list of what stereotypes the show might promote about women and men. Does anybody you know really fit the stereotype? (Probably not.)

Journal assignment:

Girls are asked to make a list of five things they really like about themselves. They will be asked to read three of these out loud at the next session.

Topic: Establishing a Positive Body Image

Session 3: Positive body image

This session teaches girls to value their appearance for its uniqueness and that attractiveness is based on factors other than physical traits and sexuality. Girls trace their bodies onto cloth and write five things they like about their bodies on the cloth. Then they identify five nonphysical traits they like about themselves and write those on the cloth. Finally, we relate the messages from the last session (hardly anybody can have the so-called perfect 10 fashion-model body) to this session (appreciate your body and your self for who you are).

Suggested topics for discussion or activity:

1. Talk with your daughter about some of the feelings, worries, or embarrassments you remember having about your body when you were her age. Share with her how those feelings might have changed over time. Also, honestly discuss your feelings about your own body.
2. Ask your daughter to show you her cloth image of herself. She will have listed five physical traits she likes about herself and five nonphysical traits she likes about herself. This is a first-rate opportunity for you to agree with what she already likes about herself and to add to her list! Remember to be positive!
3. Help your daughter decorate the cloth body outline with glitter, ribbon, yarn, etc. This activity is fun, and it gives you a chance to really build her confidence in the "positives" she listed on the cloth. Encourage her to keep adding positive personal traits to the cloth.

Journal assignment:

Girls are asked to make a list of five negative things they sometimes say to themselves (for example, "I can't do this" or "I must be such a jerk"). We will help them turn these messages around at the next meeting.

Topic: Establishing a Positive Mindset

Session 4: Rethinking self-statements

This session is designed to teach girls how they can give themselves positive messages to help them reach goals and feel good about themselves. First we teach them how to identify what self-criticism is, and then we play a game to be sure they've got the idea. We then encourage girls to set *reachable* goals, and not to set themselves up for failure by trying to be perfect all of the time.

Suggested topics for discussion or activity:

1. Ask your daughter to describe what a downward spiral is (discouraging self-

talk or put-downs). Then ask her to describe what an upward spiral is (encouraging self-talk). (Remind her to use the upward spiral whenever she can!)

2. What kinds of things do you say to yourself to help you face a challenge? Talk to your daughter about positive statements you say to yourself (for example, "I can do this" or "I'm gonna give this my best shot")

Journal assignment:

Okay. Get ready. We gave the club participants a handout and instructed them to interview you about your thoughts on dating. We did this because we want to open up the topic for discussion between you and your child. It's important that your child knows what your values and rules are. We are not going to undermine your answers in our group, but we will probably get some variation in responses, so you may hear about different families' rules after this session. We encourage you to explain that your rules apply to your house. We want you to have some advance time to figure out what your answers to the interview questions might be, so we've listed them here.

1. How old were you when you went on your first date?
2. How old do you think people should be when they go on their first date?
3. Do you think it's okay to date more than one person, or should someone date only one person at a time?
4. What do people do on a date?
5. Who should plan what to do on a date? Who should pay?
6. How should a person decide whom to go out with?
7. What made you want to go out on a date with somebody?
8. What did you feel like when you first started dating? (Were you excited, scared, happy, nervous, etc.?)
9. What do you think about guys and girls going out together in groups?

Topic: Making and Keeping Friends

Session 5: Meeting people and the qualities of a friend

During this session we help girls pick out important qualities in a friend or boyfriend. Each girl writes a "friendship want ad" to help her figure out what to look for in a friend. We also go over a list of questions (some of which you covered in the interview) to help girls come to some conclusions, like: "The kind of qualities that you look for in friendships are also the kind of qualities you will look for in dating relationships." We also describe some of the warning signs of an unhealthy dating relationship and what to do if they find themselves in such a situation.

Suggested topics for discussion or activity:

This would be a really good time to set some rules, TOGETHER, about what kinds of dating (groups only, double dates okay or not, couples dates okay but only to events, etc.) you think are appropriate for your child at this age. The earlier you start to express your values the better off this whole teenage thing is gonna go.

1. Ask your daughter what kinds of qualities she looks for in a friendship. Tell her what you look for in a friendship and why.

Journal assignment:

The girls are asked to write a very brief true story about one fight they've had with a friend of theirs who is not in this club! We don't want any names, just an example of what the fight was about and how they worked things out (or didn't work them out).

Topic: Making and Keeping Friends

Session 6: Dealing with peer pressure

This session covers a lot of material. We teach kids basic skills like how to start conversations and how to say positive things to friends. We also give them a "friendship toolbox" to use when they run into disagreements with friends. Finally, we talk about ways to deal with peer pressure and give them practice turning down temptations to engage in risky behavior.

Suggested topics for discussion or activity:

1. Relate a story from your own past about one time that a friend talked you into doing something you didn't want to do. Some questions to discuss might include: Was this person being a good friend to you? Was his or her advice good?
2. Ask your daughter to show you the toolbox she made and explain how it works. Try to come up with some sample friendship problems and use the "tools" to help figure out how to solve them.

Journal assignment:

Girls are asked to write down two problems they have run into within the last school year. These problems should be serious, but not strongly personal, deep problems. An example of the kind of problem might be "My friends were all going to this party where the kid's parents weren't home, and I wanted to go but I wasn't allowed." (Don't worry. We'll help them through a problem solving process in which they explore the possible consequences of their decisions, including what you might do if you found out they went to such a party!) An example of a problem that is important but *won't* work for our problem solving exercise is "My grandmother just died and I'm really sad." The five-step problem solving process we teach in this session is not sufficient to help them with deeper problems. We will address deeper problems in a later session

Topic: Establishing Independence

Session 7: *Problem solving strategies*

Often, teens make impulsive decisions that can have serious negative consequences. This session teaches girls how to use a basic problem solving/decision making process and gives them practice in how to avoid situations in which they will be tempted to engage in risky behaviors such as sexual activity and alcohol and drug use. We teach them a five-step method and then have them work through several problem scenarios.

Suggested topics for discussion or activity:

1. Ask your child to *teach you* the five-step problem solving process (she has a handout describing the process.) This is actually a great tool for kids *and* adults. Offer a "solvable" problem of your own to use so that you both can work through the process together. (Example: "I am thinking about applying for a new job, but I'm not sure if it's a good time to make that change right now.") Be sure you don't use a problem that is too big for the process.
2. Use the five-step process to work through a problem that you and your daughter have had some run-ins about. (Example: "I'd like to buy you the new sneakers and the shirt you asked for, but I can't afford both.")

Journal assignment:

Each group member is asked to write about one time she wishes she had spoken up for herself or someone else but didn't. (Example: "Once everyone was making fun of my friend on the bus and I wanted to defend her but I didn't say anything because I felt too scared.")

Topic: Establishing Independence

Session 8: *Assertiveness skills*

Girls are often socialized to be accommodating to others. One potentially negative result of this socialization is that girls may not assert themselves in a risky situation (for example, when someone is trying to offer them alcohol and drugs). This session teaches girls what assertiveness is and gives them practice in using assertiveness skills in a safe environment.

Suggested topics for discussion or activity:

1. Ask your child to define the following three words for you: passive, aggressive, assertive. Here is a brief definition of each so you can give her some help if she needs it.

   Passive: When you act passively you don't respect your own right to express your ideas, needs, wants, feelings, and/or opinions. You let other people make decisions for you.

   Aggressive: When you act aggressively, you disregard another person's right to be respected. An aggressive response is one that is mean, hurtful, or a put-down.

   Assertive: Being assertive means that you say what you think, feel, want, or believe in a way that is firm but not mean or disrespectful to another person. You stand up for your own rights and treat other people with respect.

2. Try to think of a time when you acted assertively when your child was around. Perhaps you needed to return an item to a store and were met with some resistance until you spoke up (politely, of course!) and demanded to see a manager. Remind your child of that incident.

Journal assignment:

We ask the girls to write down three questions or rumors they may have heard about sex. We explain that at the beginning of the next meeting we will have them put some of their questions into a box and we will answer these questions anonymously.

Topic: Let's Talk About Sex

Session 9: Sex 101 and refusal skills

Since the mid 1980s, teen birth rates in the United States have risen by 25%, and nearly twice as many females between 14 and 16 years old are sexually active than in 1982. In this session, we begin by explaining the basic facts of reproduction. We then answer questions that have been placed in the anonymous question box. We then teach girls the basics about abstinence including the following facts.

1. At age 15, about 82% of all young people have *not* had sex. (This counters the old "everybody's doing it" argument!)

2. About 48% of males and 64% of females under 17 report never having had sex.

3. Abstinence is the only absolutely positive way to avoid pregnancy and sexually transmitted diseases (STDs).

We then go over some reasons why some kids might have sex, as well as reasons why most kids choose to wait. We do some role-play exercises to help kids learn refusal skills for situations in which they may be tempted to have sex or in which they are threatened about having unwanted sex. Finally, we explain to girls the importance of protecting themselves if they do make a decision to be sexually active.

Suggested topics for discussion or activity:

1. Talk. Just try talking about sex with your child. You might want to tell a funny story about some old myth that you heard and thought was true when you were a kid. (Example: "I remember hearing that if you kissed someone you could get pregnant!") Moms: You might want to tell your daughter about what you felt like when you got your first period.

   If it's hard for you to talk about sex, you are not alone. It's okay to *tell* your child that it's hard for you to talk about, but the subject is so important that you need to. You can also:
   • Start off by talking to a good friend of yours about what you might say to your child. This gives you some practice!
   • Talk to yourself in the mirror. That way you get to check out the funny faces you unintentionally make when you say certain words!

2. Watch another TV show together. This time, see how many times sex is either referred to or acted out on screen. Then discuss whether it is depicted realistically. For instance, does anybody on TV ever worry about getting a disease? Do they act like sex is a part of a relationship or just a separate thing?

3. Ask your child if it was hard to talk about sex in the group today. Why? Why not?

4. Ask your child if she has any questions she wants to ask you. Don't just ask her once! Ask her many times over the next few weeks, months, and years. There is no such thing as having "The" sex talk and then never bringing up the subject again! Keep the lines of communication open.

Journal assignment:

We ask the club members to make a list of the names of alcohol products they see advertised in magazines or on TV tonight. Then we ask them to list and critically evaluate of, some of the media messages they think are part of these ads. (For example: Drinking makes you cool, popular, attractive, etc.)

Topic: Let's Talk About Sex

Session 10: Risky business: alcohol, drugs, and unwanted sex

Girls are beginning to smoke and drink at younger ages. In fact, one recent study showed that girls were more likely than boys to use drugs other than alcohol while in high school. In this session, the "glamour" myth surrounding substance use is put down, and we teach kids that substance use places them at high risk for unwanted sexual activity.

We have the kids pretend that they are ad executives for a company that makes alcohol products, and we ask them to design an ad that they think would get young people to drink. Then we have them draw a second ad that "talks back" critically to the first ad they created. Next, we talk about the relationship between using substances and engaging in sexual activity. We mention that substance use also increases the risks of acquiring STDs. Finally, we play a game that illustrates how quickly an STD gets passed around. We reinforce the encouragement to remain abstinent.

Suggested topics for discussion or activity:

1. Tell your child about a time when alcohol or some other substance affected your life or the life of someone you love in a negative way. (Example: A drunken driver killed a friend of yours, or your uncle died of alcohol-related liver disease.)
2. Talk about your family's rules about drinking. You may want to include some time to specifically talk about drinking and driving, as this combination is deadly. Some families design a "contract" in which their child promises to call them for a ride home if it is needed. Some of these contracts include a "clause" that says the parents won't ask questions at the time of the call, but will just arrange for a safe ride. Come up with a plan that reflects your family's values.
3. Ask your child to explain the connection between substance use and unwanted sexual activity.

Journal/workbook assignment:

Ask the girls to write down the names of three adults who they really trust (p. 84 in the workbook). What is it about these people that makes them trustworthy? Could they contact these people if they needed to talk about an important issue in their lives?

Topic: When It All Seems Like Too Much

Session 11: Seeking help, locating resources

Some problems are too big or serious for girls (or any of us!) to handle all alone. A girl who is having a hard time with a serious issue can really benefit from learning about her personal and community resources. In this session, we teach girls where they can go for help and encourage them to seek that help when they need it.

Suggested topics for discussion or activity:

1. Help your child fill in the blanks of her "Personal Yellow Pages." Suggest the names and phone numbers of adults she can trust.
2. Tell your child about a time when you needed help to solve a problem when you were younger.

Journal assignment:

The club members are asked to write about three goals they would like to achieve as adults. One goal should be about an adventure, another should be about a career, and a third about schooling. (Examples: They might want to (1) learn to surf and travel to Hawaii to do it, (2) become a veterinarian, a great mom, or both, and (3) graduate from Harvard.) At the next meeting we will talk about ways to set short term objectives in order to reach long-term goals.

Topic: Planning for the Future

Session 12: Visions for a strong future

During this session, group leaders encourage each club member to develop a positive vision of the future. Kids practice realistic goal setting, and facilitators help outline the importance of education. We review the goals the kids have recorded in their journal assignments, and we help them figure out little steps to take to make their giant dreams come true. Finally, we play a game to help them share their different goals.

Suggested topics for discussion or activity:

1. Take your child to work with you one day. Explain what you do.
2. Ask your child what kind of careers she might be interested in. Find a friend or trusted community member who is in that profession and ask if he or she would sit for an interview from your child. Help your child come up with interview questions.

3. Ask your child to show you the What I Will Be Doing handout from today's session. Encourage them to pursue these big goals and the smaller "stepping stone" goals to get there.

4. Set some goals for yourself, and then share your goals with your child, explaining how you are going to try to achieve those goals using smaller steps. You are your child's best role model. (Example: "I'm going to learn how to cook Chinese food." Small steps would include going to the library to get a book about Chinese cooking, taking a class, and visiting an oriental produce market.)

Journal assignment:

We ask all club members to write down what they liked best about the Go Grrrls club and what they liked least about it.

Topic: Planning for the Future

Session 13: Review and closure

In this session, we congratulate the girls for their hard work and let them know how much they have taught us, too. We pass out graduation certificates and celebrate the journey we have taken together.

Suggested topics for discussion or activity:

1. Ask your child if she enjoyed the program. Why or why not? What did she learn?

2. *Congratulate your child for completing the program!* Tell her how proud you are of her accomplishment.

3. *Congratulate yourself for finding time in your busy life to participate in this program with your child!*

Good luck to you both, and please call us with any comments you may have.

Parent Evaluation

Please take a moment to fill out this brief questionnaire. We appreciate your feedback, and we will use your comments to improve our program for future participants. Please circle your response to the following statements.

1. I think my child learned important skills in the Go Grrrls program.

1	2	3	4	5
(strongly disagree)	(disagree)	(neither agree nor disagree)	(agree)	(strongly agree)

2. My child talked to me about the content of the Go Grrrls meetings.

1	2	3	4	5
(strongly disagree)	(disagree)	(neither agree nor disagree)	(agree)	(strongly agree)

3. The parent curriculum helped me to understand the content and purpose of the Go Grrrls program.

1	2	3	4	5
(strongly disagree)	(disagree)	(neither agree nor disagree)	(agree)	(strongly agree)

4. I used the parent curriculum's suggested discussion/activities guide with my child.

1	2	3	4	5
(strongly disagree)	(disagree)	(neither agree nor disagree)	(agree)	(strongly agree)

5. I disapprove of the Go Grrrls program content.

1	2	3	4	5
(strongly disagree)	(disagree)	(neither agree nor disagree)	(agree)	(strongly agree)

6. I think this program will help my child make positive choices in her future.

1	2	3	4	5
(strongly disagree)	(disagree)	(neither agree nor disagree)	(agree)	(strongly agree)

7. I don't think this program helped my child at all.

1	2	3	4	5
(strongly disagree)	(disagree)	(neither agree nor disagree)	(agree)	(strongly agree)

8. Because of my child's involvement in Go Grrrls, we had an opportunity to discuss sexuality.

1	2	3	4	5
(strongly disagree)	(disagree)	(neither agree nor disagree)	(agree)	(strongly agree)

9. I would recommend the Go Grrrls program to other parents.

1	2	3	4	5
(strongly disagree)	(disagree)	(neither agree nor disagree)	(agree)	(strongly agree)

10. I learned useful information because of my child's participation in the Go Grrrls program.

1	2	3	4	5
(strongly disagree)	(disagree)	(neither agree nor disagree)	(agree)	(strongly agree)

What would you say is the most important thing your daughter learned from participating in the Go Grrrls program?

Please feel free to write any additional comments here:

Appendix H

Handouts, Other Materials, and Web Page

For additional information, updates, and Go Grrrls training, visit our Web site at:

http://www.public.asu.edu/~lecroy/gogrrrls/gogrrrls.htm

Session 2
I Am Unique!

One great way to stop worrying about what the media says we ought to be like is to explore your creativity. To help you discover what is unique and special about you, fill in the blanks of the poem below. Read your poem out loud. Share it with your family. Remember that who you are inside—your hopes, dreams, talents, skills, and ideas—are important.

My name is _____.
            (your name, backwards)

_____ dream of me at night and
(Plural favorite animal)

_____ sing my name at dawn.
(Plural favorite flower)

I am older than_____,
                (an emotion: use the noun form of the word)

and as wise as (the) _____.
                    (natural force, object, or place you love)

My name is _____.
            (your name, backwards, again)

Session 3
What I Like about My Body

Complete the following statements. Think about all the different aspects of your body that you like.

Example: *What I like about my body is that I have beautiful hands with long fingers.*

what I like about my body is _____

_____

What i like about my body is _____

_____

What I like about my body is _____

_____

What i like about my body is _____

_____

WHAT I LIKE ABOUT MY BODY IS _____

_____

WOMEN'S DISSATISFACTION WITH THEIR BODIES
Adapted from Garner (1997)

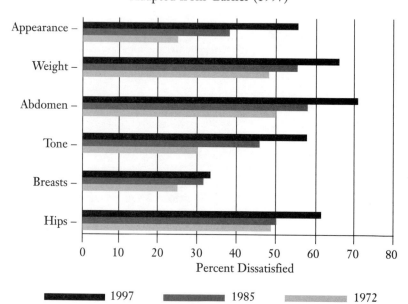

Session 4

The Downward Spiral

First you begin to set unrealistic goals:
"I have to be liked by everyone."

Then you start to use more self-criticism:
"I really messed up when I talked back to Tom, and now I'm afraid of what my other friends will think."

Next you begin to feel depressed or unhappy:
"I am sad because NOBODY likes me."

Then you use even more self-criticism:
"I don't know how to be a good friend, I can't get along with others, I'm not a very likable person."

Finally you feel even more depressed or unhappy:
"I hate myself for what I have done and I'm really feeling depressed."

Yikes! Time to turn it upside down!

Finally you feel better as a result.
"I'm happy with almost all of my other friendships and I can feel good about that."

Next you shift from self-criticism to realistic and positive thoughts:
"Even though Tom is mad at me it doesn't mean I am a bad person or that I am not worth hanging around if I don't do what he says. There are lots of good things about me as a friend."

Then you set a realistic goal.
"I want Tom to like me, but it's important for me to stick up for my own thoughts and feelings."

First you're feeling pretty low from the downward spiral you just took!
"I hate myself for what I have done and I'm really feeling depressed."

Session 4
The Upward Spiral

I Should, I Have to, I Want to: What Works Best?

Sometimes, important people in our lives give us good advice. They might say things like, "You should try to do your best", or "You should be careful when you cross a busy street." These kinds of "should" statements are fine. But other times, we say "I should" statements to ourselves that set us up for a downward spiral. You see, some "I should" statements disguise unrealistic goals that we set for ourselves. Let's take a look at one example:

I should exercise every day.

Sounds okay, right? Well, not really. To get a better idea about why this "I should" statement might take us on a downward spiral, we can change the "I should" to an "I have to." The "I should" statement above, for example, changes to:

I have to exercise every day.

But is it really true that anybody "has to" exercise every day? Of course not! And if you tell yourself you should (or you have to) exercise every day, and then you miss a day, you might feel badly and start yourself on a downward spiral like this:

I should exercise every day.

I didn't exercise today.

I am a failure because I didn't exercise every day.

So how can we set goals that will take us on an upward spiral? Easy! We can use "I want to" statements instead of "I should" and "I have to" statements. See how different it sounds when we do this with the example sentence:

I should exercise every day.

I have to exercise every day.

I want to be healthy and fit, so I will try to exercise several times each week.

Okay!

Now this is a statement that will take you on an upward spiral because it is a goal that you can really reach.

Session 4
Changing an "I Should" to an "I Want to"

Now it's time to change some "I should" statements into " I have to" statements (to see how silly they sound) and then change them into "I want" statements that will take us on the upward spiral. We finished the first one to show you how it's done.

I should get straight As in school.

I have to get straight As in school.

I want to do well in school, so I will try my best to get good grades.

I should do whatever my boyfriend wants me to.

I have to _____

I want to _____

I should be nice to everybody all of the time.

I have to _____

I want to _____

Now it's time to change one of your own "I should" statements into an "I want" statement.

I should _____

I have to _____

I want to _____

Spirals Game Cards

"I have to be liked by everybody."	"I want to have a lot of friends but not everyone will like me."
"I'm just stupid and I can't do anything right."	"Sometimes I have trouble learning new things but I can keep trying my best."
"I am depressed because I don't have any friends."	"Even though I'm not getting along with one of my friends right now, I still know that I am a good person and that I have other friendships."
"I have to get straight As."	"I try really hard to get good grades, but I don't have to get a *perfect* score on everything."
"I have to do whatever my boyfriend tells me to do."	"I care about my boyfriend's opinions, but I am smart enough to decide for myself what I need to do."
"I should be nice to everybody all of the time."	"Even though I have days when I don't feel very friendly, I am still a good person."
"*Everybody else* seems like they know how to talk to people at parties, but I just don't know what to say."	"Sometimes it is hard for me to talk to new people, but once they get to know me, they find out that I am a good person."
"I can't do this math homework so I'm not even going to try."	"This math homework is really hard, but it's okay to ask for help if I need it."

Spirals Game Cards

"If all the guys don't like me, I'm not popular enough."

"Even though some of the guys don't like me, I know that there are a lot of good things about me as a friend."

"I can accomplish a lot when I put my mind to it."

"I am happy about being able to speak up for myself even if my opinion is not popular."

"I shouldn't contradict my friends when they say something I don't agree with because they are all smarter or cooler than I am."

"I am a bad person."

"I am a good person."

"I must be stupid because I can't understand this assignment."

"Even though I wasn't invited to that party last weekend, it doesn't mean that I'm a bad person. I have good friends of my own to hang with."

"I can't get along with anybody, I'm not very likable, I must be a total jerk, and I'm never going to open my mouth to say anything again."

"Sometimes it is hard for me to talk to teachers but I know that what I have to say is important, so I speak up."

"I am proud of who I am."

"I wasn't invited to a really great party, so I must be a total geek."

"I should stay in this relationship with my boyfriend even though he hits me because I'm not sure I could get anybody better to like me."

Session 5
My Friendship Want Ad

Think about the qualities that are important for a friend to have. Then write a want ad that includes these qualities. Here is an example of a want ad:

> **Seeking a new friend: I am looking for somebody to talk with and go Rollerblading with. I'd like someone who is friendly, outgoing, and funny. I think a friend is someone who you can tell secrets to, so I have to trust you. We could talk on the phone for hours, about school, friends, guys, and life!**

_____

_____

_____

_____

_____

_____

_____

_____

_____

_____

_____

_____

_____

_____

Session 5
My Response to the Friendship Want Ad

Write a response to the friendship want ad that you received. In your response, answer the other person, and think about the qualities you would bring to the friendship. For example:

> **My response to the friendship ad: I am a very active person and I would enjoy Rollerblading and other outdoor activities, like hiking and swimming. I agree with you about wanting a friend you can trust . . . that's so important! In the past I've had friends who I trusted, but they told my other friends things I didn't want shared. I like to talk a lot, so we could talk on the phone about all kinds of things. Let's meet and we can see what happens.**

_____

_____

_____

_____

_____

_____

_____

_____

_____

_____

_____

Session 5
I Am A Friend

I am a friend
I share my thoughts and feelings with people I care about
I give others the gifts of caring and sharing

I am a friend
I let other people share their thoughts and feelings with me
I let them give me the gifts of caring and sharing

I know that friendships take time to grow
For a rose to bloom it needs water, sunlight, and time
For a friendship to grow, it needs work, patience, and care

I am a friend
I listen, I learn, I love
Every new friendship I make gives me a chance to learn and grow

I am a friend

Session 7

Did You Know? The Five Steps to Solving Problems

The key to learning how to make decisions or solve problems is to know the steps to take. Remember, for serious problems it's always a good idea to seek help from someone you trust. Here are the problem solving steps:

1. Define the problem:

What is the problem? It's a good idea to write it down. Keep it as short as you can.

2. Brainstorm choices:

The next step is to think of all the possible choices you could make to solve the problem. It's a good idea to write down as many as you can think of, and make sure you let yourself come up with some silly or outrageous choices, too! One rule during this step is that you don't eliminate any choice or criticize any idea.

3. Evaluate the choices:

This is the part where you figure out the pros and cons of each choice. It might help to put a + or - next to your brainstormed ideas.

4. Make your decision:

Now that we've evaluated the ideas, it's time to select the best idea from the list. Which one do you think would be best for you?

5. If your decision isn't working out, start back at number 1!!!

The last step is to keep an eye on how your decision is working for you. You might need to go back to the beginning . . . or, your decision might work out really great! Either way, give yourself a pat on the back for learning the art of problem solving!

Making Decisions and Solving Problems

Use this form to help you solve a problem of your own. You can write on this page, but make copies of the form on the next page so you can use the form over and over again.

Here are the steps you can use:

1. Define the problem. (What is it?)
2. Brainstorm choices. (Think of every possible solution—even silly ones! Don't criticize any of them yet!)
3. Evaluate the choices. (What are the pros and cons of each choice?)
4. Make your decision. (Select the best idea.)
5. If your decision doesn't work out, start over again at #1!

1. Define the problem.

The problem is:

_____

_____

2. Brainstorm choices. I could:	**3. Evaluate the choices.** Put a + and - beside each idea. What is positive about that choice? What is negative?	
1.	+:	-:
2.	+:	-:
3.	+:	-:
4.	+:	-:
5.	+:	-:
6.	+:	-:
7.	+:	-:
8.	+:	-:
9.	+:	-:
10.	+:	-:

4. Make your decision.

I decided to _____ because _____.

5. If your decision doesn't work out, start back at #1 and try another idea!

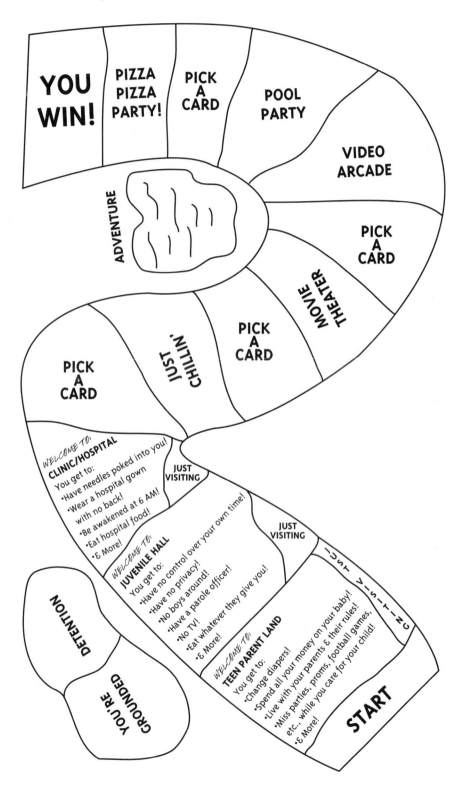

Go Grrrls Choices and Consequences Game Cards

Your friends try to get you to drink whiskey and smoke pot at a party. You do it. When you wake up the next morning, your head hurts, you feel sick, and you can't remember what you did last night. Two months later, you find out that you are pregnant. Go to Teen Parent Land.

Your folks are out of town and your friends try to talk you into having a party at your house. You tell them "no way!" Your folks are so happy with the way you kept the house that they give you a movie party with two of your friends. Go to Movie Theater. If you are already past Movie Theater, stay where you are and congratulate yourself for your good judgment.

A girl at school pisses you off and your friends tell you not to let her dis you. You beat her up after school, and she hits her head really hard on some cement. She goes to the hospital. You go to Juvenile Hall.

You go to the mall with your friend and she dares you to shoplift a silver necklace. You do it, and the store security guard catches you and calls your parents. Go to You're Grounded. Start your next turn from Juvenile Hall.

You are making out with your boyfriend, and you're both getting pretty hot and bothered. You decide to take a break to "cool down." You ask him to take a walk with you so you can talk for a while. Congratulations! He respects you so much for doing this that he invites you to go waterskiing with his family. Go to Adventure. Start your next turn at Pool Party.

You have a really hard math test tomorrow but you want to go to the mall with your friends tonight. You decide to go to the mall. You flunk your test. Move backward two spaces.

Your friend's parents are out of town and he decides to throw an after-school party with some beer and wine. You decide to go home and do your homework instead. You get an A on your social studies test. Go to the Video Arcade to celebrate.

You've known some girls from a gang for a long time, and they seem pretty cool. They tell you that you can hang with them if you rob a house for initiation. You get caught. Go to Juvenile Hall and MISS A TURN while you are assigned a parole officer.

Go Grrrls Choices and Consequences Game Cards

Your buddy has some tequila at a party you go to. He is your only ride home, and you can choose to either call your parents, call a cab, or ride home with him. You ride home with him and he crashes into a tree. Luckily, you both live, but you break your nose and your arm. Go to the Clinic/Hospital hospital and MISS A TURN while you recover.

Some older kids on your block tell you they'll pay you if you carry a package across town for them. You agree, and when you deliver it, an undercover cop arrests you for possession of cocaine. Go to Juvenile Hall.

Your buddies offer you some weed in the parking lot after school. You turn them down and go to basketball practice like you were supposed to. Your coach is so impressed with your dedication that she recommends you for a scholarship to a summer program where you get to go waterskiing and mountain climbing. Go to Adventure and start your next turn at Pool Party.

Your friend asks you to help him cheat on the science test. You tell him "no," but you will help him study. He passes the test and takes you out for pizza. Go to Pizza Party.

You have a really hard math test tomorrow and you need to study for it, but you want to go to the mall with your friends tonight. You decide to study instead. You get a B+ on your test, and your Dad takes you to the Video Arcade to celebrate.

Your boyfriend tells you that he really wants to have sex with you to prove how much he really loves you. You agree and 2 months later you realize you're pregnant. Go to Teen Parent Land.

Your friend offers you some crack and tells you that it won't hurt if you try it just once. Your heart stops when you take it. Luckily, someone nearby knows CPR and you are revived. Go to the Cllinic/Hospital.

A group of girls decide to cut school for the day. They talk you into coming, and you all go to the mall. While you're there you bump into your mom—you're busted! Go to You're Grounded. Roll a 1 or a 6 to get out. Start your next turn from Just Chillin'.

Go Grrrls Choices and Consequences Game Cards

Your boyfriend has been telling you that he is a virgin. He finally talks you into having sex with him. Two weeks later you break out in a scary-looking rash on your privates. Go to the Clinic/Hospital for treatment.*

*Don't even think about ignoring the rash! You need to seek help!

Your teacher tells you that you need to "Shape up or ship out." You suggest an unusual place for her to put a ship. Go to Detention. Roll a 1 or a 6 to get out. Start your next turn from Just Chillin'.

Two of your friends get into a big fight. One of them tries to get you to be mad at the other one, too. Instead, you give her some friendship tools to help her fix the problem. They make up and take you to a pool party to celebrate. Go to Pool Party.

Your friend tells you that you're a sissy if you won't try having sex with someone. You do. You get the HIV virus. Go to the Clinic/Hospital to get your prescriptions for the 40 pills you'll need to take every day for the rest of your life.

Session 8

Assertive, Aggressive, or Passive?

Introduction to situation #1

Okay, let's face it, sometimes you just can't help daydreaming about some cute guy. It can be hard, sometimes, to stick up for your rights when you get kind of weak in the knees every time you see him. It's really important, though, to be able to stick up for yourself. Let's see what happens in this situation.

Situation #1

A guy you really like invites you over to his house on a night when his parents aren't home. You think he's the greatest, and you'd like to go out with him, sometime, but you don't think it's a good idea to go to his house without his parents there.

> **Guy:** Hey, do you wanna come over Friday night? My folks are going out for the night, and I thought we could just hang out.
> **Girl #1:** I really like you a lot, and I want to go out with you. Let's hang at my house.
> **Girl #2:** Are you too stupid to live or what? I can't do that!
> **Girl #3:** Well, I'm not supposed to do that, but I guess I could come for a little while.

Which response is assertive? Which one is passive? Which one is aggressive? Here is a little reminder of what each word means:

Assertive:

Being assertive means that you say what you think, feel, want, or believe in a way that isn't mean or disrespectful to another person. You stand up for your own rights and treat other people with respect.

Passive:

When you act passively, you don't respect your own right to express your ideas, needs, wants, feelings, and opinions. Sometimes people act passively because they are afraid to risk the consequences if they say how they really feel or they don't know how to speak up for themselves.

Aggressive:

When you act aggressively, you disregard another person's right to be respected. An aggressive response is one that is mean, hurtful, or a put-down. You might get what you want in the short term, but in the long run you might make other people really angry and cause bigger problems for yourself later.

Introduction to situation #2

Sometimes the hardest time to be assertive is when we are with people whose feelings and opinions we really value a lot. When a girl and a guy really like each other, they might feel very tempted to have sex. It is important to practice what to do in a situation like this before it happens.

Situation #2

You have been dating a guy for about 6 months. You really like him a lot and you know he really likes you, too. In fact, one day while you are kissing each other behind the football stadium after school, he tells you that he loves you and he's sure that some day you guys are going to get married. He tells you that if you really care for him you will "go all the way."

> **Guy:** Maria, I really love you. Someday you're going to be my wife. I've been thinking. Wouldn't it really show how much we love each other if we made love?
>
> **Girl #1:** Oh, Jeremy, that's so romantic. I don't know though. You really love me, right?
>
> **Girl #2:** You absolute, incredible moron of a human being!
>
> **Girl #3:** Jeremy, I care about you a lot. That's why it's really important to me that we wait. Let's go find everybody else and cool off.

Which response is assertive? Which one is passive? Which one is aggressive? Here is a little reminder of what each word means:

Assertive:

Being assertive means that you say what you think, feel, want, or believe in a way that isn't mean or disrespectful to another person. You stand up for your own rights and treat other people with respect.

Passive:

When you act passively, you don't respect your own right to express your ideas, needs, wants, feelings, and opinions. Sometimes people act passively because they are afraid to risk the consequences if they say how they really feel or. they don't know how to speak up for themselves.

Aggressive:

When you act aggressively, you disregard another person's right to be respected. An aggressive response is one that is mean, hurtful, or a put-down. You might get what you want in the short term, but in the long run you might make other people really angry and cause bigger problems for yourself later.

Session 9

Starting My Period: One Girl's Story

When I was twelve, my mom talked to me about how I was going to develop, like about my breasts, my pubic area, and my menstruation. She told me that my period could be heavy or light like blood on my underwear, and that there's nothing to be scared of, nothing wrong with me. I was really worried about starting my period, so I was glad that we talked.

My mom also explained to me that she wanted me to know what was going to happen, because her mom never told her about menstruating, so when her period began, she hid her underwear under her bed. She had to go to her big sister for help.

Last year, two weeks after school started, in my eighth hour class my period finally began. I kinda thought I wet my pants, so I asked to use the restroom. When I got to the bathroom and realized it was my period, I just laughed and thought, "Oh my God, it finally came." I was kind of excited when it finally came, but kind of not. And I was scared that maybe it went through my jeans. I was embarrassed that somebody might have seen it. But it wasn't very heavy at all and it just went onto my underwear.

I went to the nurse's office and got a pad. After school I went to my Girls' Club and told one of the staff members what happened and she understood me perfectly. She got me a starter kit and explained everything in it. Then I called my mom and told her. I wondered whether she wouldn't be ready for me to change, and I also wondered whether I wasn't ready to change into an adolescent from a child. She got all hyper and said, "My little girl's a woman now." I was so embarrassed.

Now that I've had my period for over a year, I definitely feel different; I know I feel older. I thought my periods would be really painful but they're not. The only time it really bothers me is in the summer because I do a lot of swimming and I'm not using tampons yet. So I can't swim sometimes.

Starting my period was no problem, because I knew what was going to happen, what to do, and I could talk to someone about it. My advice to anyone else is to just let whatever happens happen and to talk to friends and family, because it makes a big difference. *

When you do start your period here are some tips to consider:

- Talk to your mom, sisters, and friends about what it was like for them to get their periods.
- Know what products you want to use.
- Practice how to use them.
- Keep some pads around the house, and maybe keep one in your locker or purse so you know you can get to them when you need them.
- Know where you can get supplies if you don't have any or run out (like in a nurse's office, bathroom, good friend, or teacher).

Session 9

Tricky Situation

You and your boyfriend have been going out for a while. From the beginning you touched and kissed a lot. Today is his birthday and you are alone together and feel very close. You begin kissing and touching and feeling really good. Your boyfriend wants to have sex with you, but you decide to tell him that you are not ready. Act this role-play out using verbal and nonverbal refusal skills.

Boyfriend: Why are you stopping? Let's do it.
Girlfriend: This feels good, but let's not have sex no.

Boyfriend: But it isn't my birthday every day, you know.
Girlfriend: Yeah, I know, but I don't think I'm ready to make that decision yet.

Boyfriend: I've never had sex before and I want my first time to be with you. You're special to me.
Girlfriend: No, not now, I'm not ready.

Boyfriend: There's no reason to wait. It will mean so much right now. What's the difference if you do it now or later?
Girlfriend: I want to wait.

Boyfriend: I thought this was what we both wanted.
Girlfriend: We both want to be close, but I don't want to have sex. How about opening your present from me? It's in my backpack.

Boyfriend: Okay.

Questions

How many times did the girl have to repeat her refusal?
What kind of nonverbal refusal skills were used?
What strategy did the girl use in the last paragraph?
Do you think you could use these skills? Why or why not?

Now, come up with some other situations that you think might be risky and role play some of the verbal and nonverbal refusal skills that you just learned.

Session 9

Having Sex: Why or Why Not

1. In the space below, list some reasons why you think some young people choose to have sex. Include reasons why you might be tempted to have sex.

_____

_____

_____

_____

_____

_____

_____

_____

_____

_____

2. In the space below, list some reasons why it is important to you, personally, to not have sex.

_____

_____

_____

_____

_____

_____

_____

_____

_____

_____

_____

Session 9

Verbal and Nonverbal Refusal Skills*

Sometimes it's hard to say no—especially to someone you care about—and to stick with it. Here are some ways that you can do it!

Verbal refusal skills

1. Say "no!" or "not now," or "stop!"
2. Repeat the refusal.
3. Suggest an alternative activity.

Nonverbal refusal skills

Body language (such as your tone of voice, gestures, the look on your face, the way you sit or stand) is an important way to communicate with or without talking. Here are some examples of body language that can help you say no:

1. Hands off: Throw your hands up in the air in a "get off of me" gesture.
2. Soldier body: Sit up or stand up stiffly like a soldier at attention and then walk away from the other person if you need to.
3. Firm voice: A strong and businesslike voice.
4. Serious expression: Your best "I mean it" face.
5. Gestures: Hand and arm movements that emphasize your point.
6. Fight back: At times, if everything else fails, you might have to use your strength to push away and protect yourself.

Session 10

My Personal Yellow Pages

Ask an adult you trust to help you make your own personal yellow pages.

Personal

Someone I trust: _____Phone: _____

Someone I trust: _____ Phone: _____

An adult I trust: _____Phone: _____

A neighbor I can call: _____Phone: _____

My doctor: _____Phone: _____

School

School nurse:_____ Phone: _____

Counselor: _____ Phone: _____

A teacher I trust: _____ Room: _____

Alcohol & Drugs

_____Phone:_____
(Has groups for teenagers who have a drug or alcohol problem)

Alcoholics Anonymous: Phone: _____
(For people who have a drinking problem)

Alateen: Phone : _____
(For children and teens who know someone with a drinking or drug problem)

_____: Phone:_____
(A place for youth to go for alcohol or drug treatment)

Counseling

My school counselor:_____ Phone:_____

_____: Phone:_____
(Offers counseling for one person or whole families)

Help on Call: _____ Phone:_____
(A 24-hour, 7-day-a-week crisis line)

_____: Phone:_____
(Not really for counseling, but a friendly person will keep you company Monday through Friday from 3:00 to 8:00 P.M.)

Violence

_____: Phone:_____
(Assistant principal at your school)

_____: Phone:_____
(Shelter for women and their children who are being harmed by someone)

_____: Phone:_____
(A place for people who have been raped or who have questions about rape)

Sexuality

Remember, try to talk to your parents whenever you can. Talk to an adult you trust. Maybe you have an aunt or uncle whom you feel comfortable talking to. Remember that sometimes other kids your own age don't have all the facts, even if they act like they do.

You can also talk to your school nurse or your own doctor. They can refer you to other sources of information. Ask them about confidentiality. Most doctors and nurses can talk to you about sexuality and keep what you say confidential, but it is important to talk with them about this first.

School nurse: _____ Room: _____Phone: _____

Doctor: _____ Phone:_____

Planned Parenthood: Phone: _____
(Where people can go for information about sexuality, birth control and sexually transmitted diseases. They also provide counselors to talk to, physical exams, and birth control supplies).

Shelters for Youth

_____: Phone:_____
(For youth who run away)

_____: Phone:_____
(A place to stay for 3 days when it gets to be too much).

Session 10

Who Can Help?

1. Sally is a 13-year-old girl who lives with her mom. Her parents recently got divorced, and Sally says that she just feels sad now whenever she's at home. She hasn't talked to her old friends in a long time because she feels embarrassed about her family breaking up, and she's afraid that if she talks to them she might start crying. She met a guy at the corner convenience store whom she kind of likes to talk to. He gave her some beer last week, and she thought it was easy to talk to him after that. All week long, she's been sneaking out the back door after her mom goes to bed, so she can meet this guy on the corner. He says he's allowed to stay out all night. Sally is starting to feel like her life is out of control. Who can help her?

In the list below, circle all of the different things that you think Sally is facing.

Depression/sadness about her parents' divorce	Using alcohol	Risky situation being with a guy she doesn't know well	School detention and suspension
Getting arrested	Eating disorders	Not talking to her old friends	Doesn't really have a serious problem

Now look at your yellow pages and list as many resources to help Sally as you possibly can.

2. Ruthie is feeling kind of scared. She has been counting calories in everything she eats and also exercising every day. She used to weigh 150 pounds but now she is down to about 100 pounds. She still thinks that she looks fat. Her friends are telling her that she looks too skinny, but Ruthie doesn't believe it. She is feeling tired and anxious all of the time. Who can help her?

In the list below, circle all of the different things that you think Ruthie is facing.

Depression/sadness about her parents' divorce	Using alcohol	Risky situation being with a guy she doesn't know well	School detention and suspension
Getting arrested	Eating disorders	Not talking to her old friends	Doesn't really have a serious problem

Now look at your yellow pages and list as many resources to help Ruthie as you possibly can.

Session II

What I Will Be Doing

To achieve big goals, we need to plan smaller steps to help us get there. Complete the following statements to help you plan the steps along the path to achieving your personal goals.

Goal #1: _____

To achieve my goal, one step I will take in the next 5 days is:

_____

To achieve my goal, one step I will take in the next 5 months is:

_____

To achieve my goal, one step I will take in the next 5 years is:

_____

Goal #2: _____

To achieve my goal, one step I will take in the next 5 days is:

_____

To achieve my goal, one step I will take in the next 5 months is:

_____

To achieve my goal, one step I will take in the next 5 years is:

_____

Session 11

What's Important to Me

There are ten statements printed on this page. Circle the three statements that you would say you are *most* concerned about. There are no "right" answers, just circle the statements that are most important to you.

1. I think people need to be more involved in protecting the natural environment: the earth, air, water, etc.

2. I think one of the most important things we could do is to help young kids learn to read, write, and do arithmetic really well.

3. I think racism is one of the biggest problems in the world today, and we need to find ways to help people get along better.

4. I think that our society treats elderly people pretty badly. We need to stop ignoring older folks and help them stay involved in life.

5. I think that people in general have a really bad impression of what teenagers are like today. We need to get the message out that most teenagers are really good people who work hard..

6. I am concerned about the way we treat animals. There are too many dogs and cats that end up in shelters and get put to sleep every year because people aren't responsible pet owners.

7. I think we need to find ways to provide mentors to young kids, to help steer them toward the right path, and to encourage them a lot.

8. I think that people in this country don't exercise their right to vote. We need to make people understand how important it is to vote.

9. I think that we need to pay more attention to people with disabilities. We need to work hard to be sure that public buildings are accessible and that people who are different don't feel left out.

10. I think the world is perfect just the way it is and there is nothing we need to do to make it better.

I chose # _____ , **#**_____, **and #** _____.

Session 11

Community Hookups

Now that you've identified some of your interests, it is time to figure out how to take action! Circle any items on the list below that you think you could do to make your community a better place. Then use your goal setting and planning skills to help you do it!

i can start a newsletter or zine about the issue i care about.

I can write a letter to the editor of the newspaper.

I can surf the Internet for sites relating to the issue I care about.

I can ask the school counselors and social studies teachers about volunteer opportunities.

i can join (or start!) a club at my school.

I CAN ASK MY PARENTS TO HOST A POTLUCK MEAL FOR THE NEIGHBORHOOD SO WE CAN ALL MEET.

I can call my local volunteer center to find out if there are places where kids my age can volunteer.

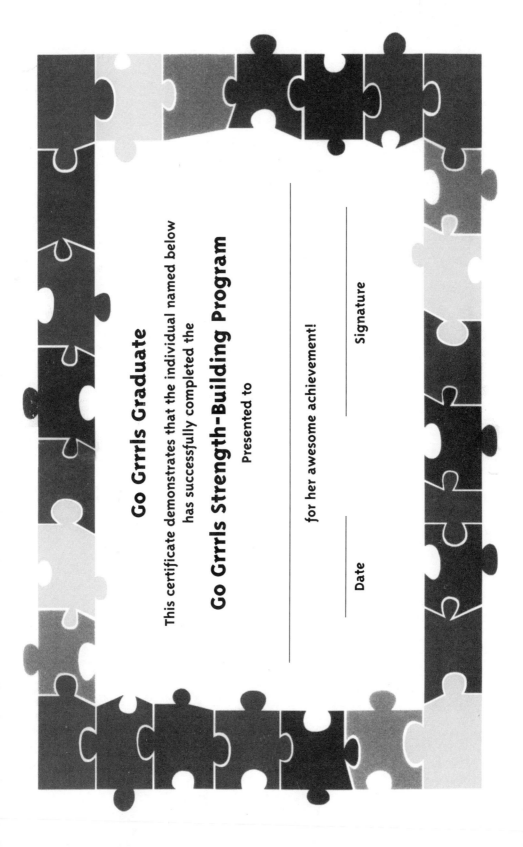

Go Grrrls Graduate

This certificate demonstrates that the individual named below
has successfully completed the

Go Grrrls Strength-Building Program

Presented to

_____

for her awesome achievement!

_____   _____
Date   Signature

References

Abner, A., & Villarosa, L. (1996). *Finding our way: The teen girls' survival guide* (pp. 97–98). New York: Harper Perennial.

Achenbauch, T. M. (1991). *Manual for the Child Behavior Checklist and 1991 Profile.* Burlington, VT: University of Vermont.

Ackerson, J., Scogin, F., McKendree-Smith, N., & Lyman, R. D. (1998). Cognitive bibliotherapy for mild and moderate adolescent depressive symptomatology. *Journal of Consulting and Clinical Psychology, 66,* 685–690.

Adams, G. (1977). Physical attractiveness research. *Human Development, 20,* 217–239.

Alan Guttmacher Institute (1994). *Sex and America's teenagers.* New York: Author.

American Psychiatric Association. (2000). *Diagnostic and statistical manual of mental disorders* (5th ed.). Washington, DC: Author.

Anderson, A., & DiDomenico, L. (1992). *International Journal of Eating Disorders, 11,* 283–287.

Arnett, J. (1992). Reckless behavior in adolescence: A developmental perspective. *Developmental Review, 12,* 339–373.

Arnett, J. (1995). Developmental contributions to adolescent reckless behavior. Paper presented at the Society for Research in Child Development, Indianapolis, IN.

Arroyo, C. G., & Zigler, E. (1995). Racial identity, academic achievement, and the psychological well-being of economically disadvantaged adolescents. *Journal of Personality and Social Psychology, 69,* 903–914.

Attie, H., & Brooks-Gunn, J. (1989). Development of eating problems in adolescent girls: A longitudinal study. *Developmental Psychology, 25,* 70–79.

Backstrand, K. (1997/ September–October). Response in Ask a Girl advice column. *New Moon,* p. 10.

Bandura, A. (1991). Self-efficacy: Impact of self-beliefs on adolescent self paths. In R. M. Lerner, A. C. Petersen, & J. Brooks-Gunn (Eds.), *Encyclopedia of adolescence* (Vol. 2, pp. 346–357). New York: Garland.

Barth, R. (1989). *Reducing the risk: Building skills to prevent pregnancy STD and HIV* (3rd ed.). Santa Cruz, CA: ETR Associates.

Barth, R., Fetro, J. V., Leland, N., & Volkan, K. (1992). Preventing adolescent pregnancy with social and cognitive skills. *Journal of Adolescent Research, 7,* 208–232.

Baruch, G. K., Biener, I., & Barnett, R. C. (1987). Women and gender in research on work and family. *American Psychologist, 42,* 130–136.

Battaglia, J., Coverdale, J. H., & Bushong, C. P. (1990). Evaluation of a mental illness awareness week program in public schools. *American Journal of Psychiatry, 147,* 324–329.

Baumrind, D. (1990). Parenting styles and adolescent development. In R. M. Lerner, A. C. Petersen, & J. Brooks-Gunn (Eds.), *Encyclopedia of adolescence* (Vol. 2, pp. 208–224). New York: Garland.

Beal, C. (1994). *Boys and girls: The development of gender roles.* New York: McGraw-Hill.

Belansky, E. S., & Clements, P. (1992). Adolescence: A crossroads for gender-role transcendence or gender-role intensification. Paper presented at the Society for Research on Adolescence, Washington, DC.

Belenky, M. F., Clinchy, B. M., & Goldberger, N. R., & Tarule, J. M. (1986). *Women's ways of knowing.* New York: Basic Books.

Bell, R. (1998). *Changing bodies, changing lives.* New York: Vintage.

Belle, D. (1988). Gender differences in children's social networks and support. In D. Belle (Ed.), *Children's social networks and social supports* (pp. 173–188). New York: Wiley.

Berg, F. (1992, July/August). Harmful weight loss practices are widespread among adolescents. *Obesity and Health,* 69–72.

Berndt, T. (1979). Developmental changes in conformity to peers and parents. *Developmental Psychology, 15,* 606–616.

Berndt, T. (1995). Friends' influence on adolescents' adjustment to school. *Child Development, 66,* 1312–1329.

Berndt, T. J., & Das, R. (1986). Children's perceptions of friendships as supportive relationships. Developmental Psychology, 22, 640–648.

Berndt, T. J., & Keefe, K. (1995). Friend's influence on adolescents' academic achievement motivation: An experiential study. *Journal of Educational Psychology, 82,* 664–670.

Bierman, K. L., & Greenberg, M. T. (1996). Social skills training in the fast track. In R. D. Peters & R. J. McMahon (Eds.), *Preventing childhood disorders, substance abuse, and delinquency* (pp. 346–357). Thousand Oaks, CA: Sage.

Bingham, M., Edmondson, J., & Stryker, S. (1993). *Choices: A teen women's journal for self awareness and personal planning.* Santa Barbara, CA: Advocacy Press.

Bingham, M., & Stryker, S. (1995). *Things will be different for my daughter: A practical guide to building her self-esteem and self-reliance.* New York: Penguin Books.

Blyth, D. A., Hill, J. P., & Thiel, K. S. (1982). Early adolescents' significant others: Grade and gender differences in perceived relationships with familial and nonfamilial adults and young people. *Journal of Youth and Adolescence, 11,* 425–450.

Bolden, T. (1998). *33 things every girl should know.* New York: Crown Publishers.

Botvin, G. J. (1985). Prevention of adolescent substance abuse through the development of personal and social competence. In T. J. Glynn, C. G. Leukefeld, & J. P. Ludford (Eds.), *Prevention of adolescent drug abuse* (pp. 8–35). Rockville, MD: National Institute on Drug Abuse, DHEW (ADM) 47.

Botvin, G. J. (1996). Substance abuse prevention through life skills training. In R.D. Peters & R.J. McMahon (Eds.), *Preventing childhood disorders, substance abuse and delinquency* (pp. 215–240). Thousand Oaks, CA: Sage.

Botvin, G. J., Batson, H. W., Witts-Vitale, S., Bess, V., Baker, E., & Dusenbury, L. (1989). A psychosocial approach to smoking for urban black youth. *Public Health Reports, 104,* 573–582.

Botvin, G. J., Dusenbury, I., Baker, E., James-Oritz, S., & Kerner, J. (1992). Smoking prevention among urban minority youth: Assessing effects of outcome and mediating variables. *Health Psychology, 11*, 290–299.

Botvin, G., Schinke, S. P., and Orlandi, M. A. (1989). Psychosocial approaches to substance abuse prevention: theoretical foundations and empirical findings. *Crisis, 10*, 62–77.

Brent, D. A. (1989). Suicide and suicidal behavior in children and adolescents. *Pediatrics in Review, 10*, 269–275.

Bretl, D. J., & Cantor, J. (1988). The portrayal of men and women in U. S. television commercials: A recent content analysis and trend over 15 years. *Sex Roles, 18*, 595–609.

Bronfenbrenner, U. (1977). Toward an experimental ecology of human development. *American Psychologist, 32*, 513–531.

Brooks-Gunn, J. (1988). Antecedent and consequences of variations in girls' maturational timing. *Journal of Adolescent Health Care, 9*, 1–9.

Brooks-Gunn, J., & Paikoff, R. L. (1993). Sex is a gamble, kissing is a game: Adolescent sexuality and health promotion. In S. Millstein, A. C. Petersen, & E. O. Nightingale (Eds.), *Promoting the health of adolescents: New directions for the twenty-first century* (pp. 180–208). New York: Oxford University Press.

Brooks-Gunn, J., & Paikoff, R. (1997). Sexuality and developmental transitions during adolescence. In J. Schulenberg, J. L. Maggs, & K. Hurrelmann (Eds.), *Health Risks & Developmental Transitions During Adolescence* (pp. 190–219). London: Cambridge University Press.

Brooks-Gunn, J., & Reiter, E. O. (1990). The role of pubertal processes. In S. S. Feldman & G. R. Elliott (Eds.), *At the threshold: The developing adolescent* (pp. 16–53). Cambridge, MA: Harvard University Press.

Brooks-Gunn, J., & Warren, M. P. (1985). The effects of delayed menarche in different contexts: Dance and nondance students. *Journal of Youth and Adolescence, 14*, 285–300.

Brown, B. B. (1990). Peer groups and peer culture. In S. S. Feldman & G. R. Elliot (Eds.), *At the threshold: The developing adolescent* (pp. 171–196). Cambridge, MA: Harvard University Press.

Brown, B. B., Eicher, S. A., & Petrie, S. (1986). The importance of peer group ("crowd") affiliation in adolescence. *Journal of Adolescence, 9*, 73–96.

Brown, L. M., & Gilligan, C. (1990). The psychology of women and the development of girls. Paper presented at the meeting of the Society for Research on Adolescence, March, Atlanta, GA.

Brown, L. M., & Gilligan, C. (1993). *Meeting at the crossroads: Women's psychology and girls development.* New York: Ballantine.

Brumberg, J. J. (1998). *The body project: An intimate history of American girls.* New York: Vintage.

Buhrmester, D. (1990). Friendship, interpersonal competence, and adjustment in preadolescence and adolescence. *Child Development, 61*, 1101–1111.

Buhrmester, D., & Furman, W. (1987). The development of companionship and intimacy. *Child Development, 58*, 1101–1113.

Bukowski, W. M., Hozas, B., & Boivin, M. (1993). Popularity, friendship, and emotional adjustment during adolescence. In B. Laursen (Ed.), *Close friendships in adolescence* (pp. 85–104). San Francisco: Jossey-Bass.

Bush, D. M., & Simmons, R. G. (1988). Gender and coping with the entry into early adolescence. In R. Barnett, L. Biener, & G. Baruch (Eds.), *Gender, women and stress* (pp. 185–217). New York: The Free Press.

Campbell, C. Y. (1988). Group raps depiction of teenagers. *Boston Globe, 44.*

Caplan, M., Weissberg, R. P., Grober, J. S., & Sivo, P. J. (1992). Social competence promotion with inner-city and suburban young adolescents: Effects on social adjustment and alcohol use. *Journal of Consulting and Clinical Psychology, 60,* 56–63.

Carlip, H. (1995). *Girl power: Young women speak out.* New York: Warner Books.

Carnegie Council on Adolescent Development. (1992). *A matter of time: Risk and opportunity in the nonschool hours.* New York: Author.

Carnegie Council on Adolescent Development. (1995). *Great transitions: Preparing adolescents for a new century.* New York: Author.

Cash, T. F. (1995). Developmental teasing about physical appearance: Retrospective descriptions and relationships with body image. *Social, Behavior, and Personality, 23,* 123–130.

Cash, T. F. (1997). *The body image workbook: An 8-step program for learning to like your looks.* Oakland, CA: New Harbinger.

Cash, T. F., Cash, D. W., & Butters, J. W. (1983). Mirror, mirror, on the wall . . .?; Contrast effects and self-evaluations of physical attractiveness. *Personality and Social Psychology Bulletin, 9,* 351–358.

Caspi, A. (1995). Puberty and the gender organization of schools: How biology and social context shape the adolescent experience. In L. J. Crockett & A. C. Crouter (Eds.), *Pathways through adolescence: Individual development in relation to social contexts* (pp. 57–74). Mahwah, NJ: Lawrence Erlbaum.

Cauce, A. M. (1986). Social networks and social competence: Exploring the effects of early adolescent friendships. *American Journal of Community Psychology, 14,* 607–628.

Centers for Disease Control and Prevention. (1995). State specific pregnancy rates among teenagers—United States, 1991–1992. *Morbidity and Mortality Weekly Report, 44,* 677–684.

Centers for Disease Control and Prevention. (1996). Facts about women and HIV/AIDS. Washington, DC: U.S. Department of Health and Human Services, Public Health Service.

Center for Population Options. (1992). *Lesbian, gay and bisexual youth: At risk and under served.* Washington, DC: Author.

Chodorow, N. (1978). *The reproduction of mothering: Psychoanalysis and the sociology of gender.* Berkeley, CA: University of California Press.

Claes, M. E. (1992). Friendship and personal adjustment during adolescence. *Journal of Adolescence, 15,* 39–53.

Clark, M. L., & Ayers, M. (1988). The role of reciprocity and proximity in junior high school friendships. *Journal of Youth and Adolescence, 17,* 403–411.

Clasen, D. R., & Brown, B. B. (1987). Understanding peer pressure in middle school. *Middle School Journal, 19,* 21–23.

Cole, D. A. (1989). Psychopathology of adolescent suicide: Hopelessness, coping beliefs, and depression. *Journal of Abnormal Psychology, 98,* 248–255.

Coles, R., & Stokes, G. (1985). *Sex and the American teenager.* New York: Harper & Row.

Collins, J. K., & Thomas, N. T. (1972). Age and susceptibility to same-sex peer pressure. *British Journal of Educational Psychology, 42,* 83–85.

Colten, M. E., & Gore, S. (1991). *Adolescent stress: Causes and consequences.* New York: Walter de Gruyter.

Colten, M. E., Gore, S., & Aseltine, R. H., Jr. (1991). The patterning of distress and disorder in a community sample of high school aged youth. In M. E. Colten & S. Gore (Eds.), *Adolescent stress: Causes and consequences* (pp. 157–180). New York: Walter de Gruyter.

Commonwealth Fund (1997). *The Commonwealth Fund survey of the health of adolescent girls.* Conducted by Louis Harris and Associates. New York: Author.

Compas, B. E., & Hammen, C. L. (1996). Child and adolescent depression: Covariation and comorbidity in development. In R. J. Haggerty, L. R. Sherrod, N. Garmezy, & M. Rutter (Eds.), *Stress, risk and resilience in children and adolescents: Process, mechanisms and interventions* (pp. 225–267). New York: Cambridge University Press.

Compas, B. E., Oppedisano, G., Conner, J. K., Gerhardt, C. A., Hinden, B. R., & Achenbach, T. M. (1997). Gender differences in depressive symptoms in adolescence: Comparison of national samples of clinically referred and nonreferred youths. *Journal of Consulting and Clinical Psychology, 65,* 617–626.

Compas, B. E., Orosan, P. G., & Grant, K. E. (1993). Adolescent stress and coping: Implications for psychopathology during adolescence. *Journal of Adolescence: Special Issue: Stress and coping in adolescence, 16,* 331–349.

Compas, B. E., & Wagner, B. M. (1991). Psychosocial stress during adolescence: Intrapersonal and interpersonal processes. In M. E. Colten and S. Gore (Eds.), *Adolescent stress: Causes and consequences* (pp. 67–86). New York: Walter de Gruyter.

Condry, J. C. (1989). *The psychology of television.* Hillsdale, NJ: Lawrence Erlbaum.

Conger, A. J., Peng, S. S., & Dunteman, G. H. (1977). *National longitudinal study of the high school class of 1972: Group profiles on self-esteem, locus of control, and life goals.* Research Triangle Park, NC: Research Triangle Institute.

Costanzo, P. R., and Shaw, M. E. (1970). Conformity as a function of self-blame. *Journal of Personality and Social Psychology, 14,* 366–374.

Costello, E. J., Costello, A. J., Edelbrock, C., Burns, B. J., Dulcan, M. K., Brent, D., & Janiszewski, S. (1988). Psychiatric disorders in pediatric primary care. *Archives of General Psychiatry, 45,* 1107–1116.

Council on Scientific Affairs, American Medical Association. (1993). Confidential health services for adolescents. *Journal of the American Medical Association, 269,* 1420–1424.

Covell, K., Dion, K. L., & Dion, K. K. (1994). Gender differences in evaluations of tobacco and alcohol advertisements. *Canadian Journal of Behavioral Science, 26,* 404–420.

Cowen, E. L., Peterson, A., Babigian, H., Izzo, L. D., & Trost, M. A. (1973). Long term follow-up of early detected vulnerable children. *Journal of Consulting and Clinical Psychology, 41,* 438–446.

Coyne, J. C., Ellard, J. H., & Smith, D. A. F. (1990). Social support, interdependence, and the dilemmas of helping. In B. R. Sarason & G. R. Pierce (Eds.), *Social support: An interactional view* (pp. 267–296). New York: Wiley.

Crockett, L. J., & Petersen, A. (1993). Adolescent development: Health risks and opportunities for health promotion. In S. G. Millstein, A. C. Petersen, & E. O. Nightingale (Eds.), *Promoting the health of adolescents* (pp. 13–37). New York: Oxford University Press.

Csikszentmihalyi, M., & Larson, R. (1984). *Being adolescent.* New York: Basic Books.

Csikszentmihalyi, M., & Larson, R. (1987). Validity and reliability of the experience-sampling method. *The Journal of Nervous and Mental Disease, 175,* 526–536.

Currie, D. H. (1997). Decoding femininity: Advertisements and their teenage readers. *Gender & Society, 11,* 453–477.

Cypress, B. K. (1984). *Health care of adolescents by office-based physicians: National Ambulatory Care Survey, 1980–1981*. DHHS, NCHS Publication, no. 99, Washington DC: US Government Printing Office.

Dee, C. (1997). *The girl's guide to life*. Boston: Little, Brown and Company.

Desmond, S., Price, J., Gray, N., & O'Connell, K. (1986). The etiology of adolescents' perceptions of their weight. *Journal of Youth and Adolescence, 15*, 461–474.

Deutsch, M., & Gerard, H. B. (1955). A study of normative and informational social influences upon social judgment. *Journal of Abnormal and Social Psychology, 51*, 629–636.

Dornbusch, S. M., Carlsmith, J. M., Duncan, P. D., Gross, R. T., Martin, J. A., Ritter, P. L., Downs, A. C., & Harrison, S. K. (1985). Embarrassing age spots or just plain ugly? Physical attractiveness stereotyping as an instrument of sexism on American television commercials. *Sex Roles, 13*, 9–19.

Dornbush, S. M., Carlsmith, J. M., Duncan, P. D., Gross, R. T., Martin, J. A., Ritter, P. L., & Siegel-Gorelick, B. (1984). Sexual maturation. Social class, and the desire to be thinner among adolescent females. *Developmental and Behavioral Pediatrics, 5*, 308–314.

Downs, A. C., & Harrison, S. K. (1985). Embarrassing age spots or just plain ugly? Physical attractiveness stereotyping as an instrument of sexism on American television commercials. *Sex Roles, 13*, 9–19.

Dreyer, P. H., Jennings, T., Johnson, L., & Evans, D. (1994). *Culture and personality in urban schools: Identity status, self-concept, and locus of control among high school students in monolingual and bilingual homes*. Paper presented at a meeting of the Society for Research on Adolescence, San Diego, CA.

Dryfoos, J. G. (1998). *Safe passage: Making it through adolescence in a risky society*. New York: Oxford University Press.

Dryfoos, J. G. (1990). *Adolescents at risk: Prevalence and prevention*. New York: Oxford University Press.

Dupont, P. I., & Jason, L. A. (1984). Assertiveness training in a preventive drug education program. *Journal of Drug Education, 14*, 369–378.

Dweck, C. S. (1975). The role of expectations and attributions in the alleviation of learned helplessness. *Journal of Personality and Social Psychology, 31*, 674–685.

Dweck, C. S., & Licht, B. G. (1980). Learned helplessness and intellectual achievement. In J. Garber & M. E. P. Seligman (Eds.), *Human helplessness: Theory and applications* (pp. 42–64). New York: Academic Press.

Eccles, J. S. (1987). Gender roles and women's achievement–related decisions. *Psychology of Women Quarterly, 11*, 135–172.

Eccles, J. S. (1994). Understanding women's educational and occupational choices: Applying the Eccles et al. model of achievement-related choices. *Psychology of Women Quarterly, 18*, 585–609.

Eccles, J. S., Barber, B., Jozefowicz, D., Malenchuk, O., & Vida, M. (1999). Self-evaluations of competence, task values, and self-esteem. In N. G. Johnson, M. C. Roberts, & J. Worell (Eds.), *Beyond appearance: A new look at adolescent girls* (pp. 53–84). Washington, DC: American Psychological Association.

Eccles, J. S., Jacobs, J., Harold, R. D., Yoon, K. S., Arbreton, A. J. A., & Freedman-Doan, C. (1993). Parents and gender role socialization. In S. Oskamp & M. Costanzo (Eds.), *Claremont symposium on applied social psychology, 1992: Gender and social psychology* (pp. 59–84). Thousand Oaks, CA: Sage.

Eder, D. (1985). The cycle of popularity: Interpersonal relations among female adolescents. *Sociology of Education, 58*, 154–165.

Eder, D. (1987). The role of teasing in adolescent peer group culture. Paper presented at the Conference on Ethnographic Approaches to Children's Worlds and Peer Cultures, Trondheim, Norway.

Eder, D., & Hallinan, M. T. (1978). Sex differences in children's friendships. *American Sociological Review, 43,* 237–250.

Eisele, L., Hertsgaard, D., & Light, H. (1986). Factors related to eating disorders in young adolescent girls. *Adolescence, 21,* 283–290.

Elias, M. J., & Clabby, J. F. (1992). *Building social problem solving skills: Guidelines from a school-based program.* San Francisco: Jossey-Bass.

Elkind, D. (1978). Understanding the young adolescent. *Adolescence, 13,* 127–134.

Elliott, D. S. (1993). Health enhancing and health compromising lifestyles. In S. G. Millstein, A. C. Petersen, & E. O. Nightingale (Eds.), *Promoting adolescent health* (pp. 119–145). New York: Oxford University Press.

Elliot, E. S., & Dweck, C. S. (1988). Goals: An approach to motivation and achievement. *Journal of Personality and Social Psychology, 54,* 5–12.

Epstein, J. L. (1983). The influence of friends on achievement and affective outcomes. In J. L. Epstein & N. L. Karweit (Eds.), *Friends in school* (pp. 177–200). New York: Academic Press,

Erikson, E. H. (1950). *Childhood and society.* New York: Norton.

Evans, E., Rutberg, J., Sather, C., & Turner, C. (1991). Content analysis of contemporary teen magazines for adolescent females. *Youth & Society, 23,* 99–120.

Evans, R., Hansen, W. B., & Mittlemark, M. B. (1977). Increasing the validity of self-reports of smoking behavior in children. *Journal of Applied Psychology, 62,* 521–523.

Fabes, R. A., & Laner, M. R. (1986). How the sexes perceive each other: Advantages and disadvantages. *Sex Roles, 15,* 129–143.

Fabian, L. J., & Thompson, J. K. (1989). Body image and eating disturbance in young females. *International Journal of Eating Disorders, 8,* 63–74.

Faust, M. S. (1983). Alternative constructions of adolescent growth. In J. Brooks-Gunn and A. C. Petersen (Eds.), *Girls at puberty: Biological and psychosocial perspectives* (pp. 105–125). New York: Plenum.

Feingold, A. (1990). Gender differences in effects of physical attractiveness on romantic attraction: A comparison across five research paradigms. *Journal of Personality and Social Psychology, 59,* 981–993.

Fisher, M., Schneider, C., & Napolitano, B. (1991). Eating attitudes, health-risk behaviors, self-esteem, and anxiety among adolescent females in a suburban high school. *Journal of Adolescent Health, 12,* 377–384.

Flanagan, T., & Jamieson, K. (1988). *Sourcebook of Criminal Justice Statistics—1987.* Washington, DC: U. S. Government Printing Office, U. S. Department of Justice, Bureau of Justice Statistics.

Fodor, I. G. (1992). *Adolescent assertiveness and social skills training: A clinical handbook.* New York: Springer.

Fordham, S., & Ogbu, J. U. (1986). Black students' school success: Coping with the " 'burden of acting white.' " *Urban Review, 18,* 810–819.

Foshee, V., & Bauman, K. (1992). Gender stereotyping and adolescent sexual behavior: A test of temporal order. *Journal of Applied Social Psychology, 22*(20), pp. 1561–1579.

Franklin, C., Grant D., Corcoran, J., Miller, P. O., & Bultman, L. (1997). Effectiveness of prevention programs for adolescent pregnancy: A meta-analysis. *Journal of Marriage and the Family, 59,* 551–567.

Fraser, K. L. (1997). Hopes, fears and the architecture of adolescence: The possible selves as polaroids and blueprints of early adolescent development. *Dissertation Abstracts International: Section B: The Sciences & Engineering, 57*(10-B), 6611.

Friday, N. (1999). *Our looks, our lives: Sex, beauty, power and the need to be seen.* New York: HarperCollins.

Furman, W., & Buhrmester, D. (1985). Children's perceptions of the personal relationships in their social networks. *Developmental Psychology, 21,* 1016–1024

Furnham, A., & Greaves, N. (1994). Gender and locus of control correlations of body image dissatisfaction. *European Journal of Personality, 8,* 183–200.

Furnham, A., & Radley, S. (1989). Sex differences in the perception of male and female shapes. *Personality and Individual Differences, 10,* 653–662.

Galambos, N. L., Petersen, A. C., Richards, M., & Gitleson, I. B. (1985). The attitudes toward women scale for adolescents (AWSA): A study of reliability and validity. *Sex Roles, 13,* 343–356.

Gans, J. E., & Blyth, D. A. (1990). *America's adolescents: How healthy are they? (AMA Profiles of Adolescent health series).* Chicago, IL: American Medical Association.

Garbarino, J., Burston, N., Raber, S., Russell, R., & Crouter, A. (1978). The social maps of children approaching adolescence: Studying the ecology of youth development. *Journal of Youth and Adolescence, 7,* 417–418.

Garland, A. F., & Zigler, E. (1993). Adolescent suicide prevention: Current research and social policy implications. *American Psychologist, 48,* 169–182.

Garner, D. M. (1997, January/February). The 1997 body image survey. *Psychology Today,* 31–84.

Geiss, F. L, Brown, V., Jennings, J., & Porter, N. (1984). TV commercials as achievement scripts for women. *Sex Roles, 10,* 513–525.

Gelman, D. (1990, Summer/Fall). A much riskier passage. *Newsweek,* 10–16.

Gibbs, J. T. (1985). City girls: Psychosocial adjustment of urban black adolescent females. *SAGE: A Scholarly Journal of Black Women, 2,* 28–36.

Gibbs, J. T. (1989). Black American adolescents. In J. T. Gibbs & L. N. Huang (Eds.), *Children of color.* San Francisco: Jossey-Bass.

Gibbs, J. T. (1990). Mental health issues of black adolescents: Implications for policy and practice. In A. R. Stiffman & L. E. Davis (Eds.), *Ethnic issues in adolescent mental health* (pp. 121–146). Newbury Park, CA: Sage.

Gibson, J. A. P., & Range, L. M. (1991). Are written reports of suicide and seeking help contagious? High schoolers' perceptions. *Journal of Applied Social Psychology, 21,* 1517–1523.

Gibson, P. (1989). *Gay male and lesbian youth suicide. Report of the secretary's task force on youth suicide, vol. 3: Prevention and intervention in youth suicide.* Rockville, MD: U.S. Department of Health and Human Services.

Gilchrist, L. D., & Schinke, S. P. (1985). Coping with contraception: Cognitive and behavioral methods with adolescents. *Cognitive Therapy and Research, 12,* 66–112.

Gilchrist, L. D., Schinke, S. P., & Blyth, B. (1985). Preventing unwanted pregnancy. In L. D. Gilchrist & S. P. Schinke (Eds.), *Preventing social and health problems through life skills training* (pp.18–33). Seattle, WA: Center for Social Welfare Research, University of Washington.

Gilligan, C. (1982). In a different voice. Cambridge, MA: Harvard University Press.

Gilligan, C. (1990). Teaching Shakespeare's sister. In C. Gilligan, N. Lyons, & T. Hanmer (Eds.), *Making connections: The relational worlds of adolescent girls at the Emma Willard School.* Cambridge, MA: Harvard University Press.

Gilligan, C., Brown, L. M., & Rogers, A. G. (1990). Psyche embedded: A place for body, relationships and culture in personality theory. In A. I. Rabin, R. A. Zucker, R. A. Emmons, & S. Frank. (Eds.), *Studying persons and lives* (pp. 86–147). New York: Springer.

Ginzberg, E. (1972). Toward a theory of occupational choice. A restatement. *Vocational Guidance Quarterly, 20,* 169–176.

Girls Incorporated (2000). *The girls bill of rights* [On-line]. Available: www.girlsinc.org/bill.html.

Gizberg, E. (1972). Toward a theory of occupational choice: A restatement. *Vocational Guidance Quarterly, 20,* 169–176.

Goodings, L. (1987). *Bitter-sweet dreams: Girls' and young women's own stories by the readers of* Just Seventeen. London: Virago Press.

Gordon, V. V. (1978). *The self-concept of black Americans.* Washington, DC: The American Sociological Association.

Gottfredson, M., & Hirschi, T. (1996). A general theory of adolescent problem behaviors: Their prevalence, consequences, and co-occurrence. In R. D. Ketterlinus & M. E. Lamb (Eds.). *Adolescent problem behaviors: Issues and research* (pp. 41–56). Hillsdale, NJ: Lawrence Erlbaum.

Gottlieb, B. H. (1991). Social support in adolescence. In M. E. Colten & S. Gore (Eds.), *Adolescent stress: Causes and consequences* (pp. 281–306). New York: Aldine de Gruyter.

Gottman, J. M., Gonso, J., & Rasmussen, B. (1979). Social interaction, social competence, and friendship in children. *Child Development, 46,* 315–336.

Gottman, J. M., & Parker, J. G. (Eds.). (1987). *Conversations with friends.* New York: Cambridge University Press.

Graber, J. A., Petersen, A. C., & Brooks-Gunn, J. (1996). Pubertal processes: Methods, measures and models. In J. A. Graber, J. Brooks-Gunn & A. C. Petersen (Eds.), *Transitions through adolescence: Interpersonal domains and context* (pp. 23–54). Mahwah, NJ: Lawrence Erlbaum.

Graham, S. (1990). Motivation in Afro-Americans. In G. L. Berry & J. K. Asamen (Eds.), *Black students: Psychosocial issues and academic achievement* (pp. 87–114). Newbury Park, CA: Sage.

Green, K., & Taormino, T. (1997). *A girl's guide to taking over the world.* New York: St. Martin's Press.

Grotevant, H. D., & Durett, M. E. (1980). Occupational knowledge about career development in adolescence. *Journal of Vocational Behavior, 17,* 171–182.

Gustavsson, N., & MacEachron, A. (1998). Violence and lesbian and gay youth. *Journal of Gay & Lesbian Social Services, 8,* 41–50.

Hall, C. (1992). Nearly half of young people lose virginity before 16. London: *The Independent,* 2.

Hall, L., & Cohn, L. (1988). *Bulimia: A guide to recovery.* Carlsbad, CA: Giurze.

Hamburg, B. A. (1974). Early adolescence: A specific and stressful stage in the life cycle. In G. V. Coelho, D. A. Hamburg, & J. E. Adams (Eds.), *Coping and adaptation* (pp. 101–124). New York: Basic Books.

Hamburg, D. A., Millstein, S. G., Mortimer, A. M., Nightingale, E. O., & Petersen, A. C. (1993). Adolescent health promotion in the twenty-first century: Current frontiers and future directions. In S. G. Millstein, A. C. Petersen, & E. O. Nightingale (Eds.), *Promoting the health of adolescents: New directions for the twenty-first century* (pp. 375–388). New York: Oxford University Press.

Hancock, E. (1989). *The girl within.* New York: Fawcett Columbine.

Handelsman, C. D., Cabral, R. J., & Weisfeld, G. E. (1987). Sources of information and adolescent sexual knowledge and behavior. *Journal of Adolescent Research, 2,* 455–463.

Hanswell, S. (1985). Adolescent friendship networks and distress in school. *Social Forces, 63,* 698–715.

Hare, B. R. (1985). *The HARE general and area specific (school, peer and home) self-esteem scale.* Unpublished manuscript.

Harter, S. (1989). Causes, correlates, and the functional role of global self-worth: A life-span perspective. In J. Kolligian & R. Sternberg (Eds.), *Perceptions of competence and incompetence across the life-span* (pp. 43–70). New Haven, CT: Yale University Press.

Harter, S. (1990). Self and identity development. In S. S. Feldman & G. R. Elliot (Eds.), *At the threshold: The developing adolescent* (pp. 352–387). Cambridge, MA: Harvard University Press.

Hartup, W. W. (1983). Peer relations. In P. H. Mussen (Ed.), *Handbook of child psychology* (Vol. 4, 103–196). New York: Wiley.

Havighurst, R. J. (1953). *Human development and education.* New York: Longmans Green.

Havighurst, R. J. (1972). *Developmental tasks and education* (3rd ed.). New York: David McKay.

Hazel, J. S., Schumaker, J. B., Sherman, J. A., & Sheldon-Wildgen, J. (1981). *Asset: A social skills program for adolescents.* Champaign, IL: Research Press.

Henderson, V. L., & Dweck, C. S. (1990). Motivation and achievement. In S. S. Feldman & G. R. Elliott (Eds.), *At the threshold: The developing adolescent* (pp. 308–329). Cambridge, MA: Harvard University Press.

Herzog, D. M., & Copeland, P. M. (1985). Eating disorders. *New England Journal of Medicine, 313,* 295.

Hetrick, E. S., & Martin, A. D. (1987). Developmental issues and their resolution for gay and lesbian adolescents. *Journal of Homosexuality, 14,* 25–42.

Hill, J. P., & Lynch, M. E. (1983). The intensification of gender-related role expectations during early adolescence. In J. Brooks-Gunn & A.C. Peterson (Eds.), *Girls at puberty: biological and psychological perspectives* (pp. 79–119). New York: Plenum.

Hodges, K. K., & Siegel, L. J. (1995). Depression in children and adolescents. In E. E. Beckham & W. R. Leber (Eds.), *Handbook of depression: Treatment, assessment and research* (pp. 517–555). New York: Guilford.

Hovell, M., Blumberg, E., Sipan, C., Hofstetter, R. C., Burkham, S., Atkins, C., & Felice, M. (1998). Skills training for pregnancy and AIDS prevention in Anglo and Latino youth. *Journal of Adolescent Health, 23,* 139–149.

Huston, A. C., & Alvarez, M. (1990). The socialization context of gender-role development in early adolescence. In R. Montemayor, G. R. Adams, & T. P. Gulotta (Eds.), *From childhood to adolescence: A transitional period?* (pp. 248–261) Newbury Park, CA: Sage.

Irwin, C. E. (1986). Why adolescent medicine? *Journal of Adolescent Health Care, 7,* 2–12.

Jackson, A. W., & Hornbeck, D. W. (1989). Educating young adolescents: Why we must restructure middle grade schools. *American Psychologist, 44,* 831–836.

Jessor, R. (1982). Problem behavior and developmental transition in adolescence. *Journal of School Health, 52,* 295–300.

Jessor, R. (1992). Risk behavior in adolescence: A psychosocial framework for understanding and action. *Developmental Review, 12,* 374–390.

Jhally, S. (1990). *Dreamworlds: Desire/sex/power in rock video* [Video]. (Available at University of Massachusetts at Amherst, Department of Communications)

Johnson, J. A. (1987). Influence of adolescent social crowds on the development of vocational identity. *Journal of Vocational Behavior, 31,* 182–199.

Johnston, A. (1997). *Girls speak out: Finding your true self.* New York: Scholastic.

Johnston, L. D., O'Malley, P. M., & Bachman, J. G. (1994). *National survey results on drug use from the Monitoring the Future study, 1975–1994.* Rockville, MD: National Institute on Drug Abuse.

Jorgensen, S. R., & Alexander, S. J. (1983). Research on adolescent pregnancy-risk: Implications for sex education programs. *Theory into Practice, 22,* 125–133.

Jukes, M. (1996). *It's a girl thing.* New York: Alfred A. Knopf.

Kahn, S. E., & Richardson, A. (1983). Evaluation of a course in sex roles for secondary school students. *Sex Roles, 9,* 431–440.

Kashani, J. H., Reid, J., & Rosenberg, T. (1989). Levels of hopelessness in children and adolescents: A developmental perspective. *Journal of Consulting and Clinical Psychology, 57,* 496–499.

Katzman, M., & Wolchik, S. (1984). Bulimia and binge eating in college women: A comparison of personality and behavior characteristics. *Journal of Consulting and Clinical Psychology, 52,* 423–428.

Kazdin, A. E. (1993). Adolescent mental health: Prevention and treatment programs. *American Psychologist, 48,* 127–141.

Keating, D. P. (1990). Adolescent thinking. In S. Feldman & G. R. Elliot (Eds.), *At the threshold: The developing adolescent* (pp. 54–90). Cambridge: Harvard University Press.

Kerr, B. (1992). *Smart girls, smart women.* Dayton, OH: Ohio University Press.

Kessler, R. C., & McLeod, J. D. (1984). Sex differences in vulnerability to undesirable life events. *American Sociological Review, 49,* 620–631.

Klaczynski, P. A., & Reese, H. W. (1991). Educational trajectory and "action orientation": Grade and track differences. *Journal of Youth and Adolescence, 20,* 441–462.

Kobocow, B., McGuire, J. M., & Blau, B. I. (1983). The influence of confidentiality conditions on self-disclosure of early adolescents. *Professional Psychology: Research and Practice, 14,* 435–475.

Koch, P. (1993). Promoting healthy sexual development during early adolescence. In R. M. Lerner (Ed.), *Early adolescence: Perspectives on research, policy and intervention* (pp. 293–307). Mahwah, NJ: Lawrence Erlbaum.

Konopka, G. (1966). *The adolescent girl in conflict.* Englewood Cliffs, NJ: Prentice-Hall.

Kovacs, M., Feinberg, T. L., Crouse-Novk, M. A., Paulauskas, S., & Finkelstein, R. (1984). Depressive disorders in childhood: A longitudinal study of the risk for a subsequent major depression. *Archives of General Psychiatry, 41,* 219–239.

Lamke, L. K. (1982). The impact of sex-role orientation on self-esteem in early adolescence. *Child Development, 53,* 1530–1535.

Larson, R., & Asmusen, L. (1991). Anger, worry, and hurt in early adolescence: An enlarging world of negative emotions. In M. E. Colten and S. Gore (Eds.), *Adolescent stress: Causes and consequences* (pp. 21–43). New York: Walter de Gruyter.

Larson, R., Csikszentimihalyi, M., & Graef, R. (1980). Mood variability and the psychosocial adjustment of adolescents. *Journal of Youth and Adolescence, 9,* 469–490.

Larson, R., & Lampman-Petraitis, C. (1989). Daily emotional stress as reported by children and adolescents. *Child Development, 60,* 1250–1260.

Larson, R., Raffaelli, M., Richards, M. H., Ham, M., & Jewell, L. (1990). The ecology of depression in early adolescence. *Journal of Abnormal Psychology, 99,* 92–102.

Larson, R., & Richards, M. H. (1991). Daily companionship in late childhood and early adolescence: Changing developmental contexts. *Child Development*, *62*, 284–300.

LeCroy, C. W. (1982). Social skills training with adolescents: A review. *Child and Youth Services*, *5*, 91–116.

LeCroy, C. W. (1994). Social skills training. In C. LeCroy (Ed.), *Handbook of child and adolescent treatment manuals*. New York: Lexington Press.

LeCroy, C. W., & Daley, J. (1997). *Girls together: Building strengths for the future pilot evaluation report*. Unpublished manuscript.

LeCroy, C. W., & Daley, J. (2000). *Experiential evaluation of the "Go Grrrls" primary prevention program for adolescent girls*. Unpublished manuscript.

LeCroy, C. W., Daley, J. M., & Milligan, K. B. (1999). Social skills for the twenty-first century. In R. Constable, S. McDonald, & J. P. Flynn (Eds.), *School social work: Practice, policy, and research perspectives* (pp. 376–390). Chicago: Lyceum Books.

Leonard, R. (1995). "I'm just a girl who can't say 'no' ": A gender difference in children's perception of refusals. *Feminism & Psychology*, *5*, 315–328.

Lerner, H. (1989). *The dance of intimacy*. New York: Harper & Row.

Lerner, R., Sorell, G., & Brackney, B. (1981). Sex differences in self-concept and self-esteem of late adolescents: A time-lag analysis. *Sex Roles*, *7*, 709–722.

Leventhan, A. (1994, February). Peer conformity during adolescence: An integration of developmental, situational, and individual characteristics. Paper presented at the meeting of the Society for Research on Adolescence, San Diego, CA.

Lever, J. (1976). Sex differences in the games children play. *Social Problems*, *23*, 478–487.

Levinson, R., Powell, B., & Steelman, L. (1986). Social location, significant others and body image among adolescents. *Social Psychology Quarterly*, *49*, 330–337.

Lewinsohn, P. M., Hops, H., Roberts, R., & Seeley, J. (1988) *Adolescent depression: Prevalence and psychosocial aspects*. Paper presented at the annual meeting of the American Public Health Association, Boston, MA.

Lewis, A. C. (1995). *Believing in ourselves: Progress and struggle in urban middle school reform*. New York: Edna McConnell Clark Foundation.

Lloyd, S. A. (1991). The dark side of courtship: Violence and sexual exploitation. *Family Relations*, *40*, 14–20.

Lochman, R. N., & Truman, J. T. (1984). Psychosocial characteristics of pregnant and nulliparous adolescents. *Adolescence*, *19*, 283–294.

Lord, S. E., & Eccles, J. S. (1994). *James revisited: The relationship of domain self-concepts and values to Black and White adolescents' self esteem*. Paper presented at the meeting of the Society for Research on Adolescence, San Diego, CA.

Lovdal, L. (1989). Sex role messages in television commercials: An update. *Sex Roles*, *21*, 715–727.

Luecke-Aleksa, D., Anderson, D. R., Collins, P. A., & Schmitt, K. L. (1995). Gender constancy and television viewing. *Developmental Psychology*, *31*, 773–780.

Lynch, M. E. (1991). Gender intensification. In R. M. Lerner, A. C. Petersen, & J. Brooks-Gunn (Eds.), *Encyclopedia of adolescence* (Vol. 1). New York: Garland.

M. F. (1997, September/October). Response in Ask a Girl advice column. *New Moon*, 10.

Maccoby, E. E., & Jacklin, C. N. (1974). *The psychology of sex differences*. Palo Alto, CA: Stanford University Press.

McGuire, K. D., & Weisz, J. R. (1982). Social cognition and behavior correlates of pre-adolescent chumships. *Child Development*, *53*, 1478–1484.

Mackoff, B. (1996). *Growing a girl: Seven strategies for raising a strong, spirited daughter.* New York: Dell.

Madaras, L., & Madaras, A. (1993). *My feelings, my self.* New York: Newmarket Press.

Magnusson, D. (1988). *Individual development from an interactional perspective.* Hillsdale, NJ: Lawrence Erlbaum.

Mann, J. (1994). *The difference.* New York: Warner Books.

Mannarino, A. P. (1980). The development of children's friendships. In H. C. Foot & A. J. Chapman (Eds.), *Friendship and social relations in children* (pp. 45–63). New York: Wiley.

Martin, K. A. (1996). *Puberty, sexuality and the self: Girls and boys at adolescence.* New York: Routledge.

Martin, M. C., & Gentry, J. W. (1997). Stuck in the model trap: The effects of beautiful models in advertisements on preadolescents and adolescents. *Journal of Advertising, 26,* 19–28.

Martin, M. C., & Kennedy, L. (1993). Advertising and social comparison: Consequences for female pre-adolescents and adolescents. *Psychology and Marketing, 10,* 513–530.

Mechanic, D. (1983). Adolescent health and illness behavior: Review of the literature and a new hypothesis for the study of stress. *Journal of Human Stress, 9,* 4–13.

Mellanby, A., Phelps, F., & Tripp, J. (1992). Sex education: More is not enough. *Journal of Adolescence, 15,* 449–466.

Millstein, S. G. (1988). *The potential of school-linked centers to promote adolescent health and development.* Washington, DC: Carnegie Council on Adolescent Development.

Millstein, S. G., & Litt, I. F. (1990). Adolescent health. In S. Feldman & G. R. Elliott (Eds.), *At the threshold: The developing adolescent.* Cambridge, MA: Harvard University Press.

Millstein, S. G., Petersen, A. C., & Nightingale, E. O. (1993). Adolescent health promotion: Rationale, goals and objectives. In S. G. Millstein, A. C. Petersen, & E. O. Nightingale (Eds.), *Promoting the health of adolescents: New direction, for the twenty-first century* (pp. 3–12). New York: Oxford University Press.

Minuchin, P. (1977). *The middle years of childhood.* Monterey, CA: Brooks/Cole.

Moore, K. A., Blumenthal, C., Sugland, B. W., Hyatt, B., Snyder, N. O., & Morrison, D. R. (1994) *State variation in rates of adolescent pregnancy and childbearing.* Washington, DC: Child Trends, Inc.

Morgan, M. (1987). Television, sex-role attitudes and sex-role behavior. *Journal of Early Adolescence, 7,* p. 169–282.

Mullis, R. L., & McKinley, K. (1989). Gender-role orientation of adolescent females: effects on self-esteem and locus of control. *Journal of Adolescent Research, 4,* 504–516.

Murphy, G. (1947). *Personality.* New York: Harper.

Myers, P. N., & Biocca, F. A. (1992). The elastic body image: the effect of television advertising and programming on body image distortions in young women. *Journal of Communication, 42,* 108–133.

National Research Council (1993). *Losing generations: Adolescents in high-risk settings.* Washington, DC: National Academy Press.

National Science Foundation (1996). *Women, minorities, and persons with physical disabilities in science and engineering.* Washington, DC: Author.

Neimark, E. D. (1982). Adolescent thought: Transition to formal operations. In B. B. Wolman (Ed.), *Handbook of developmental psychology* (pp. 214–241). Englewood Cliffs, NJ: Prentice Hall.

Newman, P. R., & Newman, B. (1997). *Childhood and adolescence*. Pacific Grove, CA: Brooks/Cole.

Nolen-Hoeksema, S. (1987). Sex differences in unipolar depression: Evidence and theory. *Psychological Bulletin, 101,* 259–282.

Nolen-Hoeksema, S. (1990). *Sex differences in depression.* Stanford, CA: Stanford University Press.

Office of Technology, U.S. Congress (1991). *Adolescent health: Vol. 1. Summary and policy options.* (Publication No. OTAH-468). Washington, DC: U.S. Government Printing Office.

O'Malley, P. M., & Bachman, J. G. (1979). Self-esteem and education: Sex and cohort comparisons among high school seniors. *Journal of Personality & Social Psychology, 37,* 1153–1159.

Orenstein, P. (1994). *School girls: Young women, self-esteem, and the confidence gap.* New York: Doubleday.

Parker, S., Nichter, M., Nichter, M., & Vuckovic, N. (1995). Body image and weight concerns among African American and white adolescent females: Differences that make a difference. *Human Organization, 54,* 103–114.

Pentz, M. A. (1985). Social competence skills and self-efficacy as determinants of substance use in adolescence. In S. Shiffman & T. A. Wills (Eds.), *Coping and substance use* (pp. 117–138). New York: Academic Press.

Pentz, M. A., Dwyer, J. H., MacKinnon, D. P., Flay, B. R., Hansen, W. B., Wang, E. Y. I., & Johnson, C. A. (1989). A multicommunity trial for primary prevention of adolescent drug abuse. *Journal of the American Medical Association, 261,* 3259–3266.

Perry, C. (1991). *The social world of adolescents: Family, peers, school, and culture.* Minneapolis, MN: University of Minnesota Division of Epidemiology.

Perry, N. J. (1992, August 10). Why is it so tough to be a girl? *Fortune,* 82–84.

Petersen, A. C. (1988). Adolescent development. In M. Rosenzweig (Ed.), *Annual Review of Psychology* (9th ed., pp. 583–607). Palo Alto, CA: Annual Reviews.

Petersen, A. C., Compas, B. E., Brooks-Gunn, J., Stemmler, M., Ey, S., & Grant, K. E. (1993). Depression in adolescence. *American Psychologist, 48,* 155–168.

Petersen, A. C., Kennedy, R. E., & Sullivan, P. (1991). Coping with adolescence. In M. E. Colten & S. Gore (Eds.), *Adolescent stress: Causes and consequences* (pp. 93–110). New York: Aldine de Gruyter.

Petersen, A. C., Sarigiani, P. A., & Kennedy, R. E. (1991). Adolescent depression: Why more girls? *Journal of Youth & Adolescence Special Issue: The emergence of depressive symptoms during adolescence, 20,* 247–271.

Petersen, A. C., & Taylor, B. (1980). The biological approach to adolescence: Biological change and psychological adaptation. In J. Adelson (Ed.), *Handbook of adolescent psychology.* New York: Wiley.

Phelps, F., Mellanby, A., & Tripp, J. (1992). So you really think you understand sex? *Education and Health, 10,* 27–31.

Phillips, L. (1998). *The girls report: What we know and need to know about growing up female.* New York: National Council for Research on Women.

Phinney, J. S., Dupont, S., Landin, J., & Onwughalu, M. (1994). *Social identity orientation, bi-cultural conflict, and coping strategies among minority adolescents.* Paper presented at the Society for Research on Adolescence, San Diego, CA.

Piaget, J. (1970). Piaget's theory. In P. H. Mussen (Ed.), *Carmichael's manual of child psychology* (3rd ed., pp. 12–33). New York: Wiley.

Pierce, K. (1990). A feminist theoretical perspective on the socialization of teenage girls through Seventeen magazine. *Sex Roles, 23*, 491–500.

Pierce, K. L. (1993). Socialization of teenage girls through teen magazine fiction: The making of a new woman or old lady? *Sex Roles, 29*, 59–68.

Pipher, M. (1994). *Reviving Ophelia: Saving the selves of adolescent girls.* New York: Putnam.

Pollay, R. W. (1986). The distorted mirror: Reflections on the unintended consequences of advertising. *Journal of Marketing, 50*, 18–36.

Pollitt, K. (1991, April 7). The smurfette principle. *New York Times Magazine*, 22–24.

Posner, J. A., LaHaye, A., & Cheifetz, P. N. (1989). Suicide notes in adolescence. *Canadian Journal of Psychiatry, 34*, 171–175.

Powell, M. (1955). Age and the sex differences in degree of conflict within certain areas of psychological adjustment. *Psychological Monographs, 69*, 14–23.

Quinn, J. (1986). Rooted in research: Effective adolescent pregnancy prevention programs. *Journal of Social Work and Human Sexuality, 5*, 99–110.

Radloff, L. S. (1991). The use of the Center for Epidemiological Studies Depression scale in adolescents and young adults. *Journal of Youth and Adolescence, 20*, 149–166.

Rauste-von Wright, M. (1989). Body image satisfaction in adolescent girls and boys: A longitudinal study. *Journal of Youth and Adolescence, 18*, 71–83.

Reisman, J. M. (1985). Friendship and its implications for mental health or social competence. *Journal of Early Adolescence, 5*, 383–391.

Resnick, M. D., & Blum, R. W. (1985). Development and personalogical correlates of adolescent sexual behavior and outcomes. *International Journal of Adolescent Medicine and Health, 1*, 293–313.

Rhodes, J. E., & Jason, L. A. (1988). *Preventing substance abuse among children and adolescents.* New York: Pergamon.

Richmond-Abbott, M. (1992). *Masculine and feminine gender roles over the life span.* New York: McGraw-Hill.

Roff, M. (1961). Childhood social interactions and young adult bad conduct. *Journal of Abnormal & Social Psychology, 63*, 333–337.

Roff, M. (1963). Childhood social interaction and young adult psychosis. *Journal of Clinical Psychology, 19*, 152–157.

Root, M. (1989). Treating the victimized bulimic: The functions of binge-purge behavior. *Journal of Interpersonal Violence, 4*, 90–100.

Rose, A. J., & Montemayor, R. (1994). The relationship between gender role orientation and perceived self-competency in male and female adolescents. *Sex Roles, 31*, 579–595.

Rosen, J. (1990). Cognitive behavior therapy with vs. without body size perception training, normal weight females with disturbed body image. *Behavior Therapy, 21*, 481–498.

Rosenberg, M. (1986). Self-concept from middle childhood through adolescence. In J. Suls & A. G. Greenwald (Eds.), *Psychological perspective on the self* (Vol. 3, pp. 271–294). Hillsdale, NJ: Lawrence Erlbaum.

Rosenberg, M., & Simmons, R. (1971). *Black and white self esteem: The urban school child.* Rose Monograph Series. Washington, DC: American Sociological Association.

Rosesler, T., & Deisher, R. (1972). Youthful male homosexuality: Homosexual experience and the process of developing homosexual identity in males aged 16 to 22 years. *Journal of the American Medical Association, 219*, 1018–1023.

Rosner, B. A., & Rierdan, J. (1994). *Adolescent girls' self-esteem: Variations in developmental trajectories.* Paper presented at the Society for Research on Adolescence, San Diego, CA.

Rowe, D. C., Rodgers, J. L., & Meseck-Bushey, S. (1990). An "epidemic" model of sexual intercourse prevalences for black and white adolescents. *Social Biology, 36,* 127–145.

Rubin, Z. (1980). *Children's friendships.* Cambridge, MA: Harvard University Press.

Russo, N. F. (1990). Overview: Forging research priorities for women's mental health. *American Psychologist, 45,* 368–374.

Rutter, M. (1995). *Psychosocial disturbance in young people: Challenges for prevention.* Cambridge, MA: Cambridge University Press.

Rutter, M., & Garmezy, N. (1983). Developmental psychopathology. In P. H. Mussen (Ed.), *Handbook of child psychology* (4th ed.). New York: Wiley.

Sanders, G. F., & Mullis, R. L. (1988). Family influences on sexual attitudes and knowledge as reported by college students. *Adolescence, 23,* 837–846.

Santrock, J. W. (1995). *Children* (4th ed.). Madison, WI: Brown & Benchmark.

Santrock, J. W. (1996). *Adolescence.* Madison, WI: Brown & Benchmark.

Sarason, B. R., Pierce, G. R., Bannerman, A., & Sarason, I. G. (1993). Investigating the antecedents of perceived social support: Parents' views of and behavior toward their children. *Journal of Personality and Social Psychology, 65,* 1071–1085.

Savin-Williams, R. (1994). Verbal and physical abuse as stressors in the lives of lesbian, gay male, and bisexual youths: Associations with school problems, running away, substance abuse, prostitution, and suicide. *Journal of Consulting and Clinical Psychology, 62,* 261–269.

Schinke, S. P., Blyth, B. J., & Gilchrist, L. D. (1981). Cognitive-behavioral prevention of adolescent pregnancy. *Journal of Counseling Psychology, 28,* 451–454.

Schnelmann, J. (1987). The ideal man or woman as described by young adolescents in Iceland and the U.S. *Sex Roles, 17,* 313–320.

Seligman, M. E. P. (1995). *The optimistic child: A program to safeguard children against depression and build lifelong resilience.* New York: Harper Perennial.

Shandler, S. (1999). *Ophelia speaks: Adolescent girls write about their search for self.* New York: Harper Perennial.

Shaver, P., Furman, W., & Buhrmester, D. (1985). Transition to college: Network changes, social skills, and loneliness. In S. Duck & D. Perlman (Eds.), *Understanding personal relationships: An interdisciplinary approach* (pp. 193–219). Academic Press.

Sherman, B. (1986). Violence and sex in music videos: TV and rock'n'roll. *Journal of Communication, 36,* 79–93.

Siegel-Gorelick, B. (1984). Sexual maturation, social class, and the desire to be thinner among adolescent females. *Developmental and Behavioral Pediatrics, 5,* 308–314.

Silberstein, L. R., & Striegel-Moore, R. (1987). Feeling fat: A woman's shame. In: H. B. Lewis (Ed.), *The role of shame in symptom formation* (pp. 89–108). Mahwah, NJ: Lawrence Erlbaum.

Simmons, C., & Wade, W. (1984). *I like to say . . . what I think.* London: Kogan Page.

Simmons, R. G. (1979). *Research in community and mental health: An annual compilation of research.* Greenwich, CT: JAI Press.

Simmons, R. G., & Blyth, D. A. (1987). *Moving into adolescence: The impact of pubertal change and school context.* New York: Aldine De Gruyter.

Simmons, R., Conger, R., & Wu, C. (1992, March). Peer group as amplifer/moderator of the stability of adolescent antisocial behavior. Paper presented at the meeting of the Society for Research on Adolescence, Washington, DC.

Slavin, L. A., & Rainer, K. L. (1990). Gender differences in emotional support and depressive symptoms among adolescents: A prospective analysis. *American Journal of Community Psychology, 18,* 407–421.

Small, S. A., Silverburg, S. B., & Kerns, D.(1993). Adolescents' perceptions of the costs and benefits of engaging in health-compromising behaviors. *Journal of Youth & Adolescence, 22,* 73–87.

Spencer, M. B., & Dornbush, S. M. (1990). Challenges in studying minority youth. In S. S. Feldman & G. R. Elliott (Eds.), *At the threshold: The developing adolescent* (pp. 123–146). Cambridge, MA: Harvard University Press.

Stake, J. E., DeVille, C. J., & Pennell, C. L. (1983). The effects of assertive training on the performance self-esteem of adolescent girls. *Journal of Youth and Adolescence, 12,* 435–442.

Steinberg, L., Dornbush, S. M., & Brown, B. B. (1992). Ethnic differences in adolescent achievement: An ecological perspective. *American Psychologist, 47,* 723–729.

Stice, E., & Heather, S. E. (1994). Adverse effects of the media portrayed thin-ideal on women and linkages to bulimia symptomology. *Journal of Social and Clinical Psychology, 13,* 288–308.

Strauss, S., & Subotnik, R. F. (1991). *Gender differences in classroom participation and achievement: An experiment involving advanced placement calculus classes.* (Part 1). Unpublished manuscript, Hunter College, New York.

Striegel-Moore, R., Silberstein, L. R., & Rodin, J. (1986). Toward an understanding of risk factors in bulimia. *American Psychologist, 41,* 246–263.

Striegel-Moore, R. H., & Cachelin, F. M. (1999). Body image concerns and disordered eating in adolescent girls: risk and protective factors. In N. G. Johnson, M. C. Roberts, and J. Worell (Eds.), *Beyond appearance: A new look at adolescent girls* (pp. 85–108). Washington, DC: American Psychological Association.

Stromme, M. P., & Stromme, A. I. (1993). *Five cries of parents.* New York: HarperCollins.

Sullivan, H. S. (1953). *The interpersonal theory of psychiatry.* New York: Norton.

Tafarodi, R., & Swann, W. B., Jr. (1995). Self-liking and self-competence as dimensions of global self-esteem: Initial validation of a measure. *Journal of Personality Assessment, 65,* 322–342.

Takanishi, R. (1993). The opportunities of adolescence—research, interventions, and policy. *American Psychologist, 48,* 85–87.

Tanenbaum, L. (1999). *Slut! Growing up female with a bad reputation.* New York: Seven Stories Press.

Thompson, J. K. (1990). *Body image disturbance: Assessment and treatment.* New York: Pergamon Press.

Thompson, J. K., Fabian, L. J., Moulton, D. O., Dunn, M. F., & Altabe, M. N. (1991). The physical appearance related teasing scale (PARTS). *Journal of Personality Assessment, 56,* 513–521.

Thompson, K. L., Bundy, K. A., & Broncheau, C. (1995). Social skills training for young adolescents: symbolic and behavioral components. *Adolescence, 30,* 723–733.

Thompson, K. L., Bundy, K. A., & Wolfe, W. R. (1996). Social skills training for young adolescents: cognitive and performance components. *Adolescence, 31*, 505–511.

Thornburg, H. (1970). Adolescence: A re-interpretation. *Adolescence, 5*, 463–484.

Thornburg, H. D. (1981). Adolescent sources of information on sex. *Journal of School Health, 51*, 274–277.

Thorton, B., & Moore, S. (1993). Physical attractiveness contrast effect: Implications for self-esteem and evaluations of the social self. *Personal and Social Psychology Bulletin, 19*, 474–480.

Tiggemann, M. (1994). Gender differences in the interrelationships between weight dissatisfaction, restraint, and self-esteem. *Sex Roles, 30*, 319–330.

Tisdale, S. (1997, July 1). The hounds of spring. *Salon* [On-line], Available: www.salonmagazine.com.

Tolman, D. L., & Higgins, T. E. (1996). How being a good girl can be bad for girls. In N. B. Maglin and D. Perry (Eds.), *Bad girls/good girls: Women, sex, and power in the nineties.* New Brunswick, NJ: Rutgers University Press.

U.S. Bureau of the Census (1995). *Statistical abstract of the United States: 1995* (115th ed.). Washington DC: U.S. Government Printing Office.

U.S. General Accounting Office (1986). *School dropouts: The extent and nature of the problem.* Report to Congressional Requestors.

Vera, E. M., Reese, L. E., Paikoff, R., & Jarrett, R. L. (1996). Contextual factors of sexual risk-taking in urban African American pre-adolescent children. In J. R. Leadbeater & N. Way (Eds.), *Urban girls: Resisting stereotypes, creating identities* (pp. 302–336). New York: New York University Press.

Wahl, E. (1988, April 8). Girls and technology: Stories of tools and power. Paper presented at the American Educational Research Association Symposium.

Wallace, J. M., & Williams, D. R. (1997). Religion and adolescent health-compromising behavior. In J. Schulenberg, J. L. Maggs, & K. Hurrelman (Eds.), *Health risks and developmental transitions during adolescence* (pp. 448–449). Cambridge, UK: Cambridge University Press.

Weiten, W., & Lloyd, M. A. (1997). *Psychology applied to modern life.* Pacific Grove, CA: Brooks/Cole.

Willemsen, T. M. (1998). Widening the gender gap: Teenage magazines for girls and boys. *Sex Roles, 38*, 85–94.

Wilson, G. T. (1996). Acceptance and change in the treatment of eating disorders and obesity. *Behavior Therapy, 27*, 417–439.

Wilson, J. W. (1987). *The truly disadvantaged: The inner city, the underclass, and public policy.* Chicago: The University of Chicago Press.

Wise, K. L., Bundy, K. A., Bundy, E. A., & Wise, L. A. (1991). Social skills training for young adolescents. *Adolescence, 26*, 233–241.

Wodarski, J. S., & Wodarski, L. A. (1993). *Curriculums and practical aspects of implementation* (pp. 95–96). Lanham, MD: University Press of America.

Wolfe, D. A., Wekerie, C., Gough, R., Reitzel-Jaffe, D., Grasley, C., Pittman, A., Lefebvre, L. & Stumpf, J. (1996). *The youth relationships manual: A group approach with adolescents for the prevention of woman abuse and the promotion of healthy relationships.* Thousand Oaks, CA: Sage.

Wylie, R. (1979). *The self-concept theory and research: Vol. 2.* Lincoln, NE: University of Nebraska Press.

Young, C. M., Sipin, S. S., & Roe, D. A. (1968). Density and skinfold measurements: Body composition of pre-adolescent girls. *Journal of American Dietetic Association, 53,* 25–31.

Youniss, J. (1980). *Parents and peers in social development: A Sullivan-Piaget perspective.* Chicago: University of Chicago Press.

Zabin, L. S. (1993). *Adolescent sexual behavior and childbearing.* Newbury Park, CA: Sage.

Zabin, L. S., Astone, N. M., & Emerson, M. R. (1993). Do adolescents want babies? The role between attitude and behavior. *Journal of Research on Adolescence, 3,* 67–86.

Index

Abner, A., 200
academic performance
  achievement motivation, 87, 88–90
  math and science, 87, 92–93
  peer influence, 51
  test anxiety, 90
access to care, 83–84, 85
Achenbach, T. M., 40, 41
achievement motivation, 87, 88–90
  in career planning, 91–93
  socioeconomic factors, 90–91
Ackerson, J., 85
Adams, G., 33
adolescence
  body image sensitivity in, 23–24
  cognitive development, 60–61
  depression risk, 39, 40–41
  developmental tasks, 4–8
  early maturation, 24–25, 35, 52, 75
  gender-role identification, 12–14
  importance of interpersonal rela-
    tionships, 46–48, 51
  middle school transition, 51–53
  negative emotions in, 36
  peer influence, 51
  self-image development in, 31–35
  see also risks of adolescence
advertising. see mass media
Alan Guttmacher Institute, 67, 75, 81
alcohol. see substance use/abuse
Alexander, S. J., 70, 74
Alvarez, M., 5
American Psychiatric Association, 28,
  29, 40
Anderson, A., 23
Arnett, J., 59

Arroyo, C. G., 91
Asmusen, L., 36, 37
assertiveness, 7
  behavioral stereotypes, 93
  parent curriculum, 231–32
  session topics and exercises,
    157–63
  skills training, 64–65, 263–64
attendance, 110
Attie, H., 24, 28, 29
attributional style, 41
Ayers, M., 56

Bachman, J. G., 32, 81
Backstrand, K., 53
Bandura, A., 13
Barth, R., 62, 70, 269
Bauman, K., 74
Baumrind, D., 92
Belansky, E. S., 5
Bell, R., 67, 72, 73, 74
Belle, D., 19, 48
Berg, F., 21
Berndt, T. J., 49, 50, 51, 56
Bierman, K. L., 62
Bingham, M., 94, 200
Biocca, F. A., 15
Blum, R. W., 74
Blyth, D. A., 2, 6, 11, 25, 33, 34, 51,
  62, 81, 93, 203
body image
  developmental context, 23–24
  disorders related to, 28t
  early maturation and, 24–25
  eating disorders and, 27–28, 29